STOP! ARMED POLICE!

Kev Lyles' painting of CO19 specialist firearms officers, commissioned in 2007 to mark the fortieth anniversary of the formation of the unit. It depicts one officer in full operational assault kit, armed with a Heckler & Koch MP5 carbine and Benelli M3 Hatton gun. The kneeling officer is in 'light order', armed with a Heckler & Koch G36 carbine

STEPHEN SMITH

STOP! ARMED POLICE!

INSIDE THE MET'S FIREARMS UNIT

ROBERT HALE • LONDON

First published in 2013 by
Robert Hale, an imprint of
The Crowood Press Ltd
Ramsbury, Marlborough
Wiltshire SN8 2HR

www.crowood.com

This impression 2017

British Library Cataloguing-in-Publication Data
A catalogue record for this book is available from the British Library.

ISBN 978-0-7198-0826-5

Typeset by Eurodesign

Printed and bound in India by Replika Press Pvt. Ltd.

Contents

Acknowledgements

I would like to thank the myriad people who have combined to make this book possible, firstly my publishers Robert Hale, for having faith in my project, in particular my editor Nikki for her kind patience and attention to detail. I would also like to thank, in no particular order: my family, for their patience, encouragement and help in many small ways over the long period of time this project has taken; Camilla O'Hare from the Met Police Branding and Copyright department for her help in explaining and navigating me through the complicated issues surrounding copyright; Paul Bickley, curator of the Met Police Crime Museum at New Scotland Yard for his help and support during my research, his assistant Keith Skinner; Neil Patterson, curator of the Met Police Historic Collection and his staff, Paul and Phil at Empress State Buildings, for their friendly help and advice. Mark Williams, the SCO19 Federation representative, has given me his friendship, help and the encouragement to see this through, even when I felt like giving up. Steve Hartshorn, his successor, has provided technical support and help on PIP and Taser. I would also like to thank that Scottish inspector Mark Adams for his level-headed advice and help when I needed it most; Steve Manning, who first said, 'you should write a book about all this stuff'; Ian and Tony for allowing me to use their fantastic artwork and drawings; Kev Lyles, the brilliant combat artist for allowing me to use one of his paintings; Pete Cox (Specialist Dog Section), JB and Simo; Steve Collins and Roger Gray for their sound advice; Steve Barrett, my sounding board from outside the job; and Black Team SFOs (my old team) for their encouragement. I also owe a big debt of thanks to Mike Waldron whose vast knowledge on the subject of the firearms department and its history was indispensable to this work, and to the old boys of D6/D11, in particular Bob Wells, Mick Weight, Ron Jarrett and Tony Grey, who are still going strong and have offered encouragement along with some good old war stories. But, of course, none of this would have been possible without the many men and women, past and present, of the Met Police firearms department under all its different titles, who have let me use photos, pictures and drawings and helped me to fill in the gaps in the accounts of incidents, equipment and training: you are all generous without fault. I cannot name you but you know who you are. Finally, I would like to thank the Metropolitan Police, in particular Ch. Supt Alistair Sutherland (head of SCO19) and Det. Supt Mark Welton also of SCO19, for their advice and help and for granting me permission to use such a fantastic collection of historic and contemporary police photographs – I hope I have done them justice.

METROPOLITAN POLICE

WANTED

FOR CRIME
FOR ROAD SAFETY
FOR EVERYTHING !

The Metropolitan Police Force wants 5,000 men of initiative and intelligence with good character and physique.

These men are wanted to prevent crime, to maintain law and order, to control traffic and prevent road accidents.

They will be the guardians, guides and friends of all law abiding citizens.

The Force offers a career of real interest with the comradeship of service life coupled with the freedom of civilian life.

It gives security of employment, good prospects of promotion and a generous pension scheme.

Excellent facilities are available for every kind of outdoor and indoor game.

The pay of a constable starts at £5 5s. a week and rises to £7 a week, plus certain allowances, and free accommodation or an allowance in lieu.

Uniform is provided free and so is medical and dental treatment.

Age limits 20—30. Height 5ft. 8ins. or over.

Apply for full particulars to any Police Station or to—
New Scotland Yard (Dept. D-5Z), London, S.W.1

Printed for the Receiver for the Metropolitan Police District, New Scotland Yard S.W.1.

An early recruitment poster for the Metropolitan Police

Dedicated to all serving and retired firearms officers
and those already at the final R.V.P.

Unofficial badge of the firearms unit SCO19

Author's Note: *legibus et armis*

I hope as you read through this book and look at the photos relating to the incidents, equipment and training, you will be left with a better understanding of the work the firearms department is involved in on a day-to-day basis.

The men and women of SCO19's specialist firearms unit provide dangerous but essential support to London's Metropolitan Police and, without this support, it could not function in its fight against organized and violent crime.

The use of firearms to tackle armed crime is seen as the ugly face of modern-day policing. This unit often finds itself on the front pages of national newspapers and has been involved in many controversial incidents through the years. Firearms in the hands of criminals and those with malicious intent will always be an issue in a bustling city such as London and that is why we must rely on the ability of the police to tackle these persons. Every officer who carries a gun recognizes the immense responsibility with which he/she has been charged and none of us takes a life lightly. It is the most awful thing, sometimes life-changing and always the beginning of a long and stressful time for all concerned. Most officers are family people themselves who understand full well the loss suffered by the loved ones of those who die at their hands.

In this book, I have attempted to cover most of the major incidents involving the unit since its inception in 1966 and to bring matters as up to date as possible. However, there are many subjects and incidents that have not been included, some because of long legal process that accompanies such matters, and some because the number of firearms operations and training aspects is so great that it makes it impossible to cover them all.

Those incidents featured in this book represent only a minute fraction of the work completed by the men and women of the unit each year, but the dedication and professionalism shown every day by these officers is remarkable. This is a unit that has earned its elite status within the police service, without a shadow of a doubt.

It is not the critic who counts: not the man who points out how the strong man stumbles or where the doer of deeds could have done better. The credit belongs to the man who is actually in the arena, whose face is marred by dust and sweat and blood, who strives valiantly, who errs and comes up short again and again, because there is no effort without error or shortcoming, but who knows the great enthusiasms, the great devotions, who spends himself for a worthy cause; who, at the best, knows, in the end, the triumph of high achievement, and who, at the worst, if he fails, at least he fails while daring greatly, so that his place shall never be with those cold and timid souls who knew neither victory nor defeat.

THEODORE ROOSEVELT, *Paris, 1910*

PART ONE:
The Wind of Change —
D6/D11 1966—1970

Looking back over the last forty-six or so years it is hard to imagine a modern police service without any form of dedicated firearms training department or specialized operational firearms wing but, before 1966, this was the case within the Metropolitan Police. (It is interesting to note that up until 1965 the death penalty still existed for murder and attempted murder.)

As society evolved after the war years, so too did its criminal fraternity. It is true that firearms-related crime, compared with today, was relatively rare, but it is still hard to believe that with less legislation and more unregistered firearms there was not more of a need within the police for a cadre of dedicated firearms professionals.

The police, contrary to their unarmed image had always had access to firearms but this was on an ad hoc basis, and up until the fateful year of

1966, any major change was just too big a mountain to climb for the Metropolitan Police.

So, what was available to the police in relation to firearms prior to 1966? Well, the training was fragmented to say the least; there were no particular rules governing the use of police firearms and it normally fell to local divisional management to interpret how it went about its training. Selected officers would be sent to firing ranges once a year to shoot off a dozen rounds or so.

The police service relied heavily on its ex-military contingent from the war who had experience with firearms, but by 1966 this pool of experience was dwindling. There were still ex-military personnel joining the police, but they did not make up as large a percentage of police personnel as they had shortly after the war.

Even those who still remained had little experience relating to pistols or revolvers. It's fair to say they were more familiar with service rifles and sub-machine guns.

Protection officers working for 'Special Branch' were another problem as they had their own particular weapons and carried out their own training, which was unregulated. They had no wish to change their training or weapons to fit in with the rest of the force.

Meanwhile, most police stations held a variety of outdated and sometimes unserviceable handguns and it fell to selected police inspectors to run the annual firearms training for their nominated officers, sometimes at open-air military ranges.

The standard of training was low; officers were usually instructed to fire two shots from the hip, making no attempt to aim or even point the weapon. Emphasis was directed more

Illustration of a D6 firearms instructor, c. 1967, using a police issue Webley & Scott .380 Mark IV revolver

at weapons handling than accuracy. Some of the recorded scores were less than thirty-three per cent hits at certain ranges.

On the plus side, some progress had been made with the completion in 1961 of a firing range at City Road police station. This meant that there was no further need to use military ranges or the City of London Police facilities (they had a firing range at Bishopsgate police station).

Another step in the right direction was a recommendation that two police inspectors per division should be sent for firearms training on army firearms instructor training courses and that all police inspectors should be trained in the use of firearms. But even after these changes, there was still no consistency shown in training or procedure and weapons and ammunition remained an issue. Even by 1964, after the five-yearly inspection of police stations, it was decided that eighty handguns from thirteen different manufacturers obtained from weapons amnesties, along with 2,000 rounds of ammunition, would be kept as an operational reserve. Although this was better than nothing and clearly a cheaper option than buying completely new weapons, it did not, unfortunately, make for an effective

arsenal. A big shake-up was well overdue but, sadly, as on many occasions, it would take a tragedy before the powers that be faced up to what was needed.

The Massacre of Foxtrot One-One
Friday 12 August 1966

At 3.15 p.m. on Friday 12 August 1966, an unmarked police car, (call sign Foxtrot One-One, from Shepherds Bush police station) driven by Police Constable Fox, with Detective Sergeant Head and trainee Detective Constable Wombwell as crew, stopped a car in Braybrook Street near Wormwood Scrubs prison in Shepherds Bush, London. The suspect vehicle, a blue Vanguard estate, containing three men, was thought to be acting suspiciously. The Vanguard was driven by John Witney, with Harry Roberts next to him and John Duddy in the back. All three men were armed with handguns and had previous convictions for serious crime.

What began as a routine matter ended in cataclysmic tragedy. The two detectives approached the Vanguard, which was stopped in front of their police vehicle. Their driver, PC Geoffrey Fox remained in the police Triumph

The crew of Foxtrot One-One, left to right: Geoffrey Fox, Christopher Head and David Wombwell

12

Scene of the massacre: the police Triumph 'Q car' stationary, its window shot through; the lifeless body of DS Head remains in the road behind the vehicle

2000 with his engine running (a normal procedure in case the suspects drove off). TDC David Wombwell began speaking with the driver, Witney, while DS Christopher Head went to the rear of the vehicle. Roberts produced an Enfield revolver, leant across Witney and shot TDC Wombwell through his left eye. He fell to the ground dead. Roberts jumped out of the vehicle, gun in hand, as DS Head attempted to run back to the Triumph. Roberts fired two shots; the second of these hit the detective sergeant in the back and he fell dying in the road a short distance from the police car. Meanwhile, Duddy had also left the Vanguard and ran up to the police car. Duddy used his Colt .380 pistol to shoot at PC Fox through the rear nearside window. He then fired two more shots (probably through the open passenger window). One of these bullets hit PC Fox in the head, killing him.

The Triumph, an automatic, now moved forward, gruesomely driving over the body of DS Head before coming to a stop. The two murderers fled back to their car and sped off.

A married couple driving in Braybrook Street saw the Vanguard speeding off; they noted the registration number and called the authorities. The response was quick. At 9 p.m., police located the owner of the blue Vanguard motor vehicle, arresting John Witney at his home in Paddington shortly afterwards. He initially stated that he had sold the vehicle to a stranger just hours before the murders, but his alibi was destroyed when police found the car the next day in a lock-up garage rented by Witney. Inside, they found three spent cartridge cases.

The story broke in newspapers' later editions and sparked outrage amongst the public, who demanded that police should be given guns and argued for the return of

13

Harry Maurice Roberts, a career criminal and murderer, born in Essex in 1936

The Standard Vanguard van used by Roberts, Duddy and Witney found in a lock-up garage

hanging for the murder of police officers. The press themselves had long been critics of the police but now were offering sympathy and understanding, running a headline in the *Daily Mirror*: 'Massacred In The Line Of Duty'. The two remaining suspects were soon given up by Witney and had their faces splashed over every front page. The nation's anger was rising at these heinous crimes perpetrated against its unarmed officers.

A few days later, John Duddy was arrested in Glasgow, leaving only Roberts outstanding. Over 500 police officers, many of them armed, were drafted in on the hunt for Harry Roberts.

Roberts had been a Borstal boy (or, as we would now say, a young offender) before completing National Service. He saw action in the Mau Mau uprising and the Malayan Emergency where he learnt jungle craft and skills that would help him to temporarily evade capture. He had recently served seven years for an armed robbery in which he and an accomplice had tied and beaten an old man about the head with a glass decanter. Their victim died of his injuries one year and three days later. If it had been just two days earlier, Roberts would have been convicted of murder and would never

have been in Braybrook Street that fateful day. He was without doubt a cruel and heartless killer.

The public were warned not to approach Roberts, who it was believed still had access to firearms, but finally, after over 6,000 recorded sightings, a break arrived in the form of information that he was seen purchasing a sleeping bag, a haversack and food supplies at a village in Essex.

Roberts had then taken the bus to the Wake Arms roundabout in the middle of Epping Forest. The hunt was on – it would be the biggest armed operation since the Sidney Street siege in 1911.

The earlier problems identified regarding weapons and training quickly came to the fore. For a start, there were too few officers trained to use firearms and even some of those displayed a complete disregard for safety and weapons awareness.

There were accounts of revolvers being handed to untrained officers who were given a five-minute familiarization and then left to 'get on with it'. Another account was given of a revolver with its hammer drawn back being pushed down the front of an officer's waistband as he nonchalantly searched through the undergrowth. Some officers were even instructed not to load their weapons until they had a definite sighting of Roberts.

All these instances only served to draw attention to the shortcomings of the Metropolitan Police and their attitudes towards armed policing. The fact that this was all done in the public eye only emphasized these points.

The search continued for two days in this fashion, but Roberts had already moved into Hertfordshire and the trail had gone cold. Rewards were posted for information leading to his arrest and the sum of £1,000 was offered. On 10 November, a young man was out hunting small game in Thorley Wood and came across a tent half buried in the undergrowth. There was a light coming from it. The man told his father, who thought it suspicious and informed the police. But after keeping observation on the tent, no one appeared, although forensics found Roberts' fingerprints on items in the tent. This sparked another manhunt with more than a hundred officers scouring the area over the next few days.

Then, on 15 November, just before noon, Sergeants Thorne and Smith were checking a disused farm building on the edge of nearby Nathan Wood, when they noticed some camping paraphernalia. They then moved some bales of hay and noticed a sleeping bag. One of the officers poked it with his rifle and Roberts emerged. He begged not to be shot, saying, 'Please don't shoot, you won't get any trouble from me, I've had enough.' Two loaded guns were recovered from his hide. The Enfield .38 used by Roberts to shoot the two officers was recovered from where it had been buried on Hampstead Heath. It was linked to Roberts by forensics.

On 12 December 1966, after a trial lasting just six days, Roberts, Witney and Duddy were convicted of the three murders and sentenced

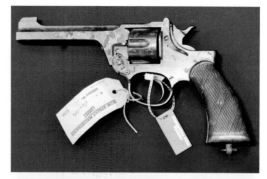

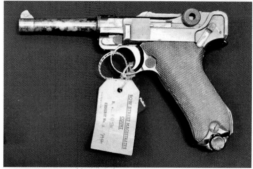

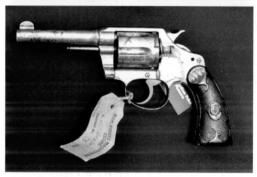

Armed to the teeth. The three firearms used by Roberts and his gang to murder the three officers. Top: Roberts' Enfield .38 revolver, used to shoot Head and Wombwell. Middle: the 9 mm Luger pistol. Bottom: the Colt .38 revolver used by Duddy to shoot driver PC Fox

to life imprisonment with a recommended minimum term of thirty years. The murders had occurred just eight months after the Murder (Abolition of Death Penalty) Act of 1965 suspended the death penalty in England, Wales and Scotland and substituted a mandatory sentence of life imprisonment.

The haystack in which Roberts was discovered hiding by the two officers

And so, for a system that was ripe for overhaul, the events of 1966 were to have huge implications, forcing changes that were long overdue in armed police organization, equipment and training. From this tragic incident the foundations were laid for a dedicated firearms training unit to be born.

Formation of the D6 Firearms Wing
2 December 1966

After the tragic deaths of Fox, Head and Wombwell, funding was quickly made available to improve and standardize the training of the Met's armed officers. But who would be given the role of setting up and running such a massive training programme? It would need to be a department with a proven track record for training large numbers of officers and it would require the administrative capacity to handle the logistics of sending hundreds of officers from all over the Met to training locations yet to be found.

In the end there was only one candidate. D6 was a department already set up to carry out the post-war 'Civil Defence Training'. (Every officer in the Met was required to attend 'war' training, in preparation for a nuclear attack on London.) The department was also responsible for running courses on radio and telecommunications.

On 2 December 1966, D6 were informed that ten firearms instructors would be attached to them to undertake all firearms training within the force.

The Firearms Wing Amoral Shield. Loosely translated, it means 'By laws and arms'

16

D6 advertised in 'Police Orders' (a police circular) for inspectors, sergeants and constables to volunteer for important specialist work. Previous experience in the handling of firearms, particularly revolvers and automatic pistols, was desirable. Successful applicants would be expected to attend a residential course at the 'Small Arms Wing' of the School of Infantry, Hythe. The course would run in January 1967.

There was a huge response, mainly from officers with ex-service backgrounds. It was from this group that ten applicants were selected. These ten men, although they could not have known it, would form the nucleus of the new firearms wing attached to D6 department.

The first battle faced by the new Firearms Wing was not against armed criminality but against one of its fellow departments: Special Branch, who were at that time responsible for protection officers and other armed officers within their department, refused to come under the umbrella, stating that they were a special case and needed their own training.

Special Branch had some powerful sponsors but common sense dictated that it was better to standardize all training, including that of the protection officers of the Special Branch, and in April 1967 they were instructed to surrender all their training to D6 (firearms training branch). The initial hurdle had been crossed and for the first time all the Metropolitan Police firearms training would come under one roof.

CS Gas: The Secret Weapon for Dealing with Armed Besieged Criminals
April 1967

CS gas (also known as tear gas) was named after its American inventors Ben Corson and Roger Stoughton in 1928 and has a long and unpronounceable twenty-four-letter chemical name.

It was seen in the USA as a law enforcement tool in riot and prison control situations and it was also used effectively in clearing tunnels in the Vietnam War in the 1960s.

In 1958, some CS gas grenades had been made available for police use and were held at army barracks in London. In the late sixties, they were introduced as a magic weapon for dealing with armed besieged criminals. Tests were carried out at Porton Down on the gas's effects when used in enclosed spaces. If employed in the right quantity, it was safe to use against humans but it made the environment they were in very uncomfortable as the gas acted as an irritant, attacking the eyes and skin. The Metropolitan Police signed up to its use in certain conditions and decided that the best people to deploy CS gas would be the instructors from the newly formed firearms training wing. So in April 1967, along with their other responsibilities, the firearms wing of D6 began trials to find a suitable CS gas delivery system. D6 eventually selected and purchased two Federal CP1.5-inch-bore gas guns, which could supposedly fire a gas grenade up to a hundred yards. In April 1967, the firearms instructors were put on a call-out system. This was, in fact, the first operational role for the firearms department. They began to develop tactics for the deployment of this gas against armed besieged criminals.

Home Office Authority to Form Training Unit
17 May 1967

In May 1967, D6 Branch received a letter of confirmation from the Secretary of State's office confirming the increase in strength of ten officers to the branch, taking into account its new role as firearms training wing. The ten firearms instructors who had already been recruited and were undergoing training were confirmed in their new roles.

The letter, countersigned by the then Police Commissioner, Sir Joseph Simpson KBE, KPFSM, was the official sanction of the new unit, which, unbeknown to its members at the time, would continue to develop and grow well into the next millennium at least.

The letter increased the fledgling department to a full complement of:

1 chief superintendent
3 superintendents
1 higher executive officer
3 clerical officers
2 inspectors
3 sergeants
5 constables

These ten instructors, now formally posted into D6 firearms wing, joined Chief Superintendent Leslie Williams and Superintendent Joe Lyons, who would head up the new wing. They were Inspectors Bob Gould (chief instructor) and Robert Roy, Sergeants Reg Gash, George Hepworth and Tom Matthews, and Constables Arthur Batten, Chris Freeland, Alec Neville, Ronald Redmond and Kenneth Colby. The other two superintendents returned back to duties within D6 after the department got off the ground, leaving the above-mentioned officers to continue the work they had begun.

It was agreed that the officers would receive an instructors' allowance. The letter also approved the purchase of twenty Lee Enfield .303 rifles, ammunition and holsters for revolvers and pistols already in service with the Metropolitan Police.

D6 Firearms Wing, now working with a small staff from temporary offices at Tintagel House on London's South Bank, sent their ten new personnel on the courses run by the army to become firearms instructors. Much of what they were taught would have to be fine-tuned for police use as it was recognized that some of

The rooms above the garages at the rear of Old Street police station were the first part of the station to be taken over by D6 firearms training branch in 1967. Later these became the force armourer's workshops

the military training and tactics would not transfer over to police usability. However, some of the discipline and strict drills were kept in the curriculum and held to be a positive addition where firearms were concerned.

The officers would also have to attend and pass an instructors' course at the recruitment training centre at Peel House in Westminster. This course had nothing to do with firearms training, but was seen as important when dealing with instructional techniques in the classroom.

When these officers returned they were eager to get started. They consulted with other firearms departments, particularly the FBI training academy in the United States who were most helpful in providing police firearms training course notes and other useful advice. From these and other sources D6 devised a training protocol and produced a manual for the first four-day 'basic defensive weapons courses', the content of which has mostly stood the test of time to this day.

Things were now moving forward fast. The foundations were being laid for a cohesive training unit with standardized weapons, ammunition and tactics.

This imposing Edwardian building, situated north of the City in Old Street, Shoreditch, was purpose-built in 1905 to house the new magistrates' court (on the left) and the new police station (on the right). It remained an operational police station until 1978 when it was given over to the firearms department as a main base. The magistrates' court remained functioning until the late 1990s and the police station served the unit until 2001

These firearms instructors were initially based in offices above the car park in the back of the yard at Old Street police station in Shoreditch until more suitable premises and training sites could be found. In time they would be given the top floor of the police station to use as offices and classrooms, and would eventually take over the whole of the police station.

PC John Ferguson, an early addition to the unit, was appointed as force armourer and moved into the rooms above the garages, which were converted to workshops. Ferguson was responsible for maintaining and servicing all the Met's weaponry.

D6 becomes D11 Firearms Branch
July 1967

In July 1967, under a force restructuring, the firearms training wing of D6 became its own separate department and was given the suffix D11. It lost its 'Civil Defence' and other non-firearms-related training roles and became a dedicated firearms training department.

Additional outdoor training spaces were urgently required from which fieldcraft (tactical awareness training) could be carried out. D11 did not have to look far as the Met had already purchased a disused Second World War prisoner of war camp in 1960 to use for police cadet training. This camp was based away from built-up areas in Epping Forest, Essex. It would be an ideal training camp and would have a long future with the department, fulfilling many of its training needs up until 2003.

Decisions had been taken to increase the number of AFOs (Authorized Firearms Officers) on each division from twenty-four to sixty. Training these hundreds of new AFOs would be the unit's first big test. Outdoor army ranges were used to supplement the few indoor police ranges that were available at that time. The job on the face of it seemed simple – D11 had to run basic firearms courses back to back until they had trained enough new officers and then they had to plan continuation training for every authorized firearms officer within the Met.

Each basic course was to be four days long. It would require two instructors for every ten students. Each student would be taught the safe handling of the weapon, aimed shooting techniques and some sense of direction

Lippitts Hill, a Second World War prisoner of war camp, was put into service for tactical training. Its location was ideal for firearms training and students spent time containing buildings (a tactic whereby armed officers would surround a building thus preventing the escape or break out of the suspect), and practising the 'call out' of armed suspects (whereby an officer would talk the suspect out from the building in a controlled and assertive manner). The site was eventually taken over by D11 and became a dedicated firearms training centre

(combat) shooting along with some basic tactics, which included the use of cover, building containment, taking the surrender of armed suspects, how to conduct slow armed searches of buildings and, of course, open-country searching (a throwback to the Harry Roberts manhunt). Throughout 1967 this small group of firearms instructors ran a huge number of courses teaching these new skills and setting a standard of excellence, which the department has tried to maintain ever since.

It wasn't long before the instructors were developing their own methods of instruction and improving on the earlier techniques; one of these was the development of the 'isosceles position' or stance (where both arms would be pushed forward, forming the sides of a triangle with the chest forming the base). This method was adopted for most of the pistol-shooting instruction, going away from single-handed aimed shooting, which had previously formed the main basis of training.

Development of Weapons and Training: Early D11
1967

Along with the new courses it also became desirable to standardize the weaponry and ammunition used throughout the Metropolitan Police. The firearms department reassessed which weapons best suited its needs. For routine use, divisional officers would still carry the Webley & Scott .380 Mark IV revolver, which had been issued to officers on the divisions of the Metropolitan Police area in 1956 and would see good service up until 1974, when it was superseded by the Smith & Wesson .38 Special model 10 revolver. However, other pistols were also introduced, such as the .38 Enfield No.2 revolver, which was used alongside the Webley from the later part of 1967.

Protection officers and those posted to fixed armed posts around London would continue using the 9 mm Walther PP semi-automatic pistol which had been in use with the police since 1960. This was reassessed after the Princess Anne kidnap incident in 1974, when it was replaced by the Smith & Wesson .38 Special model 36 revolver (which chambered five rounds) and was considered at the time to be more reliable than the Walther for protection officers and detectives (its two-inch barrel made it less conspicuous).

For training purposes D11 purchased High Standard .22 semi-automatic pistols to be used on basic firearms courses. The new instructors were also authorized to hire twenty war surplus Lee Enfield No.4 .303 rifles with iron sights. These were used by divisional rifle officers and would remain in service until 1972 when they were replaced by the Enfield L42A1 7.62 rifle, equipped with telescopic sights.

In order to test and assess whether the student had understood and learnt from the four-day basic firearms course, the student had

Above left: Drawing the Walther from the covert shoulder holster. Above middle: Drawing the Webley revolver from its police-issue canvas holster. These were standard military issue holsters painted black. Above right: Demonstrating an aimed shoot using the sitting, supported firing position

Above left: Loading the Lee Enfield No.4 rifle whilst in the prone position. Above: Demonstrating the use of cover, in this case a concrete bollard. Left: Another photo, this time depicting an officer using a motor vehicle as cover (the engine block or the wheels were his best bet)

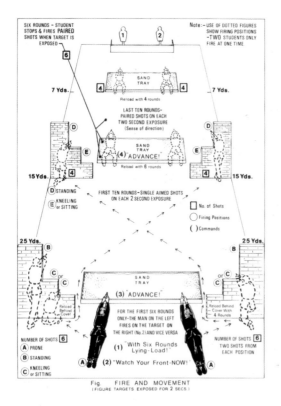

A diagram of a typical cover and movement exercise used for students on a firearms refresher

to pass a final shoot under strict scrutiny. Not only did they need to score the required amount of hits on the target, fired from a variety of positions (some in the aim and some in 'sense of direction' or combat stance), but they also had to display good weapons handling skills and weapon safety.

The instructors took great pride in their work, which has continued to this day with the pass rates for this course averaging out at ninety-two per cent.

Firearms Refresher Training

In order to maintain the balance of AFOs within the Met in the late 1960s the service needed to train between 500 and 700 new officers per year. Following basic training, it then had to run up to 10,000 half-day refresher courses for those AFOs to maintain their standard.

Some of the refresher training included cover and movement and tactical inputs. Officers would move down the range, using the points of cover, and fire whenever the targets turned to face them. This would be done in pairs, with one officer covering the target area while the other moved forward to the next piece of cover; the roles would then be reversed.

The tactical training would be alternated with a classification shoot. The officer's attendance every three months would be noted on their firearms record, along with a pass or fail. The refresher training was both challenging and thought-provoking in that it trained the officers not only to consider their surroundings and points of cover on a tactical level but also to consider the consequences of their actions in relation to the law.

Shoot-no-Shoot

Since 1968, the cutting edge of firearms training was to show the student a series of slides on a screen. The scenarios depicted on the slides would be judgemental, i.e. the student would have to decide under the pressure of an instructor shouting at him whether to shoot or not to shoot.

The variables they would have to take into account were the level of threat from the suspect, any innocent people nearby and, of course, the backdrop (meaning the line of fire behind the suspect where there might be the potential for hitting a member of the public or a fellow officer). Once they had decided whether or not to shoot, they would face a judgement on their actions. These were a long way from video games and paintballing, but this training did give the officer a little insight into the pressures they could face out on the streets.

Two examples of 'shoot-no-shoot' scenarios on slides, showing various armed threats. The student would have to take in all the details in a short space of time before deciding whether or not to shoot

In the years to come, this training would develop with the use of video, allowing the student to fire at suspects moving across a screen with a real firearm. The noise of the discharge would stop the video and the student's accuracy could be checked with a backlight illuminating the area where the round had penetrated.

Tactical Advisers' Role for D11
9 May 1969

D11 were going from strength to strength and towards the end of the decade had been called out on many occasions to advise at armed incidents and sieges.

It seemed a natural development for this tactical advisers' role to become official and so along with the CS gas role given to D11 in 1967 they could now be called out to give advice to senior officers when called upon.

A 'Police Order' (a force-wide memorandum) was issued, stating that: 'Occasions may arise when the services of a specially qualified officer are desirable. In such circumstances, the officer in command may ask for the assistance of one or more of the firearms instructors who is experienced in the use of all types of weapons'.

This was a small development, but one that opened up many doors and would eventually lead to them having a full operational role. The decade had ended on a positive note for this fledgling department, which was looking forward to meeting the 1970s head-on.

PART TWO:
Developing the Role — DII in the 1970s

As the new decade began, D11 were making a good name for themselves in domestic and international firearms training circles. They also managed to provide a huge volume of courses to maintain the increased level of training for firearms officers within the Met.

The biggest challenge facing the department was educating the senior management at divisional police stations about allowing officers to draw firearms when they were required. The unarmed stereotype image of a 'bobby on the beat', made famous by Jack Warner in the TV series *Dixon of Dock Green*, which ran from 1955–1976, still existed. Some middle and senior management frequently refused reasoned requests to arm officers, with some even making demands for the officers to carry their weapons unloaded.

Armed robberies were on the increase as the economy grew. Larger sums of money were being moved around, especially near Christmas with the savings clubs, several of which were robbed at gunpoint, causing some divisions to put out armed police cars in an attempt to stop this trend. This would have a knock-on effect on training: there grew a need to develop tactics for dealing with armed suspects in vehicles and to train armed officers on how to deploy safely from their vehicles.

The 1970s would be a challenging decade for D11 and would see them taking a full-time operational role as terrorism reached out towards London, bringing death and destruction to its streets. The unit would have to move with the times if it was to become successful in helping the Met fight armed crime and terrorism.

Advanced Firearms Training for D11 Instructors
1970

During 1970, D11 sent its instructors on SAS advanced pistol courses at Hereford to learn new skills and techniques. Other instructors were sent to the FBI training academy in Virginia for the same purpose. A rifle instructor was also sent to the military sniper course at the Skill-at-Arms Division School of Infantry. It was in the interests of D11 to have its staff learn from as many different centres of excellence as possible so that they could then amalgamate the best practices into their own training.

The First Overseas Secondment
Malawi, September 1970

D11's reputation was already spreading to faraway places and, in 1970, the first overseas secondment came in the form of a request by the Malawian government to send an instructor to train the royal bodyguards of President Dr Hastings Kamuzu Banda.

Sergeant Bob Wells was chosen for this task and dispatched to Africa. He succeeded in training eighty-five officers of the Malawian police in this and other roles. Sergeant Wells later rose to the rank of Chief Superintendent in charge of D11.

First Operational Deployment of CS Gas by D11
Cricklewood, North-west London, 29 July 1971

On 29 July 1971, local police were called to an address in Olive Road, Cricklewood, in northwest London. The occupants, Mr and Mrs McKenzie, had been stabbed to death. Police also found the body of their son-in law, Richard Simms, in the back garden. Their daughter,

Officers deployed in pairs; the officer to the right is holding the Webley 37 mm gas gun and his back-up officer has a .38 Smith & Wesson model 28 revolver

Candy, although stabbed and seriously injured, had escaped with her child.

The multiple-murderer was the McKenzie's son, Michael, who, armed with two carving knives, had barricaded himself in an upstairs room. He was said to be 'demented and berserk'.

Authority was granted by the deputy assistant commissioner of operations for CS gas to be made available at the siege. Two D11 instructors were called out and attended the scene. Michael was barricaded in the rear bedroom of the small terraced house. The officer in charge directed the D11 men to fire a CS gas round through the rear window of the bedroom but they advised that it would be better fired down into the room from the loft space. This was agreed and in due course, after all those nearby had been given respirators to wear, the gas was fired through the ceiling into the room. Michael McKenzie, in a blind panic, smashed the window, causing the uniformed officers on the landing to believe that he was attempting to escape. They began to smash their way in (against the advice of the D11 instructors).

McKenzie, who had tied two knives to his wrists with tea towels, ran at the officers, one of whom grabbed the blades with his bare hands. Both McKenzie and the injured officer pitched down the stairs. Meanwhile, a fire, caused by the discharge of the gas round, had started in the bedroom. One of the D11 officers acted quickly, running to extinguish the flames with a bucket of water.

During the struggle to subdue the knifeman, several officers had lost their respirators and were suffering the effects of the gas. The suspect was eventually placed in a straitjacket and taken away. The injured officer was seen by a doctor and made a good recovery.

The two officers who had deployed the gas were summoned back to the scene the very next day and ordered to clean up the house, as they had fired the CS gas and were responsible for its removal. They spent two days scrubbing the soft furnishings and carpets trying to get rid of the CS, which, if left, could have an adverse effect (in the form of streaming eyes, excessive nasal discharge, coughing, burning sensations and even breathing difficulties) on anyone entering the premises and disturbing the environment for months to come.

Browning Hi Power 9 mm
semi-automatic pistol

Browning 'Hi Power' 9 mm Semi-automatic Pistol
July 1971

D11 had been interested in assessing a new self-loading pistol and tried out the Browning Hi Power 9 mm. It was taken into service initially for officers escorting high-risk convoys, to give them added firepower. It would not be for another five years that it would become the standard sidearm for D11 officers.

Shotguns for CS Gas Delivery
March 1972

In March 1972, still trying to find the perfect delivery system for CS gas, D11 looked at and purchased two new types of shotgun. Shotguns were showing themselves to be far more versatile than gas guns. The many variants of shotgun cartridges allowed for smaller doses of CS gas to be fired using rounds called 'ferrets'. If necessary, multiple rounds could be fired. The models purchased were the Savage 12-bore pump-action shotgun and the Viking double-barrelled 12-bore shotgun.

Lee Enfield L42A1 Sniper Rifle
October 1972

The Second World War Lee Enfield .303 rifles had been used by the department from 1966 but were no longer fit for purpose. They were replaced by a weapon loaned by the MoD until a more suitable variant could be found. This weapon was the 7.62 Lee Enfield L42A1 sniper rifle, complete with military-grade telescopic sights. The sights alone cost the department £310 per year to hire from the MoD.

Training began immediately to update the rifle-trained officers (in the 1970s they were

The Viking double-barrelled 12-bore shotgun.
D11 purchased two of these for use in deploying
CS gas cartridge 'ferrets'

The firing points at the Gravesend range, marked out at 100 m intervals

known as 'riflemen' but in more modern times their title has changed to 'rifle officer') within the force on this new weapon. At this time rifle-trained officers were not posted into the firearms department but were brought in when required. For the main, they worked in uniform roles in the police districts and divisions. (The Met Police area of London was divided up into policing districts, and each district into divisions and sub-divisions. It was important then as it is now to spread resources throughout the police districts to get an even spread.)

There was a great need for more rifle-trained officers; they were vital for security at Heathrow Airport in case of hijackings. During 1970 there were over ninety hijackings world-wide and the fear of it happening in London was immense.

D11 advertised for thirty divisional officers to become rifle officers and they had over 900 applicants. There were marathon paper sifts and assessments before they managed to whittle it down to the final thirty.

Much of the rifle training was carried out at the MoD rifle ranges at Milton, near Gravesend in Kent. Coaches and buses would run students there from Old Street. It would be a long day

on the windswept ranges of Kent next to the River Thames.

As D11 continued with its training requirements it kept a weather eye on world events. 1972 had seen an increase in terrorist activity – not only hijackings but other atrocities such as at the Munich Olympics where the Black September Group had massacred eleven members of the Israeli team and shot dead a German police officer.

Great Britain had also seen an increase in terrorist activity, including IRA bombings and shootings of military and civilian targets. Senior members of the police were now looking at how they could react to these threats. It would not be long before other more radical changes would need to be made to the Met's firearms response and D11 were well placed to provide for these needs.

Armed Officer Shoots Two Bank Robbers
27 December 1972

PC Slimon, an officer based at Kensington on uniformed protection duties, was returning to his post at around 11.30 a.m. when he came across an armed robbery at a bank in Kensington High Street. Drawing his .38 Webley revolver from his greatcoat pocket, he entered the bank, confronting the armed gang. He was blasted by one robber with a shotgun but managed to shoot his attacker before he fell wounded on the pavement outside the bank. As the gang fled he shot another robber who pointed a gun at him. Unbeknown to police at the time, a Bulgarian tourist had also been wounded during the shoot-out by a round fired by one of the robbers.

The gang reached their stolen getaway vehicle and then switched to a changeover vehicle where they abandoned one of their wounded colleagues in the road. Two hours later, a second robber (33-year-old Robert Hart, who was shot by Slimon in the bank) was found in the seat of a stolen dune buggy on the roof of a multi-storey car park. He had bled to death. A loaded Luger pistol was recovered from his body. The remaining robbers escaped justice for the time being but, as the old police saying goes, 'they would come again'. (One of the surviving robbers was strongly suspected to be Anthony Baldessare, but more about him later.)

The wounded tourist and PC Slimon made full recoveries; Peter Slimon was awarded the George Medal for his bravery. This incident proved beyond doubt that the training given by D11 was effective – the officer had defended himself by shooting accurately and lived to tell the tale.

India House Incident, Indian High Commission, Aldwych
20 February 1973

At 9.30 a.m. three young Pakistani men (Basharat Hussain and Mohammed Hanif Hussain were aged 19 and their colleague, Dalmamar Khan, was aged just 15) forced their way into the Indian High Commission in Aldwych, London.

The motive for the attack appeared to be terrorism, stemming from the recent war between India and Pakistan in 1971 – India supposedly still held thousands of prisoners from that conflict. One of the intentions of the gang was to demand the release of these prisoners and force a meeting with the Indian Prime Minister Indira Ghandi.

The three assailants were all wearing stocking masks and were armed with a selection of weapons, which included sheath knives, a sword and two revolvers. They also had a spray containing nitric acid. They managed to secure nine hostages, who were bound, with some being randomly assaulted. One received two sword wounds to the head, fracturing his skull.

The men proceeded to smash a window and show off their hostages to horrified passers-by, threatening to kill them. Local police retreated after guns were pointed at them.

Things took a dangerous turn for the worse when one hostage, fearing for his life, pitched himself through a plate glass window to make his escape. He told police that there were armed men inside the building. The officers were from 4 Unit, SPG (Special Patrol Group), and two of them were armed with revolvers. Fearing for the safety of the other hostages they entered the building through a side door and along with two unarmed colleagues made their way down a passage. They opened a door into the foyer where they saw a commotion: one armed suspect was hiding behind a pillar while another, armed with a gun, ran towards the group of hostages, shouting that he would kill them all. An SPG officer shot him and he fell to the ground. The second armed officer moved around the side of the pillar and shouted at the second armed suspect to put his gun down. Instead, he pointed it at the officers who shot him dead.

Meanwhile, other officers arrived and overpowered the third and final suspect who was armed with a sword. It wasn't until they removed his stocking mask that they saw he was so young. Dalmamar Khan, the 15-year-old, was led away (he would later receive a sentence of three months in a youth detention centre) and the ordeal of the remaining hostages was over.

It was later found that the two guns were not real and were in fact pressed metal toy guns. Although the SPG officers had genuinely believed that they were in imminent threat of being shot they would still have to answer to the press and the general public in the coming days. The day after the incident, the *Daily Telegraph* led with a headline 'The Toy Gun Terrorists' and although the press were relatively balanced in their reporting, the coverage raised questions from police critics who asked why the police could not be taught to shoot to wound. Others suggested that the police should carry guns that fired rubber bullets.

Whilst suggestions of shooting to wound and using rubber bullets could be dismissed in most firearms incidents as being totally impractical owing to the unpredictable nature of the incidents, the need for a viable 'less lethal' (i.e. non-fatal) option was a real one. Unfortunately, it would be thirty years until a suitable alternative became available with the advent of the 'Taser' stun gun.

D11 Try Out Sterling Sub-machine Gun
April 1973

At the end of April 1973, D11 looked into purchasing a carbine to fill the gap between the pistol and the rifle. The shotgun, which had fulfilled this role, was considered in some circumstances to be indiscriminate, so an alternative was sought. The British army used the 9 mm Sterling sub-machine gun, so D11 chose to purchase a variant of this on a trial basis.

They chose the L34A1, a suppressed (silenced) version for no other reason than that it could be used in training with less hearing protection. Although this weapon was used on live operations it was not considered to be ideal, but D11 would have to wait until 1977 before a more suitable carbine would come into use in the form of the Heckler & Koch MP5.

D11 Take Delivery of the 'Enfield Enforcer' Rifle
20 December 1973

After months of waiting, the first of the new Enfield 7.62 rifles arrived. They would replace all other D11 rifles, all of which had originated from converted World War Two stock.

These new rifles were improved and modified from the Enfield L39A1s. Enfield produced these rifles at the Royal Small Arms Factory at Enfield. The new rifle gained the name the 'Enfield Enforcer' and very soon secured a good reputation as an accurate and reliable rifle, which would see many long years of service within the department.

D11 rifle instructor PC Nick Carter with the Enfield Enforcer 7.62 rifle, fitted with Pecar telescope for daylight use

Events of 1974

Whilst D11 were developing their weapons, training and tactics to keep up with events on the world stage, the UK was in the grip of yet another violent IRA campaign continuing from the bombings and atrocities of the previous year. These would have a knock-on effect within D11, which was only a year away from getting its fully operational role. Amidst these events, the Queen opened the new Metropolitan Police training college at Hendon in north-west London, known as the Peel Centre (named after the first commissioner of police). This replaced the old college in Westminster, which had been known as Peel House.

Another big change for the Met was the introduction of the 'Diplomatic Protection Group' known as the DPG, whose role would be to provide twenty-four-hour protection for all diplomatic premises in the capital. This was partly as a result of the incident the year before at the Indian High Commission.

The Attempted Kidnapping of Princess Anne
The Mall, 20 March 1974

At 7.55 p.m. on Wednesday 20 March 1974, HRH Princess Anne, her husband Captain Mark Phillips, and her lady in waiting Miss Brassey, were being driven along The Mall towards Buckingham Palace.

As their vehicle neared the junction with Marlborough Road, a white Ford Escort over-took the Rolls-Royce and swerved violently across its path. The Escort driver, Ian Ball, got out and approached the princess, who was sitting in the offside of the vehicle. Her personal protection officer, Inspector Jim Beaton (sitting in the front passenger seat) had to run around the rear of the vehicle to

get to Ball and, thinking he was just an angry motorist, did not draw his pistol.

Ball was by now opening the door to get to the princess and threatening the occupants of the car with a .38 five-shot Astra revolver. He had already told the driver not to move. He had his back to Beaton but, as Beaton approached, he turned and shot him in the shoulder. Although severely wounded, Beaton drew his 9 mm Walther PP and fired one shot before his gun jammed, most probably owing to the expended cartridge failing to eject properly. The bullet missed Ball but ended up embedded in the 'dickie seat' (a fold-down occasional seat) in front of the princess. This had the effect of distracting Ball and allowing the princess and Captain Phillips to pull the door shut, while Beaton withdrew behind the Rolls-Royce to clear his stoppage. Ball, intent on kidnapping the princess, once again tried to open the car door. He pointed his gun at her and said 'Please get out of the car.' The princess told him in no uncertain terms to go away. Ball, then seeing Beaton crouched down by the back of the car, moved towards him and pointed his revolver directly at his head, telling him to drop his gun. The pistol was still jammed and of no use and so Beaton placed the weapon on the ground and moved around to the other side of the vehicle. Miss Brassey had managed to leave the vehicle and Beaton climbed in. Ball renewed his attempts to open the car door by the princess, which Captain Phillips was now holding firmly shut.

Ball drew a second handgun (a .22 Astra revolver which chambered nine-rounds) and threatened to shoot the princess unless the door was opened. Beaton threw himself across the princess, placing his hand up to the window in front of Ball's pistol. Ball fired twice; the window shattered and although one bullet missed, the second lodged in Beaton's hand. Beaton kicked the door against Ball and tried

The aftermath: the chauffer-driven Rolls-Royce in which HRH Princess Anne was travelling along The Mall near Buckingham Palace, seen here blocked in by Balls' white Ford Escort, itself blocked by Martin's Jaguar

to get out to tackle him but Ball shot him in the stomach. The bullet passed through his intestines and lodged in his pelvis. Beaton staggered in the road and collapsed on the pavement by a tree; he would play no further part in the story.

The chauffeur, Mr Callender, now attempted to grab hold of Ball but he too was shot, the bullet entering his chest. A passer-by, journalist John McConnell, seeing what was happening, got out of his taxi and intervened, saying to Ball, 'Give me the gun old chap, don't shoot, these people are friends of mine', but Ball shot him too. The bullet entered his chest, narrowly missing his vital organs. He collapsed on the pavement, wounded.

Hearing the commotion, PC Michael Hills, who was on foot patrol in The Mall, ran to the scene. As Hills arrived he grabbed Ball by the arm and was immediately shot in the stomach. He collapsed with a bullet lodged in his liver,

but still managed to call for urgent assistance. Ball now had the door open.

A passing driver, Glenmore Martin, pulled his Jaguar across the front of Ball's Escort and got out to help, but after being threatened backed off and helped staunch the wound to PC Hills.

As Ball was attempting to drag the princess from the car, a taxi passenger named Ronald Russell went over and punched Ball in the back of the head. Ball turned and fired at Russell but missed. Russell backed off and attempted to get PC Hill's truncheon.

By now Ball had nearly succeeded in getting the princess out of the car but Captain Phillips managed to drag her back in. The Princess tried to crawl across and get out the other side of the car but Ball ran around to stop her. Russell, seeing this, ran back and again punched Ball. The pair began to struggle.

Almost as quickly as it had started, the incident ended; Ball became aware of police with sirens and blue lights arriving. He ran off, pursued by newly arrived Acting Detective Constable Peter Edmunds, who brought him down with a rugby tackle.

When the police searched Ball, they found a ransom note demanding £3 million. The terms for the release of the princess included a free pardon for any crimes Ball committed as a result of the kidnapping. In addition, he had on his person four pairs of handcuffs, two Spanish Astra pistols (identical but in two different calibres, .38 and .22) with plenty of spare ammunition for both. He had clearly been a man on a mission.

Incidentally, one of the bullets fired by Ball was recovered from the arm-rest of the Rolls-Royce, very close to the princess. She had clearly had a very narrow escape; a further round was recovered from the heel of one of the taxi-driver's shoes. In all, Ball had fired twelve times.

In May that year, Ball pleaded guilty at the Old Bailey to attempted murder, attempted kidnapping and wounding with intent. He was detained under the provisions of the Mental Health Act of 1959. When asked why he shot the officer, Ball said, 'He kept coming at me'. Indeed, the officer had been a very brave man.

Inspector Jim Beaton recovered from his wounds and was awarded the George Cross. Russell and Hills both received the George Medal while McConnell and Calendar (the royal chauffeur) along with PC Edmunds (who grappled Hill to the ground) received the Queen's Gallantry Medal.

Inspector Beaton's jammed Walther pistol caused so much concern amongst the firearms community that all police Walther pistols were replaced the following year with the Smith & Wesson model 36 revolver. The attempted kidnapping was also the catalyst for the implementation of a dedicated protection officers (or bodyguards) course, run by D11.

Stephen Smith

The Smith & Wesson model 10 revolver, in .38 calibre. This pistol chambered six rounds and was reliable and accurate. The smaller model 36 revolver, also in .38 calibre, was similar, but chambered only five rounds. Its two-inch barrel made it more concealable but less accurate

Met Police Adopt the Smith & Wesson .38 Special Models 10 and 36
October 1974

In October 1974, the Met police adopted the Smith & Wesson .38 special revolver models 10 and 36; these would replace all other police service revolvers in use at that time. It was a big shake-up and would standardize the weaponry and ammunition used by the Met across the board.

D11 would be responsible for training officers in their use and maintaining these weapons.

D11 Firearms Instructors Demonstrate Search and Containment
Late 1974

The training photos overleaf were taken some time in late 1974. The officers are armed with Smith & Wesson model 10 revolvers and some are wearing the green overt body armour as used in Northern Ireland at that time, which was part of the D11 standard equipment. The armour was constructed with heavy steel plates woven into the fabric. It would not be long before these officers would be called upon to form firearms teams and do this for real.

D11 instructors demonstrating containment of armed suspects using the Savage pump-action shotgun, which came into service with the branch in November 1972

Instructors demonstrate searching techniques. One searching officer opens the door whilst his two colleagues cover the danger points; this was bread and butter training for all AFOs

D11 instructors demonstrating urban search and containment tactics and taking the surrender of armed suspects

The Murder of PC Stephen Tibble QPM
26 February 1975

Local officers were mounting a plain-clothes, anti-burglary operation in Hammersmith, west London, when their attention was drawn to a suspect who had just left an address in Fairholme Road. This man was later identified as Liam Quinn, who was a US citizen from an Irish Republican family and who was, in fact, a member of the IRA, working as part of an Active Service Unit based on the UK mainland. When stopped, Quinn ran from the police, who gave chase.

It just so happened that off-duty PC Stephen Tibble, a 21-year-old officer of just six months service on the force, was riding past on his 175cc Honda motorcycle when he saw the chase. He stopped his bike in front of the suspect, got off and attempted to block Quinn's path. Quinn drew a revolver and shot Tibble twice in the chest. Although the other officers bravely pursued Quinn, he managed to make good his escape into the Tube system at Barons Court.

Stephen Tibble died of his wounds in hospital and a massive police manhunt began for his killer. The house Quinn had come from that day was full of bomb-making equipment, including high explosives and an automatic pistol with ammunition. Evidence found at the house linked it to an IRA Active Service Unit, which had already carried out several attacks on London and around the country. The hunt was now on to catch the other members of the ASU.

Stephen Tibble was posthumously awarded the Queen's Police Medal for gallantry, however, his family, including his young wife, would have to wait thirteen years before his killer was brought to justice.

Quinn had fled to Dublin where he was later arrested for a minor offence. Because of complications, the British police could not extradite him. Upon his release he returned to San Francisco where in 1981 the FBI arrested him. After an extradition process lasting seven years he was finally returned to the UK.

In 1988, Quinn was convicted of PC Tibble's murder and sentenced to life imprisonment with a recommendation that he serve thirty years. He was released in April 1999 under the terms of the Good Friday Agreement.

Spaghetti House Siege
28 September–4 October 1975

The peace in Knightsbridge was shattered on 28 September 1975 when three heavily armed gunmen forced their way into the Spaghetti House restaurant at No. 77 Knightsbridge, just as the staff had gathered the week's takings of £13,000.

Realizing they were being robbed, one of the managers hid the takings under a table on the restaurant floor. Eight Italian staff were led down into a small basement storeroom at gunpoint. Unbeknown to the gang a ninth member of staff had escaped as they were being moved and alerted the police. The premises were quickly surrounded by police, some of whom were armed.

A D11 firearms team was scrambled from their base at Old Street and deployed quickly to

Front aspect of the Spaghetti House restaurant, situated in busy Knightsbridge

the scene. This was the D11's first major deployment in a high-profile incident.

The gang were contained in the basement storeroom by the armed D11 officers who worked long hours in close containment positions. Tony Grey, an armed officer from the Special Patrol Group who was sent on containment at the rear of the restaurant later commented, 'I was posted with my partner into an alley behind the restaurant, and while I was standing there I could hear these voices; they were clearly coming from a grille in the wall, from an extractor fan which led into the store room, so I used my radio to suggest if we brought listening devices round it would give us an advantage.' The devices were set up and helped greatly as the siege developed. There was always the possibility of an attempted breakout by the gang whose mental state was monitored by trained personnel working closely with the hostage negotiators.

The gang's leader, Franklin Davies, claimed he was a high-ranking officer in the Black Liberation Front and assured negotiators that the gang were militants who would not be taken alive. These claims, although initially taken seriously, were downgraded as the siege developed and it became possible to listen in on the gang's conversations.

The press camped outside the restaurant and very soon every detail of the siege was reported to the nation. After the first day, one of the hostages became ill, and the negotiators were able to arrange for his release. Throughout the siege, police enjoyed a makeshift canteen set up inside the restaurant. Although their food needs were taken care of, the D11 officers were still required to wait patiently as the days passed by. They were in a constant weapons-ready state behind their improvised barricades, waiting for the suspects to surrender or attempt a breakout. The other option, never far from their minds, was the possibility of performing a hostage rescue should any of the hostages' lives be threatened. To this end, explosives had been rigged on the hinges of the cellar doors to aid a quick entry.

The highs and lows of the negotiations, brought on by the sudden changes in the mood of the gang, gave rise to many false alarms, and after six days many thought it would never end. Meanwhile, in the small storeroom that was no larger than the average person's living room, the atmosphere was becoming tense. The heat and unsanitary conditions were causing tempers to fray. Worries were swept aside when, at 3.55 a.m. on the morning of the sixth day, the remaining hostages were released. This came about after the police informed the gang that the man who set up the robbery had sold their identities to the press. Although this was not correct it did the trick. Angry at the apparent betrayal, Franklin Davies gave an abrupt announcement through the door, shouting, 'The hostages are coming out.' There followed a tense time as the hostages were walked and directed in a controlled manner until they were out of danger and in the safe custody of police and ambulance staff.

The gang, after the hostages have left, discuss what to do. This was also a tense time. Moments later, Davies, the one sitting down, shot himself, (non-fatally) probably by accident

D11 officers prepare to take the surrender of the gang who had held their hostages for six days in the tiny cellar. The officer on the left is holding a Savage pump-action shotgun

After the hostages had been moved to safety, the suspects were told to unload their weapons and place them outside the door. They pushed an antique shotgun and a vintage Steyr 9 mm automatic pistol out of the room and then after some talk of a problem with another of the guns, a shot was heard. A voice from inside the room claimed that Davies had shot himself and needed a doctor.

No doctor would be sent to the room, as this could well have been a final ploy by the gang in an effort to escape. More commands were given for the suspects to come out slowly one at a time and after a very short time, Wesley Dick and Anthony Monroe (the two unwounded suspects) emerged. They were made to lie face down on the floor and were handcuffed by the arrest team under the watchful eyes and guns of the D11 officers.

Davies had managed to shoot himself in the stomach with an antique .22 rim-fire pistol. His wound was non-fatal and was probably an accident, which occurred whilst he was attempting to unload the weapon. His gun was old and dangerous in untrained hands.

When the able-bodied suspects were safely in custody, D11 officers entered the storeroom and retrieved the firearms. Davies also had a small 8 mm automatic pistol. He was removed to hospital.

There was a general sense of relief that the hostages had all been recovered unharmed and that the gang was in custody. It had been played by the book and was seen as a great success. With the siege finally over, the Prime Minister, Harold Wilson, sent a telegram congratulating the commissioner, Sir Robert Mark, on his handling of the six-day siege, the first of its kind in Britain. The commissioner also thanked the hostages and their relatives for their patience and fortitude, and commended the press for their careful reporting of the situation – a situation that would not always repeat itself in the following decades.

In June 1976, the trial opened in an uproar at the Old Bailey when the three defendants refused to recognize the authority of the court and turned their backs on the judge. They were sent back to their cells for the duration of proceedings. The trial continued in their absence. The gang were tried for attempted robbery, having firearms with the intent to rob and imprisoning eight hostages. Davies received a sentence of twenty-one years, Anthony

Above left: An officer waits behind a make-shift barricade. He is armed with a Sterling sub-machine gun. Above: Wesley Dick emerges from the cellar door under the glare of the flood-lights

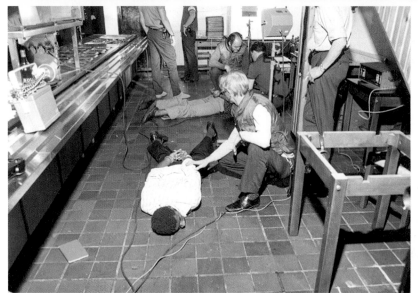

The arrest team handcuff the two suspects, Dick and Monroe, under the watchful eyes of the D11 marksman

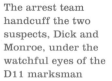

Two pistols used by Franklin Davies during the siege, recovered from the storeroom at Spaghetti House. Left: the antique .22 rim-fire revolver with folding trigger, with which Davis shot himself, seemingly by accident. Right: a Rhöner Sportwaffen SM10 8 mm automatic pistol

Monroe received seventeen and Wesley Dick eighteen years. Lillo Termine, who admitted supplying the information to the gang, received six years and Samuel Addison, who drove the getaway car, was sentenced after a re-trial that November to eleven years imprisonment.

This had been D11's first high-profile operation in the full glare of the press, who had seen the unit at work, and were quick to name them in their headlines: 'The Elite Police Firearms Unit!'

Interestingly, this was also the first incident where hi-tech listening devices, cameras and even psychiatric assessments were used to monitor the suspects and their mental state. It was a good rehearsal for the work to come in the not-too-distant future, as we shall see.

Anti-Terrorist Role for D11 Agreed by the Home Office
26 November 1975

The tragic death of PC Stephen Tibble earlier in the year led to huge changes within the D11 firearms unit. Following the public outcry about his murder and the general feeling of helplessness around catching those responsible, both for this and other atrocities, the government sought advice on dealing with terrorists and serious instances where armed and dangerous criminals had gone to ground with or without hostages.

It was accepted that the military, in the form of the SAS (Special Air Service), would attend and offer assistance if needed. However, there would always be a delay in their arrival, during which time there was no pre-planned response. So in August 1975 the Home Office agreed to proposals from D11 to form four firearms teams made up of volunteers who would each receive specialist training in CQC (close quarter combat) and other skills needed to fulfil this role.

Below is the text of the letter sent from the Home Office to Assistant Commissioner H.J.E. Hunt OBE on the 26 November 1975.

I am sorry to have taken so long to give you a formal response to your proposal for the formation of a specialist Anti-Terrorist branch comprising instructors from D11. The Home Secretary welcomes this proposal and is glad to approve it. I think we are all agreed that the Spaghetti House incident confirms the value of having these skilled officers readily available and the arrangements you propose seem a sensible means of achieving this.

I understand that you have it in mind to inform us immediately on any occasion when the unit is called out in response to a terrorist threat. We greatly value the care which is taken to inform us of major incidents, and would naturally attach particular importance to early warning of a terrorist incident, which called for this unit.

The only point on which we are uneasy is the armoured vehicle. We wonder how substantial the practical advantages of such a vehicle would be. Would the armour plating give much protection unless it were so thick as to impair the mobility of the vehicle? The Home Secretary has the impression that you already have a vehicle with some measure of protection, which though disagreeable to ride in, is fairly unobtrusive, and he wonders whether you have something more than this in mind. I am sure you will share our anxiety not to offer an opportunity for unhelpful dramatization, which could risk attracting more of a Northern Ireland image for the Metropolitan Police. If on consideration you are satisfied that a new vehicle is necessary perhaps you would come back to us with more details of what it would look like and how it would be used.

Funding would be made available to purchase specialist weapons for these officers, which included the relatively new MP5 SMG (sub-machine gun) in addition to newer shotguns to supplement the ones the department already used for deploying CS gas. The shopping list grew, with the request for personal body armour, protective clothing and other equipment.

The entire cadre of D11 instructors volunteered for these additional duties and a rigorous training regime ensued, based on the military model for CQC.

The main request was for the purchase of an armoured vehicle – this request, although agreed to, was met with some reservations on the part of the Home Office, who feared it might not meet with public approval and might make the streets of London look like the streets of Belfast.

There was no doubt that the success of the Spaghetti House siege had led to the Home Office feeling more comfortable with its decision to change the department's role to one of dual responsibility, which comprised both training and operations. The new role would mean an increase in staffing numbers and new shift patterns to cover an operational call-out team. These changes could not have come at a better or more fortuitous time. Spaghetti House would soon prove to have been a useful template for another operation that would test the department's efficacy in the extreme.

The Balcombe Street Siege
6–12 December 1975

The collapse of the IRA's 1974–1975 ceasefire triggered a wave of bombings and assassinations by four men who became known as the 'Balcombe Street Gang'. The gang became one of the most prolific IRA ASUs (Active Service Units) to carry out atrocities in mainland UK.

Following the ceasefire, they participated in at least ten murders and twenty bombings, although the total was probably much higher. Their aim was to cause as much fear and carnage as possible. Some of their acts of terror included the Guildford pub bombings in October 1974, in which four soldiers and one

The block of flats in Balcombe Street where the Balcombe Street Gang's reign of terror came to an end. Photo taken in September 2012

Stephen Smith

civilian were killed and 182 others were wounded. This tragedy was made more infamous as a result of a miscarriage of justice, when four other Irish men (who would come to be known as the Guildford Four) were wrongly convicted of the attack.

The Balcombe Street Gang had also been responsible on 7 November 1974 for throwing a bomb through the window of a pub in Woolwich, injuring twenty-eight people. They had carried out a series of other attacks on clubs, hotels, pubs and military establishments throughout London and other parts of the country, which killed and maimed scores of people.

The gang could also turn their hand to assassination if the mood took them – shooting dead author and TV personality Ross McWhirter after he and his brother had posted a reward for any information on the IRA gang.

They even set booby-trap devices, killing explosives expert Captain Roger Goad and cancer expert Professor Gordon Hamilton-Fairley (who was killed when he walked past a car under which a bomb intended for Conservative MP Sir Hugh Fraser was planted as it exploded prematurely). The gang's other methods of terror included 'drive-by' shootings and throwing bombs packed with nails and shrapnel through pub and restaurant windows.

A fifth member of the Balcombe Street Gang, Liam Quinn, was already on the run after the murder of PC Stephen Tibble. But for the four remaining members of the gang their luck was about to run out in a dramatic way. On 6 December 1975, they selected Scott's restaurant in Mount Street, Mayfair, as the target for a drive-by shooting. The gang had already attacked this restaurant earlier on 12 November when a bomb containing ball bearings was thrown through its window, killing one diner and injuring fifteen others. But this time, as the gang cruised past in their stolen

Ford Cortina, they were unaware that a massive police operation designed to catch them was in full swing.

The operation relied on flooding the West End with plain-clothed officers, paying particular attention to locations where the gang had struck before, as they had begun to set a pattern by returning to old targets and this had not gone unnoticed. These tactics paid off. The gang were spotted as they slowed down to pass the restaurant; they opened fire with a Sten gun and pistols. The car details were circulated and, as police converged on the area, two unarmed officers flagged down a taxi and followed the stolen Cortina for several streets. The gang, noticing they were being followed, abandoned their vehicle and made off on foot along Rossmore Road. The two officers followed, ignoring the shots fired at them by the gang. Two SPG (Special Patrol Group) carriers containing several officers, some of whom were armed, pulled up nearby and one cut across the front of the men. An exchange of gunfire took place between the officers and the suspects. No one was hit but several cars were damaged and windscreens were shot out. One suspect abandoned a bag that contained a Sten gun.

This intervention caused the four men to run back the way they had come, towards the two unarmed officers, who took cover in a doorway. As the gang (who were still exchanging shots with police) drew near to the two officers, an unmarked Flying Squad car drove at the men, causing them to scatter. They ran down some steps into Boston Place and then into Balcombe Street where they were momentarily lost.

When the pursuing police arrived outside the five-storey City of Westminster council flats in Balcombe Street, witnesses informed them that the men had entered the block through the basement door below the flats. The police cordoned off the area with dogs and the few armed officers already at the scene, and waited for support.

At 9.25 p.m. a search of the flats began. As police systematically moved through the building, it became apparent that the gang had forced their way into flat 22b Balcombe Street. A middle-aged couple, Post Office worker John Matthews and his wife Sheila, occupied this flat. Sheila had apparently opened her door to see what the commotion was and the gang brandishing firearms had pushed her back into the flat.

The IRA gang now held the two innocent hostages in the lounge of their flat. The police managed to gain entry, and they contained the gang and their unfortunate hostages in that one room, which faced out onto the road at the front of the block. A tense stand-off now existed. Frantic phone calls were made and a hostage negotiator was called out along with D11's relatively new anti-terrorist firearms teams, still basking in the success of the siege at Spaghetti House.

As Saturday rolled into Sunday, the police assets were all in place. D11 officers, armed with pump-action shotguns and Sterling sub-machine guns, maintained a close containment with the intention of keeping the gang bottled up in the lounge of the flat.

D11 had managed to call upon the military skills of some of their personnel in the construction of defensive points and the use of sandbags to fortify a position on the landing (known as 'Fort Sharp End'), which looked into the hallway of the flat through the open front door, with an oblique view of the lounge door. The lounge would be known colloquially as 'the stronghold', meaning a fortified place. During the night, officers had accessed the flat from a scaffold, which had been erected in the rear garden. They entered through a bedroom window taking great care not to make any noise

that would alert the terrorists to their presence. Listening devices were placed on the door of the stronghold, and as an early warning system the police attached string to the door handle. They realized that this could not be seen clearly so, after looking around the flat, they found a model of a witch on a broomstick in the kitchen, which they hung from the string. It was simple but effective – if the witch twitched, it would warn the officers at Fort Sharp End that that the door was being opened.

Divisional rifle officers manned sandbagged observation points at premises across the street, overlooking the distinctive narrow balcony of number 22b. It was here that the negotiating team, including Peter Imbert who was later to become Sir Peter Imbert, Met Police Commissioner, were also based.

During Sunday morning a telephone was lowered onto the balcony, along with a portable toilet, food and water. The negotiations had begun in earnest. The gang, after stating they were members of the IRA, demanded a plane to fly them to Ireland. This request was robustly turned down and a long war of nerves began.

While D11 officers familiarized themselves with the layout of the flats and studied photos of the hostages, the SAS arrived and were shown around. They were still relatively unknown in public circles, although their presence would not have been a surprise to the IRA Active Service Unit under siege in flat 22b.

The siege continued for six long days. One cannot begin to imagine what it must have been like for the Matthews couple, cramped in one room with four desperate men, not knowing how it would all end.

After careful and patient negotiations, on Friday 12 December at 2.12 p.m., Mrs Matthews appeared on the balcony and was directed to safety by D11 officers who were waiting for her at the other end of the balcony, accessed from the adjoining flat. Two hours later, one of the

Mrs Matthews looks back at one of her hooded IRA captors as she moves along the balcony

One hooded IRA gunman looks on as hostage Mr Matthews is released. After a period of time the IRA gang came out one by one

IRA members came out with his hands in the air and was talked at gunpoint along the balcony, using the same route as Mrs Matthews. Then, Mr Matthews and the three remaining IRA men followed one by one, moving tentatively along the narrow balcony where, with the exception of Mr Matthews, they were led into captivity. Hoods covered the heads of the terrorists so that they could not be photographed by the awaiting press as they were led away by police.

The press would not be denied and showed photos of the surrendering terrorists under the guns of two D11 marksmen as they were led away. They feasted on the story and speculated about the new police unit that the *Daily Mail* had christened 'the Blue Berets'.

The four IRA members known now as the Balcombe Street Gang: Martin O'Connell, Eddie Butler, Harry Duggan and Hugh Doherty, all stood trial at the Old Bailey charged with twenty-five counts, including murder, causing explosions with intent to endanger life, possessing firearms with intent to endanger life, assault, unlawfully detaining persons and conspiracy to cause explosions in the United Kingdom.

The stash of weapons recovered both in flat 22b and at other premises used by the gang amounted to a Sten gun, an Armalite rifle, two .30 calibre M1 carbines, three Smith & Wesson .357 magnum revolvers, two Colt revolvers and two other pistols. Tests carried out on these weapons proved that they had been used in murders and shootings around the capital including the murder of Ross McWhirter only nine days before the siege at Balcombe Street began.

Three of the unarmed officers who had initially chased the IRA gang into Balcombe Street (Inspector John Purnell, DI Henry Dowsell and PS Murtagh McVeigh) were awarded the George Medal for their bravery on that day. Mr and Mrs Matthews, who had acted with dignity throughout their ordeal, presented the witch doll, now affectionately known as 'Witchy-Poo', mounted in a case with a personal inscription to D11 as a token of gratitude for their assistance.

Developments in Training and Equipment

After the success of the Spaghetti House and Balcombe Street sieges, D11 continued to take their additional roles and responsibilities seriously and engaged in tactical training for further major firearms operations. However, they were brought back down to earth with

While one officer provides cover another puts his back into pushing them forward. The officer is wearing one of the first police ballistic helmets issued to the department; these were used up until the early 1990s

some less mainstream firearms work, which included having to deal with an escaped bullock that had run amok on the edge of the Epping Forest, injuring a cyclist. The unfortunate animal had to be destroyed to prevent further danger to the public.

Meanwhile, D11's training role continued to increase with the demand from other police agencies who were dealing with sustained terrorist campaigns. During this period, D11 personnel kept a watchful eye on what was happening on the international stage as well as with other police forces in Britain.

D11 Portable Ballistic Shield and Rescue System

1976

In Leicester in 1975, a deranged man had shot, among others, two police officers during a domestic siege. One had been killed instantly and the other was wounded. The emergency services could not retrieve this wounded officer without drawing fire from the gunman, so the injured policewoman had to wait until the siege was concluded before she could be treated for

extensive gunshot wounds.

It was with this incident in mind that the D11 officers came up with the design to build two versatile ballistic shield systems for retrieving wounded or injured persons trapped by hostile fire. They were constructed from welded steel plates capable of stopping penetration from small arms fire. These systems, although heavy and unwieldy, would enable officers to barricade corridors or passageways both inside buildings or out in the open. Small windows of bulletproof glass were included in the shields to provide vision, augmented by hinged openings from which officers could fire if necessary.

The shields were portable, i.e. on wheels, allowing them to be pushed into position or pulled back to enable emergency services to remove a wounded person on a stretcher. The two armoured systems could be enlarged with the addition of side panels, and a trailer was purchased to transport them to armed incidents. This would be towed behind the operational team kit van. The two heavy, thick, steel-plated shields were christened 'Alpha' and 'Omega', with Alpha being the larger of the two. Training in their use was rehearsed and practised and in their time they were considered to be cutting-edge technology, giving the department more tactical options at armed sieges.

Basic Firearms Training: Taking the Surrender
1976

On basic firearms courses, students were put through their paces under the watchful eyes of their D11 instructors. They were required to successfully take the surrender of an armed suspect by talking to them from a position of cover. By giving clear audible commands they would tell the suspect to slowly take their firearm by the barrel and place it on the ground; they would then direct them to step away from the weapon. The suspect would then be talked into a safe location where they could be approached by a colleague whilst the first officer provided firearms cover. The second officer would handcuff the suspect.

It may sound simple but the instructors knew every trick in the book, such as using any opportunity to escape, if they thought they were not being dominated and controlled enough. They were adept at concealing weapons and generally being awkward and obtuse if the student officer's instructions were not clear and concise. However well prepared the student, they would always be left with some valuable learning points after this part of the course.

D11 Hydraulic Door-opening Ram
1977

Police had always had difficulty in gaining access through substantial or heavily fortified doors. In 1977, an experimental piece of equipment came on the market. This was bought into service by D11 and was basically an Acrow-Prop, (an adjustable scaffold pole used to brace walls and ceilings) which, when it was braced against brickwork and hydraulic fluid was manually pumped into it, caused the telescopic arm to extend. This in turn exerted huge poundage of force onto the small surface against which it had been placed. The weaker surface (hopefully the door) would then give way, thus gaining entry for the firearms team into the premises.

D11 officers deploy the ram for tactical training on a door in the basement at Old Street. The ram took some setting up and was renowned for leaking fluid

45

Although it was a noisy and cumbersome piece of equipment, it did the job and eventually led to more effective versions in the following decades, a form of which is still in use today.

D11 Humane Cage
October 1977

Another innovation, developed out of necessity for an ongoing operation, was the D11 Humane Cage. It was the brainchild of a serving D11 instructor and was built with great urgency at one of the Metropolitan Police garages at Merton in Surrey. The following story is typical of the problem-solving that went on within D11 in an effort to overcome difficult situations.

On 24 October 1977 police and bailiffs attended a first floor council flat at Worthington House, Myddleton Passage, Islington, to carry out an eviction of a tenant called Stuart Brickell, following disputes with his landlord over rent. As officers went to the flat, Brickell, a 43-year-old keep-fit fanatic who had armed himself with a stiletto knife, a machete and a cutthroat razor, attacked them. In the following moments, Brickell managed to fracture a superintendent's skull and stab a sergeant in the stomach, also slashing his head. In the ensuing stand-off, Brickell threatened anyone who came near his flat with the same treatment. By 7 p.m. that day, Brickell had barricaded himself in the small bedroom of his flat, where he was now contained.

Although this was not considered to be a firearms situation *per se* as there were no hostages and the suspect had no access to firearms, the local commander asked D11 for help and advice because of the violence shown to his officers. He also wished to discuss the possible use of CS gas. He made sure that it was understood by the officers from D11, that under no circumstances was Brickell to be harmed. He even suggested that they may have to go in unarmed, but this was not an option they would readily agree to.

After the Commander decided against the use of CS gas, one of the men, Sergeant Alex Moir, suggested to the Commander that if they could use some sort of wire mesh cage which could be fed into the room to restrict Brickell's movement, along with using a sort of 'snake stick' device to pin his arm to the wall, they could achieve his arrest without anyone getting hurt. A few hours later, the Commander came back to them saying, 'If you can get down to Merton garage, the technical support staff will make one for you.' The officers drove off to get the ball rolling.

Meanwhile, in the main bedroom, one of the D11 officers discovered that Brickell had constructed some sort of gas bomb in an old trunk, using a plastic bag full of gas with a cigarette lighter attached. The officer had noticed a strong smell of gas coming from the trunk. It was possibly planned as a booby-trap but, thankfully, the gas had mostly escaped and the device did not explode when the trunk was opened. Police now played the waiting game, attempting to negotiate Brickell into surrender without much success. Four days passed by. The window to the bedroom was boarded over to stop Brickell jumping out and attacking people, but there was now the added worry that he might overdose on the tablets he had in his room as his mental state deteriorated.

The wire cage system arrived at the siege in the early hours of 29 October, just after Brickell had attempted to force his way out over the police barricade at the bedroom door. (The officers had managed to force him back into the room.) From that point, for the safety of everyone, the cage was secured across the doorframe, effectively turning his room into a cell.

Those in control were still trying to talk Brickell into surrender, but they were worried he might commit suicide if the police made an aggressive move. It was decided that the cage would only be used as a last resort.

By 2 November, after nine days of confinement in the tiny room, Brickell's health had started to decline. He had refused food and water from day one and those in charge of the siege decided it was time to act to save his life. D11 were given the go-ahead to use the purpose-built humane cage. Later that day the slow process of hooking out any obstructions, such as furniture, began whilst fending Brickell off with poles.

Eventually the room was clear enough to begin feeding in the wire panels. After the first two sections had been pushed forward, Brickell nearly managed to jump over the top with his machete, only just missing the cage inventor's skull. Eventually, after manipulating their man against a wall, officers pinned him there. His arm was forced against the wall and the machete was removed from danger. Brickell was restrained and removed into custody. The local commander was pleased with the service he had received from D11 along with the outcome, and the D11 officers were pleased that they had found yet another tactical option for their growing toolkit.

Brickell was charged with causing grievous bodily harm to two officers and later at the Old Bailey he received a five-year prison sentence.

The Humane Cage was taken to many sieges but never used again. The tactic, however, was developed and was used successfully many times in the form of police riot shields instead of wire mesh panels to pin dangerous suspects against a wall so as to disarm them.

Of course, other less than lethal tactical options now exist in the form of Tasers, but these old methods worked in their day, thanks to the officers thinking outside the box.

Kevlar Body Armour
June 1977

By June 1977 great improvements had been made in the development of the body armour used by both the military and police. Gone were the heavy steel plates, replaced with a relatively new invention: Kevlar. Introduced in 1977, it afforded lighter and in most cases improved ballistic protection.

Drawing of a D11 shotgunner wearing early Kevlar body armour with groin protector. He is carrying a Remington 870 pump-action 12-bore shotgun with folding stock and 7-shot magazine, along with his Browning 9 mm semi-automatic pistol in holster

D11 Get the MP5 1977

Late in 1977 the first of the new 9 mm Heckler & Koch MP5 SMGs arrived with the force armourer at his workshops in the back of Old Street police station. These had been promised when the department received its anti-terrorist role back in 1975.

The Heckler & Koch MP5 SMG, shown here with retractable stock and thirty-round box magazine. This weapon would see more service as a single-shot carbine, both at Heathrow Airport in 1986 and later in 1988 with PT17

For first time in the department's short history it had managed to secure for itself the most up-to date weaponry. It did not know it at the time, but this brand of carbine would come to be the favoured primary weapon of every Special Forces and SWAT unit in the Western world, and would go on to serve the firearms department well for the next four decades. Initially, it was put into service with the fairly new operational teams and taken out occasionally on armed operations and sieges for use as a close containment weapon. It was also used during the protection of high-risk convoys, such as those with high-value loads, or escorting dangerous prisoners to and from court.

In time, the MP5 would be issued in its various forms to other armed departments within the Metropolitan Police, including, in its carbine form Heathrow Airport, the DPG, close protection officers and, later in the 1990s, as the primary weapon of the SO19 Armed Response Vehicle crews. Over time, it would become the weapon used in the majority of police-related shooting incidents and, owing to its accuracy, ease of use and reliability, it became the favoured weapon among nearly all firearms officers.

In April 1977 as well as the MP5 SMG, the D11 instructors also took delivery of the Smith & Wesson .357 magnum Model 28 revolver, which had a larger frame than the now-standard model 10 revolver, used throughout the rest of the force.

The D11 Armoured Land Rover arrives 1979

In the late 1970s the promise of a suitable armoured vehicle for the burgeoning firearms department came to fruition. The earlier concerns voiced in the Home Office report regarding emulating the heavily armed appearance of our troops in Northern Ireland seemed to have been forgotten as the department took delivery of one of the new armoured Land Rovers.

The Land Rover could seat six fully kitted D11 officers; two in the front and four in the rear. It was fitted with all the bells and buttons the instructors of D11 had asked for, including a loud PA (personal address) system with speakers fitted onto the roof for calling on armed suspects to surrender from the protection of the vehicle's thick armour plating. The vehicle also boasted several opening gun-ports, which provided all-round firing positions. The armour would protect against a bomb blast and penetration from up to 7.62 calibre ammunition. The armoured glass in the windscreen and rear door was also designed to stop multiple hits from that same calibre.

A towbar was fitted for use in removing blocking obstacles or vehicles on an approach to an armed incident. It was also effectively used many times by attaching a hook and posting this through the letterbox of a front door. The door could then be dragged from its hinges. The vehicle would also provide the option for retrieving wounded victims under fire by manoeuvring between the armed threat and the wounded victim, who could then be picked up and placed in the back before being transported to safety, thus superseding the earlier cumbersome ballistic shield system.

The new vehicle was well received by the department. It was to see much use over the coming years at all the major sieges and would become a relatively common sight on the streets of London.

D11 Early Abseil Training
1979

The ever-rising height of the capital's skyline increased the already growing need for abseil-trained officers within the set-up of D11. A training programme was commenced in 1979 with the help of Ron Skinner, the head of physical training at Hendon police college. Ropes were set up on the roofs of the buildings and officers began a very basic form of descent. The danger of using an abseil option was driven home when an officer fractured both his legs during this early training.

D11 Arrest IRA Cell: Operation 'Otis', Holland Park
11 December 1979

By December 1979, information had come to light relating to an elaborate plot to spring IRA

Michael J. Waldren

D11 officers take the plunge in this very basic introduction to abseiling at Hendon police college

quartermaster Brian Keenan from Brixton Prison in south London using a helicopter. Keenan had been one of the central organizers of IRA activities during the time that the Balcombe Street Gang were active. He was due to be charged with conspiracy to cause explosions and firearms offences. Anti-Terrorist branch officers had identified his conspirators and the locations they were using as safe houses and were intent on foiling this attempted breakout. Operation 'Otis' was the name given to the co-ordinated raids on addresses around the country, one of which was in London.

At 3.30 a.m. on 11 December, using rifle officers to cover their approach, two D11 firearms teams moved into position in Holland Park, west London. A rapid entry was made into the apartment being used as a safe house and the operation was a complete success. The police arrested not only the three IRA men they had been hoping to find (Robert Storey, Richard Glenholmes and Robert Campbell) but also Gerald Tuite, who was wanted for bombing attacks on London. Among the evidence recovered, which included a map of Brixton prison, they also found two loaded Browning pistols and 196 rounds of ammunition.

Gerald Tuite later escaped from prison before he could face trial (he was re-arrested in 1983 in the Republic of Ireland and was sentenced to ten years imprisonment). Storey was acquitted after a retrial but Glenholmes and Campbell received five years for their part in the escape plot and ten years for firearms offences. Keenan was sentenced to eighteen years imprisonment in 1980 but after his release on parole he became a key player in the peace process.

This was yet another high-profile anti-terrorist operation that D11 had successfully carried, once more improving their standing within the anti-terrorist community.

PART THREE:
Bloodied — D11/PT17
in the 1980s

The 1980s were to be even more challenging for the staff of D11 than the previous decade, and the coming years would see the SAS showcase a hostage rescue operation that D11 could only dream of, for now at least.

The department would continue to develop training and tactics as the demand for armed officers increased once again. They would experience their first hostage rescue operation with the first operational rounds fired. The massive increase of 'cash-in-transit' armed robberies would lead to a spate of shootings including the department's first fatal shooting. They would undergo their first major organizational change in 1987, going from D11 to PT17 (Personnel and Training). They would feel the full force of trial by media as their workload increased and drew the attention of the nation's press.

The Romeo Siege, Tottenham
7 January 1980

The year began with a domestic siege at Greenfield Road in Tottenham, after a 41-year-old Italian waiter, Carmello Pinelle, forced his way into the flat occupied by his ex-girlfriend Georgina Philipides, who lived there with her young son.

Pinelle was hoping to win her back, but just in case this failed he took with him a loaded revolver. As he forced his way through the upstairs window, local police arrived. Pinelle opened fire, firing several rounds but thankfully missing the officers. They contained the house and managed to rescue the child through a window at the rear of the flat.

D11 were called in along with hostage negotiators and other support services. There followed a nine-hour siege, which ended peacefully with two D11 officers entering the flat via ladders and arresting Pinelle. His hostage was unharmed. Pinelle received seven years imprisonment for his crimes (he had previously served eleven years in Naples for murder).

The papers called it the 'Romeo Siege', and the *Daily Express,* having missed the action photo it wanted, decided to tamper with an image to make it more interesting for readers. The game was given away when the officer in

Taking the surrender

Compliant suspects ready to be searched and handcuffed whilst covered by an armed officer

Training photograph illustrating how dangerous it is when approaching a suspect vehicle. An officer should never assume an apparently empty vehicle is clear of armed suspects

the photo noticed that he was not only at the top of the ladder but also standing in the street below. This would not be the only time the press would manipulate photographs of firearms officers to make them look more interesting. In later years an article showed a rifle that had magically appeared in an officer's hands after a shooting incident in Woolwich.

Vehicle Stops and Use of Cover, Lippitts Hill Firearms Training Centre
1980

An important aspect of firearms continuation training was, and still is, to instruct officers on how to become proficient in dealing with armed suspects in vehicles. The photograph at

Photo taken from one of the rifle positions at the rear of the embassy

the bottom of the previous page was taken to assist students' understanding of the correct tactics and ability to identify the pitfalls of doing things incorrectly.

Iranian Embassy Siege
30 April–5 May 1980

London in the 1970s had been no stranger to terrorism and atrocities in the form of IRA bombings and assassinations, but it would be fair to say that London and the rest of the country was shocked when an internal dispute in Iran, relating to a small area in the south of the country known as Arabistan (now the Khuzestan province), bubbled over onto the streets of London.

On 30 April 1980, six terrorists belonging to a group who called themselves the Democratic Revolutionary Movement for the Liberation of Arabistan (dedicated to gaining independence for this small state in Iran) bundled their way into the Iranian Embassy at Princes Gate, Kensington. PC Trevor Lock, the armed DPG officer on duty at the embassy, was taken by surprise, overpowered and swept inside. The

men pulled out sub-machine guns and pistols, firing them into the walls and ceilings of the building. The terrorists were ignorant of the fact that PC Lock had a .38 Smith & Wesson revolver in his coat pocket. He wisely kept this his secret.

The alarms were activated, which triggered a chain of responses from the police. Within minutes, the embassy, a huge Victorian terraced villa with multiple levels, was surrounded by armed DPG officers.

The terrorists inside now gathered up twenty-six hostages, including PC Lock and two BBC sound engineers who were there on visa enquiries. Eighteen of these hostages were Iranian embassy staff. Within hours, dialogue with the terrorists was set up and hostage negotiators began their work. The group demanded the release of ninety political prisoners in Iran within twenty-four hours and the end of mass executions in their province. They also demanded that an aircraft be put at their disposal and threatened that if the police attempted a rescue, they would blow up the building and everyone in it.

D11 officers were rushed in with as many

personnel as they could muster. An inner cordon of armed officers was formed at the front and rear of the embassy. Armed dog-handlers from Heathrow Airport and their counter-terrorist attack dogs were placed at strategic points and force rifle officers were called in from their division to take up positions in buildings overlooking the many windows and openings of the embassy.

The surrounding buildings were evacuated. Trained police hostage negotiators and interpreters worked in shifts. The situation was highly volatile. A hotline was established with the Cabinet Office briefing room and the SAS were put on immediate standby. Unarmed police were bussed in to maintain cordons and prevent the gathering crowds of Iranian students (who had descended on the area from all over the country to voice their support for Ayatollah Khomeini, and condemn the takeover of the embassy) from storming the embassy themselves.

D11, meanwhile, were preparing for the long haul. Positions were maintained around the clock, and officers were ever aware of the possibility of a breakout. Along with other responsibilities, D11 took on the tasks of regular food drops to the embassy.

During the next few days, delicate negotiations took place with the terrorists. PC Lock

The waiting game: a force rifle officer keeps observation on the embassy

was used as an intermediary. During those first few days, five of the hostages were released. PC Lock managed to pass out a message saying that, if it came to it, he would use his revolver to shoot the first terrorist with a machine gun, and then try to barricade himself and the hostages inside a room.

During the long days of the siege, one of the D11 officers in a rifle observation point took the time to feed and care for a nesting duck. The nest, containing seventeen eggs, was on the window ledge of 18 Princes Gate, overlooking the embassy. Happy for a distraction from the serious nature of the siege, the *Daily Express* took on the story, featuring it in their paper. This became a bit of light-hearted relief amongst the D11 personnel who used a picture of the duck as a sign outside their control room. Thankfully, the duck lived through her experience not troubled by her brief celebrity status.

Meanwhile, in the background, the SAS were rehearsing hard, using plywood mock-ups of the rooms in case they were needed to assault the embassy. It was discovered that the lower windows were constructed of armoured glass and so explosive charges would be needed if they were ever to gain entry. The hostage negotiators were ever hopeful that it would not come to that.

Sadly, notwithstanding all the efforts of the negotiators, the siege deteriorated and on 5 May, after passing many deadlines, the terrorists showed their deadly intent. At 1.15 p.m. shots were heard from inside the embassy, followed at 6.42 p.m. by more shots.

A few minutes later the body of the Iranian press attaché, Abbas Lavasani, was dumped out of the front door. Whilst this was happening the leader of the group Salim Towfigh, known as Oan, informed police over the telephone that a hostage would be killed every hour until their demands were met. (It was believed that a second hostage had already been killed inside.)

This activity set in motion a chain of events from which there was no return. William Whitelaw, the Home Secretary, authorized the military to be committed and so the deputy assistant commissioner, John Dellow, who was in charge of the operation, handed formal control of the incident to Lieutenant Colonel Mike Rose. This was done on a handwritten sheet of paper, timed at 7.07 p.m.

As negotiators talked to Oan, confirming a coach was on its way to take the terrorists to the airport, D11 officers moved forward in close containment positions in support of the impending assault. At 7.24 p.m., using a huge explosion above the glass atrium roof covering a second floor landing as a form of distraction, up to thirty-five SAS troopers began their assault on the embassy. The assault teams abseiled from the roof while others stormed the lower floors. Various entry points were used on different levels, guaranteeing the assault teams' entry into the building.

As the assaulters flooded through, clearing the rooms, a different kind of struggle was taking place in the minister's room on the second floor.

PC Lock had managed to overpower one of the terrorists, known as Oan, who was acting as the group's leader. He had wrestled him to

SAS troopers move into final assault positions after carefully roping off from the embassy roof

the floor as the doors burst open and two CS gas grenades were tossed in. Oan broke free and was attempting to retrieve his machine pistol, to which he had a grenade attached. PC Lock was told to get out of the way as two SAS troopers fired at Oan – he was struck fifteen times; the SAS were taking no chances. Four more terrorists were killed as the determined troopers swept through the building, one of them as he prepared a grenade to throw amongst the hostages. The whole assault, code-named Operation 'Nimrod', lasted just seventeen minutes from start to finish.

The SAS troopers secured the hostages in the building and they were then passed from trooper to trooper down the stairs and out onto the lawn at the back of the embassy. The sixth and final terrorist was discovered hiding amongst the women on the lawn. Armed cover was maintained on the hostages until all their identities could be confirmed.

The firepower bought into the Iranian Embassy by the terrorists included two Polish 9 mm WZ63 machine pistols, a Browning Hi Power 9 mm pistol and a .38 Astra revolver. They also had several hand grenades and claimed to have explosives.

During the assault, one hostage had been killed and two wounded by the terrorists, and all but one of the terrorists had been killed by the SAS. All the other hostages were rescued unharmed. Despite the tragic loss of life, the operation was heralded as a huge success – things were deemed to have gone as well as could realistically have been hoped. As the assault team were spirited away, the now burning embassy building was handed back to the control of the police.

The surviving terrorist, Fowzi Nejad, later received thirty years imprisonment. (When he was finally released from prison in 2008, he was granted political asylum to remain in the UK.) PC Trevor Lock was awarded the George Medal

The grisly aftermath: the bodies lie in the room where they were shot by the SAS

along with the Freedom of the City of London (a symbolic award dating back to 1237, allowing the holder to enjoy certain trade privileges within the City of London, such as the right to earn money and own land!).

The SAS and the government received congratulations from around the world, and terrorists would think twice before bringing their disputes into the UK (for a while at least). But what of D11? What did they take away from the experience?

In the world of siege intervention, the SAS were now the undisputed masters. It would not be for another twenty years that D11 would have the personnel, the training and the motivation to mount such an assault themselves with any chance of success. However, one very positive thing to come out of this incident was a lasting relationship between D11 and Special Forces that would prove useful to both parties over the coming years, with a steady flow of ideas between the two expanding organizations ensuing. D11 had seen the vision of the future and would strive to improve its training, tactics and weaponry to secure its destiny as a force protecting the capital.

High Risk Convoys and Court Protection
1980s

Another role that D11 was required to provide was that of armed escort to high-risk convoys. Under normal circumstances, the SEG (Special Escort Group, especially trained by D11 for escorting VIPs, high-profile prisoners or large cash value deliveries) would carry out this duty. However, if there was an identified threat, or the possibility of suspects who had access to exceptional firepower, then it would fall to D11 to provide the escort. The majority of this type of work was court-runs: escorting prison vans with high-profile prisoners to the Old Bailey or other local magistrates' courts for committals and applications.

This was the case in the 1980s when several IRA terror cells had been arrested after prolonged campaigns in the capital. Each week they would have to go before a magistrate to remand them in custody. This was a security nightmare and great thought was put into how best to achieve this.

The court chosen was the small magistrates' court in Kennington known as South Lambeth

A D11 officer dressed in operational uniform circa 1987, prepped for a high-risk escort of IRA prisoners to SWMC. He is wearing heavyweight body armour with added ceramic plates. He has a back-to-back radio set and is carrying a Heckler & Koch M93 5.56 carbine and a Browning 9 mm pistol.

route from the prison to the court. Once near the location, the leading vehicle would deploy its officers around the court building whilst watching and waiting for any sign of attack.

Over the nine years of these activities, no attacks or attempted break-outs were made although intelligence was received that the court had been placed on IRA hit lists.

The Waldorf Shooting and its Consequences
14 January 1983

The build-up to this incident reached back five months to August 1982, when David Martin, a 36-year-old violent criminal from London, stole twenty-four handguns and ammunition in a burglary. He later shot and wounded a security guard in a robbery. Days later, he broke into a recording studio. Police were called and, when challenged, Martin pulled out a concealed gun and shot one of the officers (whose life was saved by emergency surgery in hospital). Martin escaped.

His girlfriend was followed in the hope that she would lead police to their man. Martin had previously evaded police capture by dressing as a woman. Armed with this information, the police were prepared the next time he turned up outside his girlfriend's flat in Kensington. Martin was in a stolen VW Golf, was dressed as a woman and was wearing high-heeled shoes. As police moved in, he fled. They caught up with him in Oxford Street and during the struggle Martin pulled a gun from his handbag and threatened the officers. One officer drew his pistol and shot Martin in the neck. He was taken to hospital in custody. His wound was not serious and he later appeared at Marylebone Magistrates' Court charged with the attempted murder of a police officer. During his stay in the cells, he somehow managed to pick a lock and escape across a roof. Another huge manhunt had begun.

Magistrates' Court. It was chosen because of its 'out of the way location'. It also lent itself to protection for attack, with high brick walls and flat roofs where armed officers could keep watch. Directly opposite was a large police residential section house.

Each week the court would be searched and isolated from the public, the street would be cleared of parked vehicles and local armed officers would be positioned around and inside the court and on its roof. Once this was complete the convoy of police and prison vans would leave Wormwood Scrubs and take a varied

Police continued surveillance on Martin's girlfriend and on 14 January 1983 they identified her as the rear seat passenger in a yellow Mini with two other men. One of the officers believed David Martin was the front seat passenger. He had long hair and fitted the description well. As the Mini was held in traffic, PC Finch, who could identify Martin from an earlier encounter, was sent forward to confirm whether it was him in the car. As Finch approached the Mini the driver looked at him and said something to the passenger, who reached behind him as if to get something from the back seat.

Believing that it was Martin and that he was going for a gun, PC Finch opened fire with his revolver, firing three pairs of shots (his first pair hit the rear tyre, the other two pairs he fired directly at the front seat passenger). Two other officers ran to assist. One, DC Deane, believed it must be David Martin and fired five shots through the rear window; the third officer, DC Jardine, fired two shots as the suspect attempted to crawl out through the driver's door. Meanwhile, PC Finch, who had by now run around to the driver's side, hit the suspect with his empty revolver in an attempt to firmly neutralize the threat he presented.

This aggressive and, some would say over the top, reaction from the armed officers underlines the threat that David Martin was perceived to be. The fact that no one else in the car was hit was partly down to the fact that the driver, Lester Purdy, fled from the vehicle during the shooting. Martin's girlfriend must have ducked down across the rear seat.

As things quietened down, the police still believed they had got their man, but as others arrived it became apparent that the man they had shot was not David Martin but a freelance film producer called Stephen Waldorf. He had been hit five times as officers attempted to shoot him whilst avoiding the other passengers in the Mini.

Weeks later, Martin's girlfriend co-operated with police and arranged for them to meet Martin at a restaurant. After yet another spectacular chase, this time into the Underground system, Martin was arrested as he surfaced above ground. His life on the run was over.

On 11 October 1983, David Martin was convicted of trying to murder PC Carr. He received twenty-five years imprisonment. After six months, on 13 March 1984, Martin was found hanging in his cell.

On 19 October 1983, two of the police surveillance officers, PC Finch and DC Jardine, were tried at the Old Bailey for the attempted murder of Stephen Waldorf and for wounding with intent to cause grievous bodily harm. Both officers were found 'not guilty', the jury accepting that at the time they were in fear for their lives and therefore used reasonable force.

Stephen Waldorf was reportedly awarded £120,000 from the Metropolitan Police and went on to give radio interviews and make TV appearances, talking about his close encounter with death at the hands of London's armed police.

As for the consequences this incident would have on London's armed police, it forced the Home Office to send each chief constable new 'Guidelines for the Issue and Use of Firearms by Police'. These were to be implemented strictly and immediately. Firearms could now only be issued to police on authority of ACPO (commander) rank, or by a superintendent, in an emergency where life was at risk. Basic firearms courses would be increased from one to two weeks long with new emphasis on Section 3 of the Criminal Law Act of 1967, published in the Home Office guidelines, which hadn't necessarily applied to police using firearms, but would from now on.

The main emphasis was as follows:

Every officer to whom a weapon is issued must be strictly warned that it is to be used only as a last resort where conventional methods have been tried and failed, or must, from the nature of the circumstances obtaining, be unlikely to succeed if tried.

They may be used, for example, when it is apparent that a police officer cannot achieve the lawful purpose of preventing loss, or further loss, of life by any other means.

This legislation would be studied and learnt by every officer authorized to carry a firearm. A reminder would be printed on the back of the officer's firearms authorization card and carried at all times. All future investigations into police-related shootings would be judged by these rules.

A Most Depressing Job: Multiple Murder in South Croydon
17 December 1983

At around 6 p.m. on Saturday 18 December 1983, the day after the IRA exploded a huge car bomb outside Harrods in central London (killing six, and injuring ninety-nine others), police were called to a residential family home in Crest Road, south Croydon. The alarm was raised after a young man who would later be identified as Geoffrey Green staggered, seriously wounded, from the house, having been shot twice in the stomach.

Local police arrived but did not enter the house, wisely choosing to maintain observation from a discreet distance. Information gleaned from the victim was worrying. Apparently the victim's brother, Graham (who had recently been dismissed from the police as unsuitable after failing his probationary period) had shot him after a minor dispute. Three other people

were still inside the house with Graham. Checks revealed that Graham held a firearms licence for several handguns and ammunition. A D11 firearms team was called out from Old Street.

Upon their arrival at the three-bed semi-detached house, D11 officers were instructed to wait and observe. Reports of a curtain moving in an upstairs bedroom gave the impression that there was someone inside. Attempts were made to establish contact using the telephone and loudhailers but there was no response. Listening devices were installed by C7 (the technical support department), but no evidence of any living soul in the house was heard. So at 2 a.m. a decision was made to allow a six-man D11 team with a police support dog to enter and search the house. Permission to break through the patio doors at the rear of the house was given. (This was a precaution in case of booby traps or an ambush.) The team set up around the patio doors and on a given signal the glass was smashed. The noise of the breaking glass was loud and prolonged but was met with an eerie silence.

This was no rapid entry. The chosen tactic was to search through the house slowly and safely, covering all the angles and danger points. Foremost in the minds of the D11 officers was the fact that someone had already been shot by this suspect. As far as they knew, he was armed and dangerous and somewhere in this house.

As the team moved through into the front room they saw two young men, one dressed in a suit on the sofa, and the other wearing an outdoor coat on the floor. Upon closer examination they were both found to be dead from gunshot wounds. One was later identified as Gregory Green, aged 20, and the other was a friend, Michael Skinner, aged 19.

The search moved into the hallway. An officer covered the stairs with a Remington shotgun at the ready as his colleagues continued into the kitchen. In the doorway of the kitchen they came across the body of an elderly man who had been shot in the back at close range. This was Geoffrey Green senior, the father of the wounded escapee. The team checked for signs of life, but there were none. The police noticed a pile of rubble in the middle of the kitchen floor but there was still no sign of the suspected shooter.

They moved back out into the hallway and up the stairs. It was in one of the bedrooms that they found the fourth and final body. He was lying on his back with obvious signs of ballistic trauma to his head. A handgun lay nearby and Sony Walkman headphones were still in place on his head. He bore the signs of a self-inflicted wound. This was Graham Green, the ex-cop and gun enthusiast who had served in the police at Tooting police station in south London for less than two years.

The team searched the rest of the house. Although they found no more bodies, they did discover a hoard of firearms and ammunition, most legally held by Graham Green, with the exception of one Heckler & Koch 9 mm pistol. There was also a massive stockpile of water and food along with survival magazines and even a tunnel dug in the garage leading from the inspection pit and going under the house (hence the rubble in the kitchen). It would appear that Graham Green was prepared for Armageddon.

Green (who, since leaving the police had worked as a security guard in a department store), for reasons known only to himself, had shot and wounded his brother Geoffrey who ran from the house and then systematically shot his father, his brother Gregory and their friend Michael Skinner before turning his Smith & Wesson .357 magnum on himself.

The inquest jury returned verdicts of murder and suicide. This incident was not widely reported, owing to the interest shown in the Harrods bombing which filled the news that same weekend. One officer, looking back over a firearms career of twenty-five years, said, 'Of all the incidents I have been involved with and the awful things I have seen, this one was the most depressing.'

Libyan People's Bureau Siege
17–27 April 1984

On the morning of 17 April 1984, a political demonstration was taking place outside the Libyan People's Bureau in St James Square, Westminster, in central London. The demonstration had been organized by the Libyan National Salvation Front in protest at the execution of two students who had criticized Colonel Gaddafi.

About seventy-five protesters were in attendance behind metal crowd barriers.

Two months earlier, the Libyan Embassy, which was at that time known as the Libyan People's Bureau, had been taken over by a group of students loyal to Gaddafi, who had assumed control of the embassy with the tacit approval of the Libyan government. The vast majority of workers in the bureau were not professional diplomats.

Gaddafi loyalists who worked in the bureau informed police that they intended to mount a counter-demonstration. They assumed a position behind barriers directly outside the building. Both groups were exchanging chants and opinions and some were waving placards and banners. Loud music was played from open windows in the bureau in an attempt to drown out the noise of the protesting demonstrators. The demonstration was lightly policed by uniformed officers and was seen as a routine crowd control operation.

At 10.15 a.m., the chanting was interrupted by the distinctive sound of automatic gunfire. Individuals in the group opposite the bureau

A D11 armoured Land Rover provides protection for officers on containment at 'Point 6' in St James Square

began to collapse to the ground. One of them was 25-year-old PC Yvonne Fletcher who had been shot in the back. The bullet had travelled down into her stomach.

The gunfire appeared to have come from a first floor window of the bureau itself. In the ensuing panic, the square was evacuated. Fellow officers attempted to help their fallen comrade. In total, eleven other members of the crowd were taken to hospital with gunshot wounds. Sadly, Yvonne Fletcher died from her injuries shortly after arrival in hospital.

Libyan radio reported that the embassy was stormed and that those inside the building had fired back in self-defence against 'a most horrible terrorist action'.

Armed DPG (Diplomatic Protection Group) officers quickly contained the bureau. Technical support and D11 specialist teams were sent for. The shooter (or shooters) were still believed to be in the Libyan People's Bureau and this was not thought to be a hostage situation. All that could be confirmed by contacting the bureau was that the occupants within had claimed diplomatic immunity. A crisis response committee was called to attend COBR (the Cabinet Office Briefing Rooms), as some

serious political negotiations were about to take place. Once again Britain's capital had been used as a world stage to play out foreign power struggles, but this time it had cost the police one of their own.

There was a short delay in D11 attending the scene, owing to some internal politics regarding who should have primacy over the armed operation. Should it be the DPG, who were responsible for all diplomatic premises, or D11 who had the experience and training for armed sieges? In the end, it was agreed that D11 would deploy in support of the DPG. An eleven-day siege was now underway as politicians considered how best to end the stand-off.

Gaddafi claimed that the People's Bureau was under attack from British forces, and Libyan soldiers surrounded the British Embassy in Tripoli in response. The situation was escalating. The public outcry led by the national papers was immense. The *Daily Express* ran a headline 'Killed in Action', showing a photo of fellow officers crowded around the wounded Yvonne Fletcher.

D11 officers were employed in many roles during the siege. They were instrumental in showing the SAS the surrounding buildings

Watch and wait: D11 officers observe goings-on at the bureau. On the right, a force rifle officer waits in readiness

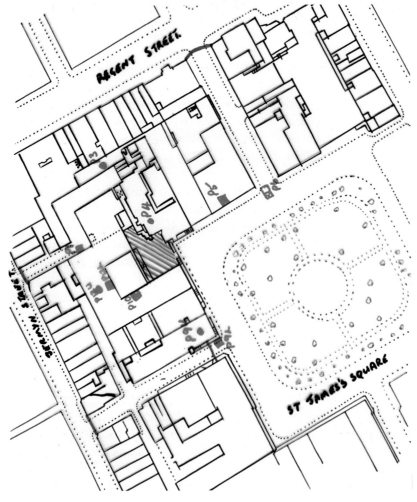

D11 plans showing an aerial view. Rifle and containment points are shown in red

and approaches in case there was the need for an assault on the premises. This was soon ruled out as it became apparent that there would be a political solution.

It was with great anguish that the British public and the officers surrounding the bureau received the news that the government intended to allow all those inside free passage back to Libya with full diplomatic privileges. The mood of the general public seemed to be such that it would have welcomed a full-blown assault on the building to bring the killers to justice, but that was not to be. There was a bigger picture, and the safety of British nationals in Libya, who were being held as bargaining chips, had to be considered. The need for oil was also a serious concern. It was a bitter pill to swallow for those involved in or affected by the siege and it was a high price to pay for any government who wanted to walk away with a clear conscience.

D11 officers and force rifle officers now supplemented the DPG officers in a containment of the bureau, and a daily routine of watching and waiting was taking place as all awaited the final agreement to end this débâcle.

D11 officers worked hard formulating viable surrender plans, which had to be agreed through intermediaries as acceptable by the

The occupants of the Libyan People's Bureau leave under the watchful eyes of the D11 marksmen

Libyans. All this took time. There was a lot of frustration at the apparent inactivity and most officers were suspicious of the Libyans in the bureau, believing that, given the opportunity, they would use their pending surrender to somehow embarrass the government and make Britain look like an aggressor.

Finally, on 27 April an acceptable ending was negotiated, and Britain reluctantly let PC Fletcher's killer go free. All thirty occupants of the building would be led away in groups of five, walking two metres apart. They could each have their personal belongings in a clear plastic bag. This would be inspected for weapons. The searching seemed pretty pointless as the staff were allowed to load large cases full of so-called diplomatic documents, which would not be searched or checked.

The surrender was carried out with trademark professionalism and restraint by D11. The Libyans left under the watchful eyes of its officers, who were armed with shotguns. These were held pointing upwards, but ready just in case.

As the plane lifted off with the killer on board, a period of diplomatic separation began with Libya. For the officers of D11, there was no celebration of a job well done, only a feeling of sadness and frustration. However, once again they had been at the forefront of a major armed incident and had performed extremely well under pressure.

The official inquest into PC Yvonne Fletcher's death concluded that she had been killed by shots from a Sterling sub-machine gun fired from the first floor of the Libyan Embassy. There would be many upsetting conspiracy theories in the years to follow, some suggesting that the shots were, in fact, fired from another building, but it would not be for another thirty-seven years and the overthrow of the Gaddafi regime in 2011 that there was any real light at the end of the tunnel regarding finding Yvonne

PC Yvonne Fletcher's police hat, which remained where she had fallen for days after her shooting and became a poignant reminder of the futility of her death. Two weeks after she was killed, the Police Memorial Trust was set up, sponsored by UK film director Michael Winner. Yvonne was to be honoured as the first recipient in the form of a monument erected where she had fallen

Fletcher's killers. New Scotland Yard are still hopeful of finding new leads and bringing her killers to justice.

The Anthony Baldessare Manhunt
15 August 1984–26 January 1985

On 15 August 1984 career armed robber Anthony Baldessare and his accomplice Patrick Murray robbed a Group 4 security van, which was delivering to the Lloyds Bank in Station Road, Petts Wood, Kent. This was the last robbery in a series committed by the duo, which had netted £41,500 in raids across south-east London over the previous few months.

On this occasion, PC Coxan, a police dog handler, was in the bank cashing a cheque. He saw what was happening and sent his dog, Yerba, after the men as they made off. Yerba ran towards Baldessare, who levelled his .38 Colt revolver at the dog and fired, hitting it twice in the head. As the police dog lay in the road,

Baldessare fired again into the dog's back. As PC Coxan attempted to tackle the robbers himself, Patrick Murray, who was still with Baldessare, pointed his gun at the constable and said, indicating towards the now-dead police dog, 'You will get the same'.

Despite Yerba and PC Coxan's intervention, the two robbers made it to their getaway car. Other police officers arrived but, following a desperate car chase, the robbers managed to escape. Although there must have been more deserving criminals on the loose, Baldessare had, by shooting a police dog during an armed robbery, catapulted himself to the top of the most wanted list and was now the subject of a nationwide manhunt.

In October 1984, Patrick Murray was tracked down and arrested at Gatwick Airport whilst attempting to board a flight for Tenerife. His partner, Anthony Baldessare, was not so easy to trace and it would be another three months before police caught up with him.

The scene of the Petts Wood robbery, cordoned off by police. The body of Yerba, the police dog shot by Baldessare, lies partially covered in the road

In January 1985, the Regional Crime Squad traced Baldessare to a top-floor attic flat in Gleneldon Road, Streatham, only a stone's throw from Streatham police station. This quiet south London suburban street was about to find itself in the glare of the public's press as police moved in to make the arrest of Britain's most wanted criminal.

Anthony Phillip Baldessare was born in south London in 1939 and, by the age of 15, he had been arrested on four occasions for petty crimes, the last one involving possession of a stolen rifle and ammunition.

By the age of 20 he had progressed to assaults and a malicious wounding and by the age of 21 he had his first conviction for conspiracy to rob, possession of an offensive weapon and taking a motor vehicle, which sealed his fate as a career criminal.

There followed many spells in prison for other serious crimes, including robbery and possession of firearms and ammunition, along with many ancillary offences. He was released

from a five-year prison sentence in 1982 and continued his life of crime (including the Group 4 robbery of August 1984) until 26 January 1985 when he found himself alone in his hideout, besieged by armed police in Gleneldon Road, Streatham. The last violent chapter in his life was about to play out.

On the morning of Thursday 24 January 1985, officers from D11 had arrived and moved into containment positions around the flat. The flat, in the attic of a large, Edwardian mid-terraced house on four levels, was fairly easy to control once the occupants in the lower level flats had been evacuated. (This had all been done by the time the first phone call was made into the premises at 9.11 a.m. that day.)

The first attempt to call found the line engaged, but persistent efforts by a detective inspector who knew Baldessare bore fruit just five minutes later. Baldessare was informed that he was surrounded and he was invited to give himself up. He replied that he would think about it but wanted to make some more calls first. Time progressed and it soon became apparent that the incident would not be concluded quickly.

Over eighty residents were evacuated to a nearby church hall to sit the siege out. Within the hour, siege negotiators were on their way, along with technical support services. More calls were made to the flat and Baldessare stated that he wanted to speak with his wife before giving himself up.

The press became interested and within the hour an attempt was made by Thames TV to speak on the phone with Baldessare. Shortly after midday, sounds could be heard that were believed to be Baldessare testing a firearm. In fact, it later transpired that he had shot the head off a statue in his lounge. When questioned over this, he declared that he was fearful of not being taken alive. The negotiator attempted to reassure him. By 4 p.m. that day, his wife had been fetched to Streatham police station, where she was allowed to speak with him.

The negotiating cell was now set up on the ground floor of the house with D11 firearms officers on standby in the flat directly below Baldessare's. They were playing the waiting game. Various sightings of Baldessare were made at windows of the flat. Information had previously been sought as to the layout of the flat and the types and numbers of locks on the doors and windows as the D11 officers planned for the possibility of an entry. It soon became clear that there was only one way in and one way out.

In the early hours of Friday morning at 1.05 a.m. contact was lost until 7.05 a.m., when sounds of movement were heard from inside the flat. Baldessare's wife, under police control, managed to speak with him, after which she described him as being fatalistic.

D11 officers prepared a surrender plan and considered the use of CS gas. Respirators were supplied to the police negotiators who were situated in one of the flats below. Things were getting desperate for Baldessare, who had become anxious and intimated that if police wanted him they should come in and get him. Although D11 now had the keys to the flat, they suspected that Baldessare had booby-trapped the doors and windows. It was believed that he wanted to die in a shoot-out, taking police officers with him. This was not going to be allowed to happen if at all possible.

Later that day at around 11.20 p.m., after speaking with a solicitor, Baldessare informed police that he was going to burn the money he had in the flat on the grounds that it was the proceeds of crime. A short time later, thick smoke was seen coming from the skylight in the flat. The fire brigade were put on standby but were not required as the smoke had lessened by 1.30 a.m.

D11 officers could hear 'bumps and thuds' and optics were drilled through the walls to try to find out what was going on. There was the sound of furniture being moved about and then a muffled shot was heard from inside the flat. One officer claimed to have heard what he thought were feet drumming on the floor directly after the shot. The police negotiators attempted to call Baldessare on the phone but there was no answer.

Initial probes indicated barricades inside the flat. It was decided to wait until more information was obtained, as there was always the risk that it was a trap, with Baldessare waiting to ambush officers when they made an entry.

It was not until 12.41 p.m. on the Saturday that the probes had a visual into the lounge and could confirm an apparently lifeless body on the lounge floor.

Still cautious about the possibility of booby traps, officers planned to effect entry through the walls supporting the adjoining roof. A large hole was knocked through the wall and a police

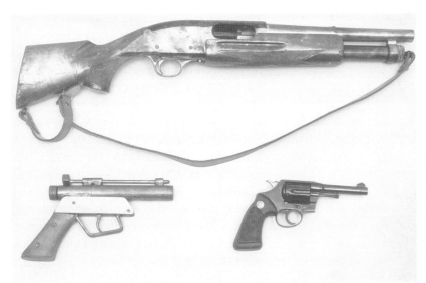

Baldessare's armoury, found in his flat. Top: a Fusil Rapide Brevete 12-bore pump-action sawn-off shotgun. Left: a homemade 12-bore pistol. Right: a Colt .38 Special Police Positive revolver

dog was sent in, followed by armed D11 officers who searched through the flat. They found Baldessare lying dead on his back in the lounge, with the .38 Colt Special Police Positive revolver he had used to shoot Yerba lying a few feet away. It was loaded with five rounds, with one empty chamber under the hammer. Baldessare had shot himself in the chest.

As the officers searched through the flat, they were left in no doubt of Baldessare's intent. Loaded weapons had been positioned strategically behind makeshift barricades enabling him to effect a fighting retreat through the flat. This was a desperate man intent on stopping the police from taking him alive. In the sink were the smouldering remains of his ill-gotten gains.

The siege had lasted two-and-a-half days and as the detectives moved through the flat gathering evidence, Gleneldon Road was allowed to return to normality. At the inquest in Southwark in March 1985, the court was informed that Baldessare had wanted to die in a shootout with officers and had been frustrated by the police tactics. The verdict was that Baldessare had killed himself.

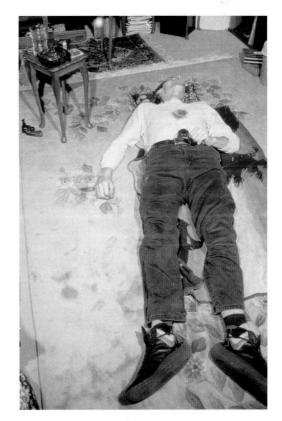

The apparently lifeless body of Anthony Baldessare lay on the lounge floor. He had shot himself in the chest

D11 Uniform and Equipment
1985

A drawing of a D11 officer in the uniform of the period around 1985. He carries a 9 mm MP5 SD (silenced) SMG with wooden foregrip, and a 9 mm Browning Hi Power semi-automatic pistol. The officer pictured is a wearing a dark blue, quick-release assault vest (over his lightweight body armour) in which he carries his back-to-back radio set, with wired-in earpiece and PTT (Press To Talk) switch, spare magazines for both weapons and a Schermuly (Green Meanie) distraction grenade. He is also issued with a field dressing for gunshot wounds. You will notice that he is wearing the D11 blue beret with dark blue shirt and black police trousers

Philbeach Gardens – Van Siege
20–22 March 1985

At 6 a.m. on Wednesday 20 March 1985, detectives who were looking for one James Alexander Baigrie attended a bedsit flat in Philbeach Gardens, Earls Court, about a hundred yards from the Earls Court Exhibition Centre in south-west London. Baigrie, aged 35, had escaped from high-security Saughton Prison in Edinburgh on 16 October 1983, where he was serving life for the murder of Edinburgh barman Ron Flockhart, whom he had shot in the back with a shotgun during a bungled pub robbery.

At the time of his arrest he had been dubbed 'Scotland's most wanted criminal'. Known to be a fitness fanatic from Kelty, Fife, in Scotland, Baigrie has been described as a loner and a hard man. He had served just fifteen months of his sentence before he cut through the bars of his prison window using a smuggled hacksaw; he then edged out along a narrow ledge and climbed sixty feet down a drainpipe to make good his escape.

The London detectives had been tipped off that Baigrie was now going under the name of Brian Robertson and was working as a part-time labourer for a Kilburn construction company, whilst living with a flatmate at the Earls Court address.

The detectives, some of them armed, entered the flat – a typical rough bedsit, used by casual workers. They found his flatmate present, but had just missed Baigrie. They found a pile of fitness and gun magazines in the space where he had until recently been sleeping. As the detectives left the premises one of them decided to check out a white builder's van parked in the street outside the flat. He noticed it belonged to the construction company that Baigrie supposedly worked for.

The officer opened the rear doors of the van

Aerial view of Philbeach Gardens, Earls Court

and was surprised by a man who emerged from under an orange blanket, brandishing a sawn-off 12-bore shotgun. Baigrie made threats to shoot the officer who dived out of the way and ran for cover. He was heard to shout, 'Watch it, he's got a shooter.'

The streets and surrounding area were cordoned off. The locals were told to stay away from their windows and evacuated where necessary. Just before 8 a.m., a D11 firearms team was called out from Old Street. They were in position at Philbeach Gardens within the hour in close containment, where they remained for the duration.

Many attempts were made to talk Baigrie from the van but nothing was heard until just after 3 p.m. when he shouted from the van, 'All you want is to send me back to prison.' True as this was, attempts would still have to be made to reason by negotiation with this desperate man.

Baigrie placed empty cement bags over the back windows, blocking out any view inside the van. Police on containment also believed that he was fortifying the inside of the van using bags of sand and cement. D11 officers main-

tained round the clock armed containment of the vehicle. Floodlights were put in place to illuminate the van and an armoured police Land Rover was parked nearby as part of the containment. However, pressure was mounting from the local community whose day to day running was being interrupted. Questions were being asked of the senior management as to how long the police would allow the siege to continue. The knock-on effect to the flow of traffic around this busy area of London was becoming an issue.

An experienced negotiator, one of the best, was brought in, namely Detective Chief Superintendent Dave Veness, who had been the negotiator at both the Iranian Embassy and Libyan People's Bureau sieges. But before a dialogue could be established he would need a direct phone line. Later that evening, after some shouted negotiating, Baigrie agreed to hang a bucket out of the rear window of the van on the end of a broom handle. A D11 officer then tentatively placed a portable telephone in the bucket, which Baigrie retrieved. Negotiations continued, now using the phone, but it was strongly suspected that Baigrie (known to be a drug user) had been taking amphetamines from a stash he had with him in the van. He had not eaten since before the siege began and had only water from a bottle he kept in the van for a leaking radiator. The uppers could cause delirium and panic and their effect would be compounded by a lack of food and drink.

The D11 officers had been specifically briefed that, if he came out on foot, police dogs would be used and resorting to firearms would only take place if he came out with the shotgun. In the event of him driving the van they were not to open fire as the street had been blocked off. (It was later found that he could not have got through into the cab area as the opening he had made was too small.)

The police psychologist brought in to gauge

Baigrie's mood swings was becoming worried. This was compounded when, at just before 10 p.m., after telling police that he would rather die than be taken alive, Baigrie cut the wire to the phone line. It was feared that in his drug-induced state he would force a confrontation. It was known that he had over twenty cartridges for his shotgun.

It all came to a head late on Thursday evening, when Baigrie broke a partition panel to gain access into the cab of the van. A decision was made to force the issue before he could take the initiative, in the hope of getting him to surrender. This would be achieved by firing CS gas rounds, called 'ferret' rounds, from a shotgun into the van through the rear windows. Simultaneously, calls for Baigrie to surrender would be shouted through a loud-hailer.

At 1.40 a.m. a D11 officer fired two ferret rounds into the van and as the gas filled the van, a call for Baigrie to surrender was made. There was no response and a few seconds later there was a muffled shot heard from inside the van. Tense moments then passed before two D11 officers wearing coveralls, body armour and respirators were sent forward. They forced grappling hooks through the windows and signalled the armoured Land Rover to pull the back doors off. With a loud rending the doors came away, revealing a smoke and dust filled van. As the smoke from the gas cleared, they could make out the body of the killer James Baigrie lying prostrate in the back of the van. He had shot himself in the head with his shotgun. The forty-four-hour siege was over.

During the months that followed, the police tactics used during the siege were criticized from many quarters. Allegations that police caused Baigrie to shoot himself and that they should have waited longer were made. The *Evening Standard* ran with a headline on 22 March that asked: 'Why Did Siege End In

The rear of the builder's van where James Baigrie spent the last forty-four hours of his life. His body is partially covered at the back by a blanket

Death? The police came back and defended their actions, stating that their first priority was the safety of the public and residents who lived nearby. It was a no-win situation for Commander Perret of 'B' district who had been in overall command and had been just days off his retirement when the incident occurred. He must have taken some solace when, in May 1985, the inquest jury at Westminster gave their decision that Baigrie 'killed himself at a siege in March'. With a rider, they added 'that they approved of the police tactics which have been criticised by the national council of civil liberties'.

Two other men were charged with assisting Baigrie to avoid arrest, one of whom was his flatmate from Philbeach Gardens.

Cherry Groce
September 1985

On 28 September 1985, local armed officers led by Inspector Douglas Lovelock attended the address of Michael Groce who was believed to have been involved in a robbery and discharging a shotgun at another address in Brixton two days earlier. He was believed to be 'armed and dangerous'. The front door was forced open and Inspector Lovelock led the officers into the poorly lit hall area. He kicked open the door into the lounge and entered the lit room, but Michael Groce was not at home. Instead, his mother Dorothy 'Cherry' Groce, surprised by this intrusion, ran towards Inspector Lovelock. According to his later testimony, Lovelock was startled by the sudden movement, causing him to tense up and fire his Smith & Wesson model 10 revolver once. The round entered Mrs Groce's body and lodged near her spine. She survived but was tragically paralysed from the waist down.

Following the shooting, there were two nights of rioting in Brixton with over 200 arrests made. Inspector Lovelock faced charges of unlawful and malicious wounding. His defence successfully claimed that Mrs Groce's injury was an accident and he was acquitted in January 1987.

The Home Secretary, Douglas Hurd, set up a working party to look into the facts surrounding the incident and explore how such a tragedy could be avoided in the future. Leslie Curtis, the chairman of the police federation for England and Wales, gave an interview to the BBC saying, 'It was important officers were given rigorous training in the use of firearms.' He added, 'At the end of the day, you have placed the gun in the hands of a human being – you will never eradicate the (occasional) mistake that occurs.'

Cherry Groce died in 2011, aged 63 years. Her son Michael was arrested many times following the shooting, serving several terms of imprisonment for serious offences. He now writes poetry and is involved in work within the community in Brixton.

The Northolt Siege, Gallery Gardens
25–26 December 1985

On Boxing Day 1985, the TV news carried live images of armed officers storming a flat in Northolt. At first glance, the rescue appeared inept and ill-timed and although the operation finished with the rescue of a child who had been terrorized for twenty-nine hours it left one perplexed at how a situation had been allowed to deteriorate to such a degree before an intervention was authorized. It wasn't until the following years that all the facts would emerge and one could better understand the dilemma that the D11 firearms team found themselves in on that day in December 1985.

The protagonist of this sad story was Errol Anthony Walker, born in Jamaica in 1956. He had travelled across to England around 1968 where he began a career of crime, committing burglaries and thefts. In 1982, Walker married Marlene, the mother of his child, but instead of settling down he continued his life of crime, embarking on a series of armed robberies. Walker was eventually arrested that same year after forcing his way into the home of three elderly people, where they were terrorized and robbed in an ordeal lasting forty-five minutes.

Walker was charged with robbery, possession of a firearm and false imprisonment, and he asked for twenty-six other offences to be taken into consideration. (This was a common practice during court cases as it allowed the criminal to have a clean break, as well as clearing up many other reported crimes for the police. In most cases it had little or no effect on the length of sentence awarded.) At his Old Bailey trial, Walker received a sentence of just five years imprisonment. This was considered short for the eighties, but the fact that he had turned Queen's evidence, helping to convict his accomplices, would have helped somewhat.

Walker was released in 1985 and set up

home in Northolt, but was soon back in trouble with the police, being arrested for theft, for which he was bailed. Walker, now an official police informer, would always be looked upon as a potential source of information; some informers no doubt enjoyed their special relationship with the police, wrongly believing they were untouchable.

It was no secret to the neighbours that Walker was a violent and aggressive husband – this violence came to a head in November 1985 when his wife Marlene went out with her step-sister Jacqueline. As Marlene returned home around midnight, Walker assaulted her and locked her in a room (a pattern of behaviour that he would go on to repeat). She managed to escape from a window and called the police from a phone box. They attended but Marlene was advised to pursue a summons for common assault (a far cry, one would hope, from the reaction she would receive today, but sadly this first chance of an intervention was missed).

After hospital treatment she was still fearful and stayed at her step-sister's in nearby Poynter Court, Gallery Gardens. She managed to retrieve her daughter and both stayed with Jacqueline, who also had a daughter, 4-year-old Carlene. On 1 December Walker enticed Marlene back to the family home where he tied her up and raped her. He released her on the condition that she did not report him to the police. But as soon as she was free she attended a firm of solicitors and made a statement concerning her assault and rape. During the following weeks, Walker visited her at Poynter Court to see his daughter. He was never allowed in, but he did manage to see his child at the door.

On Christmas Eve, Jacqueline hosted a party at her flat in Poynter Court. Errol arrived uninvited. He wanted Marlene to go back with him to open her Christmas presents. To avoid a scene, she agreed, but once there, Walker produced a knife. He raped her several times, telling her he would kill her when he had finished. At one point, when Walker put the knife down, she managed to pick it up and demanded the key to the locked room. Unfortunately, Walker wrestled the knife from her and beat her violently.

As Christmas morning arrived, Walker told Marlene he wanted his daughter back. Marlene agreed to accompany him in his car to Poynter Court to collect her. Upon arrival, Walker sent her up to get their daughter but instead she told Jacqueline what had happened and went to a neighbour's flat to phone the police. She made the allegation of rape to police in a call that was tape-recorded.

Local police responded, sending two officers to Poynter Court. As they arrived they saw Walker climbing through the kitchen window of Jacqueline's flat holding a large knife. He took hold of Jacqueline, threatening to cut her unless the police got his wife to come back.

One officer went to get Marlene. The other stayed, attempting to reason with Walker. It was to no avail as, within minutes, Jacqueline was pushed from the kitchen window out onto the balcony. She had been slashed and stabbed

View of the front of Poynter Court; the flat is on the top level. An armoured police Land Rover is still *in situ* outside

repeatedly by Walker. Jacqueline was evacuated to hospital where she was pronounced dead on arrival.

Meanwhile, back in the flat, Walker had Jacqueline's 4-year-old daughter Carlene, along with his own daughter. Things were at a critical state.

Police dog handlers arrived, along with two local authorized firearms officers. The fire brigade attended and planned how they would catch a child should Walker drop one from the third floor window at the rear of the flat. All these resources were in place by noon. A D11 firearms team had also been called out. Meanwhile, the two young police officers were left on the balcony to do the talking. They attempted to reason with Walker whose volatile state ebbed and flowed as the mood took him.

Officers brought his wife, Marlene, to the flat in an attempt to persuade Walker to release the two girls. Walker nearly succeeded in dragging her inside through the kitchen window. His failure only enraged him more and he held Carlene out of the window, threatening to kill her. A short time later, he passed his own daughter out through the kitchen window to waiting police, but refused to give up Carlene.

Not only did he refuse to let her go but he displayed his sadistic traits: putting her on the floor, he slashed at her fingers with his knife. He then dangled her from the rear window, allowing her blood to drip onto the waiting fire crews below. He also made threats to the police on the balcony that he intended to kill the girl.

One brave young officer, who spent many hours trying to reason with Walker, stated that she saw him display nothing but sheer violence as he held a ten-inch carving knife.

At one time he tied Carlene to a chair with flex around her neck and hit her so hard that she was barely conscious. He put a plastic bag over her head as if to suffocate her, but the officer managed to persuade him to remove it.

Bandages were offered to Walker to dress the child's wounds but he refused them, saying she could bleed to death.

During the negotiations Walker was handed a police radio in order to help communicate, but instead he used this to beat the child. He even cut the electric cable to the kettle and threatened to electrocute her with the exposed wire. These facts, although relayed to senior officers, appeared not to have been passed to the D11 firearms team when they arrived.

The question of whether or not two local police AFOs who were originally on the balcony would have been justified in taking action to save the child after what they had witnessed remains to be seen but, regardless, senior officers now appeared intent on negotiating the incident to a non-violent conclusion. In their defence, there was every reason to believe that

View along the fourth level walkway towards the flat. Note the abandoned riot shield in the bottom right of the photo

Walker would have killed the child if any entry had been made into the flat, but the young female officer outside the flat later stated that she believed Walker would have killed the child anyway, if nothing had been done.

At some point a riot shield was bought near to the flat to help protect the officers should Walker come out. The trained negotiators left the two officers to communicate with Walker outside the flat as they were doing such a good job but at 7.15 p.m. they were finally withdrawn.

Earlier that day, officers from D11 had arrived and made assessments of the situation. They presented the senior officers in charge with the following tactical options: 1) try to talk him out, 2) manoeuvre him into a position where police could intervene between Walker and the child, 3) shoot him, 4) respond with appropriate force if Walker attacked the child.

A rifle position was set up in a flat opposite but the officer was under strict instructions not to fire unless he was commanded to do so. The remainder of the team set up and prepared. Negotiations were mainly carried out through the kitchen window on the balcony with the D11 team ensconced in flats on either side.

They were 'stood-to' many times during the afternoon and evening, but the final order to go in was never given, even though threats and assaults on the child persisted.

As Christmas evening drew to a close, it was decided to continue negotiations over the telephone. The D11 team was pulled further back to either end of the balcony, so as not to antagonize Walker who was still making demands that he wanted Marlene in exchange for the child.

During the night, Walker constructed a barricade inside the kitchen window, using an internal door he had removed and a refrigerator. This would make any entry into the flat more difficult. Also during the night, the D11 team was changed over; they were briefed but once again no details of the child's injuries were given to the officers. The officers were told that Walker had appeared on the balcony with a rag soaked in what he claimed was the girl's blood but that it was believed to be jam or tomato ketchup. They were told in no uncertain terms that if this should happen again they were not to intervene.

Walker was now free to come out onto the balcony and at one point sat the child on the edge of the handrail. The D11 officers formulated a plan to rescue the child should it present itself but permission to implement this was refused. The officers kept their plan just in case it was needed. One later commented that it was better to have a plan in mind than no plan at all!

Negotiations between the police and Walker continued. He was allowed to walk along the balcony unmolested for short periods of time. He even dictated terms with the negotiators who, at his request, once again bought Marlene to the flat to talk with him face to face. He ordered her, with the agreement of the negotiators, to walk between either end of the

Errol Walker leans menacingly out of the front door with a knife taped to his left hand

balcony and throw the sledgehammers put there by D11 over the wall. This was done without any warning and it was only by luck that these heavy objects missed the firefighters waiting three floors below. It was now noticed that Walker had tied the ten-inch kitchen knife to his left hand using a lady's headscarf.

It was one such excursion onto the balcony that led to the rescue being attempted. As Walker approached a flat where he knew police to be hiding, he put his face to the glass, taunting them. The officers inside made up their minds that if he came back again they would grab him. Walker then decided to collect the riot shield, which had been left the other end of the balcony, as he could use this to help fortify the flat. The officers in the flats either side were effectively blind to his movements but were receiving a commentary from the observation point opposite. Going by this commentary, the officers in one of the flats sprung their trap, thinking Walker was nearby, only to see him at the opposite end of the balcony. Apparently there had been a misunderstanding. It was now a race to the front door. Walker had the edge. He also had the riot shield.

The three officers were committed; there was no turning back. Walker was running back to the flat. The officers had a lot of ground to make up and Walker got to the front door marginally before them. Throwing the shield at the leading officer momentarily slowed them down, allowing him time to open the door. Once Walker was inside the flat, he slammed the door shut in their faces. As their colleagues arrived they took a moment to reorganize. One officer hit the door with the sledgehammer, but the door would not give. Over the radio came the order to withdraw. This was not an option as Walker was shouting, 'She dies! She dies!'

Two stun grenades, known at the time as 'Green Meanies' (owing to the fact that they were green and had a very loud detonation), were tossed through the bathroom and kitchen windows. In the massive explosions that followed, debris, including broken glass, was thrown out. Smoke and dust hung in the air as the officers made their entry as best they could. This was now a question of life and death for the young hostage.

The first officer forced his way through the kitchen window, clambering over the obstacles

Each stun grenade detonation produced a massive flash with an extremely loud percussion

The lounge, where Walker stabbed Carlene in the neck, before he was shot by an armed officer

left by Walker to delay them. The entire flat was in darkness and there was furniture and other household items strewn about. The first officer inside the flat, revolver in hand, made his way from the kitchen and into the lounge, where he could just make out Walker on his back on the sofa holding the child across his chest as a human shield. He stabbed the child in the neck.

The officer shouted, 'Drop it, you bastard!' Receiving no response, he fired his revolver. The area he had to aim at was the shoulder and only half of Walker's head. He later said, when giving evidence at Walker's trial, 'I fired a pair of shots into his shoulder; when this appeared to have no effect I fired one at his temple.' In fact, of the first two rounds fired, one had entered the sofa, and the other hit Walker in the armpit. The third was fired as Walker hunched up; it hit his shoulder and ricocheted into the side of his head. The officer grabbed the child – she had Walker's knife protruding from her neck. The knife fell out as the officer left the flat with the child cradled in his arms, and he rushed down the stairs to the waiting ambulance.

To the armed officers left in the flat Walker appeared to be dead, but after a few moments his eyes blinked open. He was alive. He pleaded with the officers to kill him – they declined and he was taken to hospital where he survived his wounds.

The firearms team were taken to Southall police station where they were seen two hours later by the senior police officer who had been in charge of the siege. He explained to them that his first reaction had been to throw the book at them for wilfully disobeying his commands. He added that, at the time of the assault, he was giving a press conference on camera with his back to the flats, stating that they were working towards a negotiated peaceful settlement when he was interrupted by one of the press asking why there were armed police running along the balcony. He had replied that there had been frequent movements on the balcony and that nothing happened without his knowledge – this was followed by the stun grenades detonating. The press conference had ended abruptly.

His decision not to discipline the officers had been influenced by the fact that the child, although seriously injured, would survive and that Walker would also live. At the subsequent press conference, he fully supported the officer's actions.

It seems unbelievable under these circumstances, but at that time the police were concerned about sparking a repeat of the violence experienced on the Broadwater Farm Estate just two months earlier and feared that storming the flat would cause community friction. It is also fair to say that up to this time there had never been a siege where the firearms department had stormed a building to rescue a hostage in London and so caution, in case the attempt ended in failure, along with the death of the hostage and hostage taker, was the byword. (The capabilities of D11 in this field were known only to a privileged few at this time. They were yet to be tried and tested. Although they had been present at many sieges, you would have to look back to the SPG officers entering the Indian High Commission in Aldwych thirteen years earlier for an example of armed police in London going in to rescue hostages.)

Of course, management appeared to have overlooked the fact that the crowds gathering at the foot of the block were protesting about the *lack* of police action, not an excess of it.

The medical report on Carlene highlighted that she was in deep shock and could not have been expected to live much longer without medical attention.

Carlene did recover, although she would never forget her terrible experience at the hands of Errol Walker, and was understandably scarred by the tragic death of her mother.

At the Old Bailey in December 1986, Walker's defence of diminished responsibility was rejected and he was sentenced to life imprisonment for murder, false imprisonment, two counts of wounding with intent, threats to kill and attempted murder. (There was no mention of the rapes at the trial; perhaps it was thought that prosecuting over these would have been unnecessarily distressing for Marlene at an already hugely traumatic time.) The judge Mr Justice Alliott told Walker, 'You knifed the toddler on three occasions causing sickening injuries. They were monstrous attacks.'

The Northolt siege, as it became known, was an important event in the history of the firearms unit, not only because it was the first incident where one of its officers had discharged shots to save a life, but because it proved that the unit had matured and shown it was capable of doing what was necessary to protect the public.

The Met's senior management had also learnt some valuable lessons in siege strategy, the main one being that not all sieges, domestic or otherwise, could be brought to safe conclusions by talking alone, and that when this point was reached they had a viable alternative.

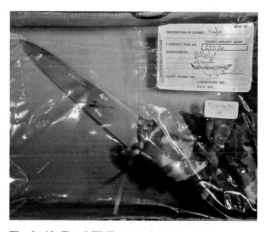

The knife Errol Walker used to murder Jacqueline and wound her 4-year-old daughter. Walker fastened the kitchen knife to his wrist using the blue headscarf

Overt Weapons Carriage at Heathrow Airport
20 February 1986

D11 officers were first deployed to patrol Heathrow Airport following the terrorist attacks in Vienna and Rome over the New Year of 1986 when nineteen people were killed. The idea was primarily to provide a high-profile, visible armed presence to reassure the public and to act as a deterrent against any terrorist attacks. These patrols were continued until local officers could be trained in the use of the MP5. A similar armed presence has been maintained at all British airports since this date.

The training and weapon types used continue to be assessed; heavier calibre weapons are now available for airport officers and have become a common sight to us all when travelling. Overt carriage was a major change in the stance of the Metropolitan Police, which had, since 1976, demanded that police firearms be hidden from public view. Outside of the airport this would remain the case almost until the turn of the century.

The papers had a field day with the change to overt carriage, as they were able to photograph D11 officers patrolling the terminals armed with Heckler & Koch MP5 SMGs, and report that London's police were using SAS machine guns to battle terrorism. Even the local commander was concerned about these machine guns, and sent a memo to all D11 officers, reminding them of their rules of engagement. He added, 'In addition the Heckler & Koch sub machine gun MUST NOT be used in the fully Automatic Mode.' He was worrying unnecessarily, as the D11 officers would far prefer the accuracy of firing on 'single-shot' mode to that of firing on 'fully automatic' in a crowded airport terminal.

Despite early unease about open carriage and the initial outcry in the papers, the public soon became used to seeing heavily armed officers at their airport terminals.

D11 Becomes PT17 (Personnel and Training)
9 January 1987

After yet another force restructuring, 'D' department was re-branded 'PT' (Personnel and Training). The firearms department moved with it, as training was still considered its main role. The department was given the title PT17.

In June that year a further eighteen operational officers would join the department on the three newly formed level 2 teams. These new additions brought the operational strength of the department up to one chief superintendent, one superintendent, one chief inspector, six inspectors, fifteen sergeants and fifty-four constables.

The unit now boasted six level 1 firearms teams (made up of instructors) three level 2 firearms teams, an operational support staff and a permanent instructional staff, based at Lippitts Hill. The level 1 teams would now rotate between operational duties and instructional duties.

PT17 Level 1 Teams Abseil Training at Empty Commercial Premises
1987

PT17 officers wearing respirators and hoods during abseil training in an empty office complex

One of the extra skills the level 1 officers had to master was tactical rope work, including abseiling and fast roping (deploying down a thick rope up to seventy feet long.) Training locations were sought and many empty or disused office buildings were used to rehearse and train in.

Level 2 Firearms Teams Go Live
1 June 1987

It had taken nearly two years to implement the recommendations of the working party set up by the Home Secretary Douglas Hurd (to look into police training and tactics) following the accidental shooting by police of Cherry Groce.

In March 1987, applications were sought from officers of PC and Sergeant rank to attend selection for a place on the new PT17 level 2 firearms teams. These teams would be run in conjunction with the existing level 1 specialist team.

Following the working party's recommendations, the new level 2 teams would take over all pre-planned firearms operations, which had previously been carried out by local divisional AFOs, including the type of police operation in which Mrs Groce was shot. They would be trained to a higher standard than divisional AFOs and so could hopefully avoid mistakes and accidents, and they would also be able to relieve the workload of the level 1 teams by carrying out the less complicated day to day operations, some of which were resource- and time-intensive.

The management of PT17 decided on three level 2 teams. The selection process for these new officers would be tough and thorough, and the selected officers would undergo an intensive three-week residential course at Lippitts Hill firearms training centre, focusing on weapon handling, slow armed building searches and siege control/containment, which would allow them to assist at sieges whilst the level 1 officers dealt with any hostage intervention. Many of those selected went on to have long and distinguished careers within the firearms department, becoming national firearms instructors and specialist firearms officers.

Level 2 selections involved various agility and balance tests on the assault course

High ropes test, to weed out any candidates with heights issues

Level 2 selection involved myriad tests, some physical and some mental. Candidates were expected to work in teams to solve problems, like building bridges or moving a large object across a course. They were constantly assessed over a two-day period. The ideal student was one who was physically fit, competent with firearms and had a good knowledge of the law around firearms (tested by an exam on the first day).

The level 2 system was an instant success across the Met. Local police commanders were keen to use the new teams who were inundated with work. The 'bread and butter' armed operations, which included the arrest of persons wanted in connection with armed crime, were conducted in the early hours of the morning. The use of these teams provided a much safer option than those available prior to

Applicants spent a morning on the ranges at Lippitts Hill, being tested under the watchful eye of PT17 instructors – they had to achieve ninety per cent accuracy and have faultless weapons handling. Nerves got the better of a lot of people, who were not invited back

The new level 2 firearms teams worked in a mixture of uniform and plain clothes as the work demanded. They were restricted with weapons to the MP5 A2 carbine and initially the .38 Smith & Wesson model 10 revolver, but progressed to using the 9 mm Glock semi-auto

their formation. The officers on the level 2 teams became experts in these early morning 'dig-outs' (armed call-outs) and slow search operations.

It was a sound grounding for those officers with the inclination to progress within the department to become firearms instructors and level 1 team operators.

Level 2 teams also went on to work on low-level ambush operations and to provide hostage reception at sieges for their level 1 colleagues. They were even adept at running control rooms at major armed incidents. In short, they improved the ability of the Met Police firearms department to function more efficiently.

Surrounded by woodland: the Royal Arsenal Co-operative Society, a former abattoir, now a meatpacking factory in Plumstead, south-east London

Shooting at the 'Abattoir', Operation 'Kincraig'
9 July 1987

For over seven months leading up to July 1987, No. 9 RCS (Regional Crime Squad), which was based in Dulwich, had been gathering intelligence on a violent gang of robbers suspected of committing a series of offences in south London and the Home Counties. The gang had discharged firearms during these robberies. On one occasion a security guard had been shot and wounded and on another the gang had fired at the pursuing police. The RCS were worried that the gang would kill someone before very long.

In July 1987, they received information that the gang were planning a wages snatch at premises in Plumstead. It was to be during a Securicor delivery at the RACS (Royal Arsenal Co-operative Society) meatpacking factory in Garland Road, Plumstead, in south-east London. The premises, an old abattoir, lent itself not only as an easy target for the would-be armed robbers but as an excellent site for the police to ambush and arrest them.

Planning began in earnest around setting an ambush at this location. Consideration was given to the propensity to violence of the gang and their ready access to firearms. Because of the fear that they may have inside agents either within the factory, or the security company, it was considered prudent not to involve either at this stage.

Now all that remained was to find out when the robbery would take place.

This question was soon answered when, on Thursday 8 July, members of the gang were observed stealing a white Ford Granada 2.8i saloon motor vehicle from Edmonton High

Street. This was the final piece in the jigsaw and plans were put into place to use a firearms team from PT17 to carry out the ambush.

A reconnaissance was carried out by the firearms team, and the decision was made to use a jump-off vehicle – a delivery van that would not look out of place parked in the loading bay near to where the delivery was expected to take place.

The plan was simple: plain clothes CROPs (Covert Rural Observation Post officers) would lie in wait in positions in the woods and on a nearby golf course to give warning of the gang's approach. Once the Securicor wages delivery commenced, armed PT17 officers would wait until the gang committed themselves and then deploy from the jump-off van.

Attempts to arrest the robbers in the open area, before they could threaten the guards, would be made. Failing that, officers would deal with any threat using such force as was reasonable. RCS officers in unmarked vehicles would act in support and deal with any getaway vehicle. A cut-off vehicle (an armoured police Land Rover) would be used to block an escape route down a track to a farmyard in Shooters Hill Road. If the padlock to this gate had been cropped (cut) overnight it would be an indication that the robbery would take place the following day. Police dog handlers were also in reserve along with the ASU (Air Support Unit) and an ambulance.

The very next day, it was noted that the padlock had indeed been cropped and, at around 7 a.m., the officers inside the jump-off van were driven to their location by RCS officers and parked adjacent to a wall, with their roller shutters facing towards the loading area. At the last minute, they had decided to inform the Co-op supervisor, but had not told him the full extent of their purpose. He agreed to keep his lorries parked at the other end of the yard, and direct the Securicor delivery van to a space

overlooked by the jump-off van. One driver failed to receive these instructions and near to the critical time parked his lorry in a way that completely obstructed the team's view of the delivery area!

Officers kept observation through spy holes that had been drilled in the roller shutter. One of these officers had the additional role of covering his colleagues while they deployed from the back of the van. This officer was equipped with a Browning pistol and a long ballistic shield. This shield was a new acquisition and had never before been deployed on an armed operation.

After a short while in position, the team received radio transmissions from the CROP officers that the three suspects were present in the woods and were carrying a heavy bag. They came so close to the officer that they nearly tripped over him. From this point he was unable to report their movements. In the meantime, the conventional surveillance officers noted that the stolen getaway car was being driven locally, apparently watching for police activity.

At 8 a.m., after a long period of radio silence, the arrival of the Securicor vehicle was announced. The officers saw the van reverse into the loading bay and out of the view of the team and the CROP officer (hidden from view by the lorry) at the same time that they saw the getaway car, which had followed the van in, carry out a three-point turn in preparation for a quick exit.

Seconds later, the shield officer watching through his spyhole was aware of a blur of movement across his field of vision from right to left towards the Securicor van. He could not be sure of what he had seen, but had to make a split-second decision. He called the attack, and the roller shutters were thrown open, only to reveal an empty expanse of concrete in front of them. Checks on the radio revealed that no one

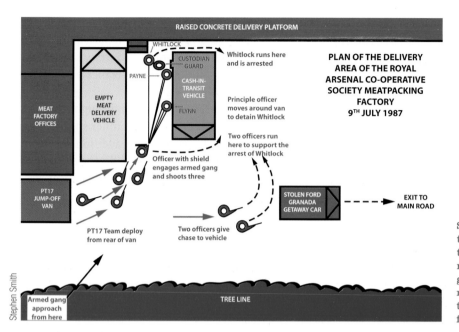

PLAN OF THE DELIVERY AREA OF THE ROYAL ARSENAL CO-OPERATIVE SOCIETY MEATPACKING FACTORY 9TH JULY 1987

RAISED CONCRETE DELIVERY PLATFORM

WHITLOCK

CUSTODIAN GUARD

PAYNE

CASH-IN-TRANSIT VEHICLE

FLYNN

EMPTY MEAT DELIVERY VEHICLE

MEAT FACTORY OFFICES

Whitlock runs here and is arrested

Principle officer moves around van to detain Whitlock

Two officers run here to support the arrest of Whitlock

Officer with shield engages armed gang and shoots three

PT17 JUMP-OFF VAN

PT17 Team deploy from rear of van

Two officers give chase to vehicle

STOLEN FORD GRANADA GETAWAY CAR

EXIT TO MAIN ROAD

Stephen Smith

Armed gang approach from here

TREE LINE

Sketch showing the positions of the police, the robbers and the guard just moment before the shots were fired

else including the CROP officer had seen any movement.

The shield officer leapt out onto the concrete, squinting as his eyes adjusted to the bright sunshine. He ran forwards towards to where they knew the van to be (behind the big lorry). The rest of the team followed, not sure if they had deployed too early. There was no going back.

As the shield officer moved around the back of the Co-op lorry towards the cab of the Securicor van into a space no more than three metres wide, he was confronted with something resembling a scene from a movie. The robbers were going about their work, oblivious to the arrival of the armed police. Two of the three had their backs to the advancing officers. They were all armed and wearing dark clothing, including balaclavas. The closest, Michael Flynn, was on his tip-toes, peering through a small grilled port behind the driver's window. In his right hand he held a long-barrelled stainless steel Smith & Wesson .357 magnum revolver, with which he was threatening the guard inside.

Nicholas Payne was pointing his Franchi 6-shot 12-bore automatic shotgun at the midriff of a guard who was at the rear of the van. He was banging on the side of the van with his elbow and demanding that cash be passed out to them through the money chute or the guard would be shot. Derek Whitlock (the furthest away and the only robber actually facing the officer) held his sawn-off Browning semi-automatic shotgun to the head of the terrified guard. Whitlock, the guard and Payne were in a tight cluster, making it very difficult for the officer to engage the robbers without the guard being struck. It was a life-changing moment for all concerned.

As the shield officer faced the masked gunmen, his team leader's voice burst out over a loudspeaker system. (This was a portable, belt-worn device on trial with the unit.) A shout of 'Armed police! Armed police!' echoed around the parked vehicles. The officer had no time himself to shout a challenge; as to do so would have caused a delay, which would put his life and that of the guard in danger. (His training and standing instructions were clear on that point: 'A firearm may be fired when it is apparent that the police cannot achieve their lawful purpose of preventing loss or further loss of life by any other means; if it is reasonable to do so, an oral warning is to be given before opening fire.')

At that moment, all hell broke loose. Flynn turned his head and looked directly at the officer. Their eyes met and Flynn began to turn his shoulders, as if to spin around. In that fraction of a second, the officer fired two shots, hitting Flynn twice in the back.

Before Flynn had hit the ground the officer turned his attention to Payne, who was about to take on the officer with his shotgun. It was a case of kill or be killed. Before he could do any damage with this devastating weapon, Payne too was shot twice, one round striking his right arm and the other his right shoulder, exiting his throat. He collapsed to the ground.

Whitlock attempted to duck into cover behind the van; he still had his shotgun and was a threat to the officers and the guard who remained frozen to the spot where he stood. The officer fired once at Whitlock but, conscious of the risk of hitting the guard, he held his fire and moved across the front of the van to cut off the third robber's escape.

Other officers now played their part. During the time it had taken the first officer to engage all three suspects at the van (estimated to be less than two seconds), two other officers, both armed with Remington 870 pump-action shotguns, having failed in their attempt to detain the getaway car, turned their attention towards Derek Whitlock, who was now hopelessly outgunned, had thrown his shotgun away and was shouting 'Don't shoot! Don't shoot!' as he lay prostrate on the ground.

The principal officer, having discarded his heavy shield, moved forward to secure Whitlock with plasticuffs. It was then that the robber

complained of being in great pain and they noticed he had received a single gunshot wound to the right of his torso. The bullet was later found to be lodged near his spine. All five of the rounds fired by the officer had found their mark.

The officers now focused their attention on the two men who lay motionless in the space between the vehicles. They were both dead or close to death and there was nothing the officers could do for them. The paramedics were called forward to deal with Whitlock and confirmed the two men on the ground were dead. They were left *in situ* for the time being.

Meanwhile, another drama was playing out nearby. The driver of the getaway vehicle, Richard Parfett, hearing the shots and seeing the police activity, drove for his life, somehow managing to evade the cut-off team. He was pursued for half a mile before crashing into a wall, where he was detained. On the seat next to him police found a radio scanner tuned into the local police radio frequency. He had been listening to the radio traffic.

Whilst the RCS officers awaited transport with their prisoner, a local lady asked whether they would all like a cup of tea. They replied, 'We do, but he doesn't', referring to their disgraced charge.

Whitlock is stood against the Securicor van under the watchful eyes of armed officers. It was here they discovered he had been wounded

The bodies of the two armed robbers, Flynn and Payne, remain *in situ*. The practice of automatically handcuffing wounded suspects was reconsidered after this incident, with consideration being given to the extent of the suspect's wounds

The following day, on 10 July, the *Sun* newspaper ran with a headline that read: 'The Equaliser', together with a large photograph of a Browning semi-automatic pistol. The article went on to state wrongly that officers must 'only shoot to disable'. MP Sir Eldon Griffiths was quoted as saying, 'A wounded gunman is much more dangerous than a dead one, both to the police and members of the public. Police would have been wrong yesterday if they had not opened fire.'

At the robbers' trial, Derek Whitlock (aged 24) was sentenced to fifteen years for his part in the robbery and getaway driver Richard Parfett (also 24) received eight years imprisonment. At the inquest held at Lambeth the following year, whilst giving evidence, the officer who fired the shots said: 'The men did not respond by surrendering. Their immediate reaction to me put me in fear for both myself and the guards. I felt that my life and the lives of my colleagues behind me, and certainly the security guards, were at risk if I did not open fire.' He added, 'I just get paid to do a job. I am not in the habit of doing reckless things.'

The jury passed lawful killing verdicts, unanimously on Nicholas Payne (29) from Erith, and with a seven-to-two majority on Michael Flynn (24) from Catford. The officer who had shot the robbers had been named in the papers and even received death threats. The police force did not know what to do with this officer, or how to react to the press hailing him as some kind of lone ranger. Needless to say, his future was unsure for a while; this was all new ground for the unit.

Although this was by no means the first fatal shooting by officers from the Metropolitan Police, the 'Abattoir shooting' as it became known within the department, was the first occasion where PT17's own officers had fatally shot suspects on an armed operation. It was also the department's first involving multiple suspects. Many lessons and training points were learned from this incident, the main one being the speed at which these situations unfold and the importance of training that helps officers assess situations quickly and react decisively, using reasonable force. The principle of 'action beating reaction' is an important one in police work. Officers who wait too long to assess a situation may not leave themselves enough time to react effectively if there are multiple suspects with hostile intent.

This incident also highlighted the limitations of the police shotgun in close-quarter confrontations where hostages or other innocent members of the public are present. The shotgun was the mainstay of police firearms teams at the time and was carried by the majority of officers on Operation 'Kincraig'. Had that been the only weapon confronting the suspects it is more likely that the guard would have been wounded by the spread of shot.

The Hungerford Massacre
19 August 1987

Levels 1 and 2 PT17 firearms teams were scrambled out of their base at Old Street on 19 August 1987 to assist local police at a small market town in Berkshire called Hungerford. The peace and tranquillity of this English idyll had been shattered after a gun enthusiast called Michael Ryan walked through the town shooting people at random, killing sixteen (including his own mother) and wounding a further fifteen, using firearms that he legally owned. These included semi-automatic pistols, shotguns, an M1 carbine and an AK47 assault rifle (up until this incident a licence holder could own this type of assault rifle if it had been converted to fire single shots only, although with its large magazine capacity the gun could still be fired as fast as the shooter could pull the trigger – to devastating effect). Ryan was eventually cornered in a school building where, after a short stand-off with police, he shot himself with his Beretta 9 mm pistol. By the time PT17 officers arrived in their call-out ladder van and armoured Land Rover there was not a lot for them to do but offer assistance to the stunned local police and population.

Just as the shooting of Cherry Groce caused changes in police firearms training and the formation of the level 2 firearms teams, the Hungerford massacre would force the government to overhaul gun laws, in particular the private ownership of assault rifles and other large calibre rifles, and place restrictions on automatic shotguns. It stopped short of restricting ownership of semi-automatic pistols even though Ryan had used these to kill several of his victims. This incident would be seen as the catalyst for the nationwide use of armed response vehicles in the years that followed.

Level 1 Team Assaulters: Equipment and Training
1987

Little has changed in terms of the equipment and weapons of PT17 since 1987. There have, however, been refinements in the ballistic properties and weight of the helmets and body armour available. The department has also worked hard to find ways to improve its tactics and training facilities.

A level 1 team take time off from training to pose for a team photo. This picture, taken around 1986, shows the lighter grey coveralls, which were replaced by dark blue around this time. Interestingly, at the time of writing, SFO teams are looking at moving back to this shade of colour of operational coveralls in place of the dark blue ones currently used

House Assault Demonstration, MPFTC Lippitts Hill
1987

From the early 1980s, the department had been developing its CQC skills in line with the military model, sending instructors away on courses with Special Forces and adapting tactics to fit within what was permitted under civilian law (i.e. mainly Section 3 of the Criminal Law Act of 1967, which focused on the use of reasonable force).

The training and tactics were developed and, on a regular basis, rehearsed and performed for the benefit of senior officers' courses, including the hostage negotiator's course, in which the new negotiators would experience what it was like to be on the receiving end of a full-blown PT17 house assault.

Once in position the officers wait for the words 'attack, attack, attack'

As the distraction devices are detonated the PT17 assaulters make their entry

Below: The hostages and suspects are led out, having been plasticuffed then placed on the ground

The Last of the 'Old-time Blaggers' – Operation 'Turkey': The Woolwich Shooting
23 November 1987

In early November 1987, an informant contacted SO8 Flying Squad and offered information regarding a group of suspects who were planning an armed robbery. He was able to name three of the men: Ronald Easterbrook (aged 56), Gary Wilson (aged 34) and Anthony Ash (aged 49). All had previous convictions for serious offences. Gary Wilson, even with convictions for robbery, was the novice of the gang. Anthony Ash had twenty-two convictions, including one in 1987 for having an insecure load on a motor vehicle, which had resulted in the death of two Kent police officers, PCs Malcolm Boakes and John Ryan, who were crushed to death in their car whilst on their way in to work.

Easterbrook was an even more hardened criminal. In 1958, when he was 27, he was tackled by a police officer whilst committing a burglary. He shot the officer in the face. PC Henry Stevens was later awarded the George Cross for pursuing Easterbrook and attempting

Inside the Bejam's store, looking towards the cash office. Sensibly, the staff were compliant with the robbers

to detain him after being shot. He had disarmed Easterbrook and wrestled his jacket from him, allowing police to identify and later arrest him.

Further information about the planned robbery in 1987 mentioned access to an AK47 assault rifle and an intention to steal a £1 million haul by hijacking a security van. Plans were made to keep the suspects under observation until it was ascertained that they were in possession of a 'Happy Bag' (a robbery kit, including guns) or until there was material evidence that they were intent on carrying out an armed robbery.

On Saturday 21 November 1987, the informant again made contact. This information resulted in an armed operation commencing on Monday 23 November. Involved in this operation were SO8 officers along with fourteen PT17 firearms officers. These included one inspector (on his first firearms operation), three sergeants and ten constables. They were split between five unmarked vehicles; all were armed with handguns and had further access to two Remington pump-action shotguns and one Heckler & Koch M93 5.56 calibre rifle.

The day began at 7.15 a.m. when the three suspects left a house in Peckham in a gold Mercedes. SO8 and PT17 mobilized and at 9.10 a.m. the three men were seen to collect a silver BMW, which was registered as stolen, from a lock-up garage. They set off in convoy under police surveillance, and the convoy trailed across Blackheath towards Woolwich.

Ash and Easterbrook parked the Mercedes in Sunbury Street and walked away. Four PT17 officers remained by this vehicle. Still no Happy Bag or weapons had been seen. Ash and Easterbrook then walked a quarter of a mile to a pedestrian precinct at Hare Street and entered a Bejam's supermarket where Ash pushed a trolley around the store. SO8 wrongly suspected that the pair were just looking at delivery times and that this was, in fact, only a reconnaissance.

A security van pulled up outside the store and a guard walked in. The safe was opened and £10,400 cash was handed over. Ash moved with deliberation, drew a revolver and threatened a female member of staff. The money was immediately handed to Easterbrook. The two men fled the store with the bag of cash. Before an arrest could be made, the robbers had jumped into a silver BMW on stolen plates with Wilson driving and sped off.

Unaware that they were heading into a trap, the BMW arrived in the garage area in nearby Sunbury Street (which contained lock-up garages) and it stopped by a wall. Just the other side of the wall, parked on the street, was their changeover vehicle, the gold Mercedes.

As Anthony Ash began to emerge from the rear nearside door, he was still clutching the revolver he had used in the robbery. The waiting police officers who were left near the changeover vehicle as a contingency shouted challenges of 'Armed police!' Two other armed officers joined them from a gunship (see page 95) that had followed the gang from the scene of the robbery, one armed with the 5.56 Heckler & Koch M93 rifle.

Ash spoke briefly to Easterbrook, who remained in the rear of the vehicle. Ash then climbed out with the gun in his hand. He moved, crouching, towards the front of the vehicle. Whilst Ash was moving forward, Easterbrook leaned across the back seat, stuck his hand out of the window and fired six shots at the PT17 inspector and sergeant who were positioned at the end of the wall.

The first round hit the inspector just below the left knee; the bullet luckily passed straight through. His fire was returned by five of the six officers, including the wounded inspector. The rounds either missed or failed to penetrate the vehicle but succeeded in keeping Easterbrook pinned down in the back of the car.

As Ash came up from behind the bonnet of the car, ready to fire, he was engaged by a single officer who fired two rounds, the second of which entered the sleeve of Ash's raincoat, before travelling up the inside of his arm and into the left side of his chest. Ash fell backwards and dropped the gun. He was dead.

Easterbrook's revolver was empty and he was unable to access more rounds from his pockets

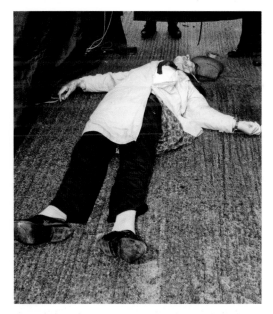

The aftermath: the abandoned getaway car. Anthony Ash's body lies under a tarpaulin at the front of the vehicle

The body of Anthony Ash, fatally shot by armed police as he tried to open fire on them from behind the car

because his jeans were too tight. Who knows what went through his mind at this point, having just seen his fellow gang member gunned down at the front of the car. So, at an appropriate lull in the shooting, he surrendered, as did Gary Wilson, who had spent the whole shoot-out cowering in the well of the front seat.

In summary, one police officer was shot in the leg, eighteen shots were fired by five police officers and six were fired at police by just one suspect. From the time of the first shot being fired to the surrender there were just twenty-five seconds. Ironically, it was Easterbrook's shot that had wounded the officer but it was Ash who paid with his life.

The press made the most of this story. The *Sun*, true to form, ran an attention-grabbing headline that screamed: 'Exit A Hood' (referring to the demise of Anthony Ash, a well-known London villain). The picture was of Ash, his head covered with a tarpaulin as he lay dead, still wearing his light-coloured raincoat.

The *Daily Mail* went one stage further, printing the front page headline: 'Ambush'. Unlike the other papers, they were not happy with a post-shooting photograph showing several armed officers around the vehicle and body of Ash, so they decided to re-touch the picture, adding an extra rifle into the hands of a PT17 officer.

This could have fuelled conspiracy theorists alleging that if police lied about the presence of certain weapons they could be lying about other details. Thankfully, the fabrication was spotted and the paper published a full apology in their next edition.

This was a high-profile case, made more so by the fact that the aftermath had been filmed by an embedded TV crew doing a documentary on the Flying Squad, which incidentally featured as evidence in the trial.

On the first day of his Old Bailey trial, Easterbrook attempted to blow up the prison van taking him back to the remand prison by using a small amount of Semtex-type explosive. This failed to open the hatch but gave him a nasty headache. It was never discovered how he obtained the explosive.

At the trial, Easterbrook defended himself and tried to convince the jury that PT17 and SO8 had conspired to murder him and his colleagues. He also alleged that PT17 had a 'shoot to kill' policy and claimed that he opened

Unperturbed: the embedded TV crew carried on filming footage for their documentary *Flying Squad*

92

fire in self-defence. His claims were rejected and he later received four terms of life imprisonment. Wilson was cleared of robbery but was sentenced to seven years imprisonment for theft.

After a campaign by friends of the family, £10,000 was raised to pay for legal representation at the inquest of Anthony Ash, but an unscrupulous person stole the money, leaving the family to represent their own case. Eventually, a verdict of justifiable homicide was announced.

The wounded police inspector made a full recovery and later returned to operational duty, a little embarrassed, not because he was the first-ever PT17 officer to be wounded but because it was on his first-ever armed operation.

Little is known about Gary Wilson's trajectory after sentencing, but Easterbrook lost his appeal against his sentence and died in prison in May 2009. The press lamented the passing of what they described as the last of the 'old-time blaggers'.

'Order to Engage': First Directed Rifle Shooting, Maiden Lane WC2
2 Dec 1988

On the evening of Thursday 1 December 1988, in the busy West End of London, tourists and drinkers were about to get more than they had bargained for after a domestic incident in the Chandos pub near Trafalgar Square spilled out onto the surrounding streets.

Around 10.15 p.m. a tourist was talking to a girl in the pub when her boyfriend burst in holding a revolver and accused the man of 'messing with his missus'. He pointed the handgun at the tourist's face and forced him outside onto the busy streets. It was the beginning of a three-hour nightmare for this unfortunate man whose only crime was talk to a girl in a pub.

The boyfriend, Michael Rose, a skinhead known locally as 'Mental Mickey', owing to his irrational behaviour and the fact that he had a screwdriver tattooed on his head, had been living rough on the Embankment prior to this incident. Rose now forced his unfortunate victim to walk the streets with a gun held to his head. He must have been terrified by Rose who was a fearsome-looking man, obviously deranged and under the influence of drugs and alcohol.

The incident being in the West End of London, police were quickly on the scene, alerted by the commotion, and they began shadowing the pair as they moved through the West End towards Maiden Lane, WC2. This was a spontaneous armed incident and, because of the time of day, scrambling a PT17 firearms team from home could take up to an hour. (Until 1991 there was no stand-by twenty-four-hour firearms cover.) There were, however, other options open to the local police commanders. The DPG (Diplomatic Protection Group) operated at premises all over central London and were armed. They also ran their own armed response vehicle, call sign 'Ranger 500'. This vehicle was manned by two DPG rifle officers, both of whom were equipped with Ruger Mini 14 .223 carbines. They were assigned to give support to local officers. Another fortunate piece of luck was the availability of the then police commander, Dave Veness, head of the Protection Command and also the most senior hostage negotiator within the police service. He had achieved fame after his handling of the Iranian Embassy siege back in 1980.

Commander Veness took control of the incident. What was foremost in his mind at this time was the fear that the suspect might run amok as had happened recently in Germany, where lack of decisive police action had apparently contributed to the deaths of two teenagers, one of whom was taken hostage in similar circumstances. A police officer had also died in the ensuing pursuit across the city.

Negotiations were being carried out using a loudhailer. Meanwhile, the behaviour of the gunman appeared to be getting more irrational. He had retreated into the doorway of Corpus Christi Church in Maiden Lane and was demanding that a taxi be sent to him. As Rose became more and more agitated he shouted, 'Where is my taxi? I want to get going. I'm going to count to thirty.' He then began counting down from thirty, intimating that he would shoot his hostage when he reached zero.

Commander Veness gave the order over the police radio to his rifle officers: 'Order to engage if you've got a clear line of sight.'

A last-ditch effort to negotiate commenced, but the countdown continued. As Michael Rose neared the end of this countdown, he edged out to have a look down the street, still clinging onto his hostage with the gun held firmly to his head. Then, just before 1 a.m. a single shot rang out. Rose fell back into the church doorway, allowing his hostage to run free into the safe hands of the waiting police.

Rose had been hit through his chest, the bullet exiting out of his back. He was lucky the round had missed his vital organs, but even after being shot, as police approached, he still had the energy to throw a milk bottle at them.

After a night in Westminster Hospital, Rose was off the critical list and police had discovered that the revolver he had terrorized hundreds of West End revellers with was a replica. He recovered from his wounds and on 2 November 1989 he received a lengthy prison sentence for kidnap and firearms offences.

The *Evening Standard* led on 2 December with the headline: 'Gunman Felled From 120 Yards'. Although the distance cannot be confirmed, when you take into account the shadows and gloomy lighting conditions, it was an amazing piece of accuracy with a small calibre carbine.

Although this incident was not directly related to the firearms department it is significant in that it was the first directed sniper option ever used in London. The officer who fired at Rose had recently transferred from PT17 into the DPG. The senior officer who made the call to engage stood by his decision. Commander Veness would later rise to the rank of assistant commissioner and would be knighted by the Queen in his retirement year in 2005.

Operation 'Char', Harrow: PT17 Officer Wins the Queen's Gallantry Medal
13 April 1989

Towards the end of 1988, Flying Squad officers were investigating a series of armed robberies of bank premises and security delivery vehicles in north London. They named the investigation Operation 'Char'. The gang appeared to have up to eight members; any mix or number of those eight could be involved in the next robbery. The identities of some were known to the Flying Squad, and they were busy trying to gather more intelligence and identify the others. Although some of the intelligence was sketchy, the gang's modus operandi was not: they were using blocking vehicles and vans fitted with battering rams to smash open doors and gain access to the cash contained within armoured vehicles. They were no strangers to firearms – on one occasion when a police car chased them and forced them to stop, they calmly got out and made the unarmed officer kneel on the ground as they shot out the tyres of the police car. This was a determined and dangerous group of criminals.

After months of work the Flying Squad discovered that the gang was indeed made up of eight individuals, any one of whom could be called upon to commit these robberies, and they only knew the identities of three of the men.

Things came to a head when the police received a tip-off that the gang were planning to rob premises in Rayners Lane, Harrow, but they did not have much else to go on. A decision was made to recruit the help of local uniformed officers to find possible getaway vehicles laid down by the gang in preparation for the robbery. It was known that up to fourteen vehicles of the type the gang favoured had been stolen over the past few days; if the police could locate any of these they might have a chance of catching these men at work.

On the evening of 12 April, after a protracted search, a stolen red Ford Sierra was located parked in a side road off the main thoroughfare near Rayners Lane. Other stolen vehicles were also found to be parked-up in the area. They all needed to be watched.

The Flying Squad once again called upon PT17 for armed support. The officers from these two specialist units would combine to form crews of 'gunships' more commonly known in firearms circles now as CARVs (Covert Armed Response Vehicles.) Each gunship would have four officers – two armed PT17 officers and two unarmed Flying Squad officers. One of the Flying Squad officers would drive the gunship, the other would map-read and operate the radios, while the PT17 officers in the rear waited in readiness to deploy with their firearms and detain any armed suspects. A Flying Squad detective would then come forward and formally arrest the suspects.

The plan was that three such gunships would remain in the area ready to respond should the gang be spotted. The Flying Squad believed that the gang would target the National Westminster Bank in Rayners Lane, but unbeknown to police the gang had their sights set on a nearby Post Office that had over

£76,000 in its safe ready for pension day.

On Thursday 13 April 1989, the wheels were set in motion for what would turn out to be the biggest shoot-out the firearms department had been involved with since its inception in 1966.

Shortly before 9 a.m. the officers in the gunships began to hear radio traffic concerning the team of robbers who were spotted at the rear of the Rayners Lane Post Office in a stolen Ford Escort van. They had bolted a steel joist to the floor of the van, which protruded out of the rear.

On this day the gang was made up of three members. James Farrell, aged 52, (a career armed robber who had recently been released from prison after serving ten years of an eighteen-year sentence) was wearing a black crash helmet. Terrence Dewsnap, aged 48, (himself no stranger to prison having served six years inside for serious criminal offences) was wearing a white crash helmet. Finally, John Gorman, aged 49 (who had a robbery and firearms offences record stretching back three decades) was wearing a black balaclava. They used the van as a battering ram, reversing it into the rear doors of what they believed was the Post Office. However, their plan was not foolproof: they had rammed the wrong doors. Their van was now wedged against a staircase in the building next door to their intended target. They quickly aborted the robbery attempt and ran to their stolen Ford Sierra getaway car, which was parked nearby.

At 8.57 a.m. one of the gunships turned up a service road near to the Post Office and saw the three men run to the red Ford Sierra, get in and drive off at speed. They gave chase towards Harrow but after a brief pursuit the car turned into Thackeray Close, which led to a dead end in a garage area. They stopped next to a fence line but, as the officers began to deploy, drove off. They eventually abandoned the Sierra by a footbridge that crossed over the Rayners Lane Tube line.

Gorman, armed with a sawn-off shotgun, Dewsnap, armed with a 9 mm Luger pistol and Farrell who was carrying a .45 calibre Colt revolver were in no mood for giving in without a fight.

As they ran up the stairs and crossed the footbridge one officer was right on their heels. As they ran down the alleyway on the other side he drew back slightly as at least one of the men opened fire on him but, undeterred, the brave officer would not give up.

As the three men cleared the alley into Twyford Road, Gorman passed Farrell his sawn-off shotgun. He was intending to drive the getaway vehicle. Upon reaching this vehicle (a stolen Ford Granada), parked only a few metres away from the exit, Farrell stopped by the passenger door on the pavement side of the vehicle. He turned and waited a split second for the officer to exit the alleyway. (One can only

Stephen Smith

Twyford Road, looking from the alleyway leading from the footbridge. The second officer opened fire from behind a decorative concrete wall. The fence and privet hedge were not there in 1989. Visitors to the scene can still see the damage caused by rounds striking the wall on the right

Stephen Smith

The footbridge over which the two officers chased the gang. The getaway car was parked on the other side of the bridge in Twyford Road. (Photos taken in 2012)

assume that, at that point, he had made his decision to fight it out with police in the hope of escaping after the officer had been killed or disabled.) Meanwhile, Gorman and Dewsnap had run to the driver's side of the car. Dewsnap remained at the rear offside corner of the car and turned to face the officer. Gorman did not have time to get in the car before all hell broke loose.

As the officer emerged from the alleyway still shouting 'Stop! Armed police!', he was met by a blast from Farrell's powerful Colt .45 revolver. As Farrell continued to fire at the officer from only seven metres away, the officer pushed his Glock 17 pistol out in front of him and began shooting back. He did not stop until Farrell, who was still wearing the black crash helmet, fell to the ground, shot twice in the chest. He would die of his wounds later in hospital.

Realizing he was still in mortal danger the officer now turned to face the second threat. Dewsnap had already been shooting at the officer and was now only five metres away. The officer managed to fire just two rounds before he felt a searing pain in his ankle. It did not at first register with him that he had been shot; his brain told him he had snapped his ankle on the kerb. The pain was intense (the bullet from Dewsnap's Luger had penetrated the officer's shin just above the ankle and exited through the back of his heel) but he did not have time to dwell on his injury. As he fell back into a sitting position he once again pushed his Glock out in front of him and fired until the threat went away. This time it was Dewsnap in his white crash helmet who fell to the ground; he was fatally wounded, hit once in the leg and twice in the chest, with one round rupturing his aorta.

The officer rolled over onto his right side to gain vision around the side of the car. But he was now a spectator as his colleague fired from the alleyway, using his 5.56 H&K rifle to shoot through the windows of the car at Gorman who

Action photo, taken during the shootout from across the road, showing Gorman crouching by the side of the car, with Dewsnap on the ground in his white crash helmet

was still a threat as he crouched beside the car. The shotgun dropped by Dewsnap was within arm's reach. Gorman was hit with a glancing blow on the side of his head and then hit in his arm, the round penetrating into the side of his body. He had had enough and surrendered. From the time the police gunship had picked up the getaway car to the time the last shots were fired, just over five minutes had passed.

Gorman was taken to hospital where he survived his wounds. When the scene was examined it was found that during this exchange the gang had fired over twenty rounds at police, who had returned fire with eighteen rounds. The wounded PT17 officer was placed in an ambulance at the scene and checked over; an ambulance man carefully removed his left sock and was surprised when a 9 mm bullet head fell out onto the floor of the ambulance. It was kept for evidence. The ambulance man commented that he was due to start training as a police officer at Hendon the following Monday and was now having second thoughts. As he was transported to hospital, the officer reassured him that it was not always like this. The wounded officer went on to make a good recovery.

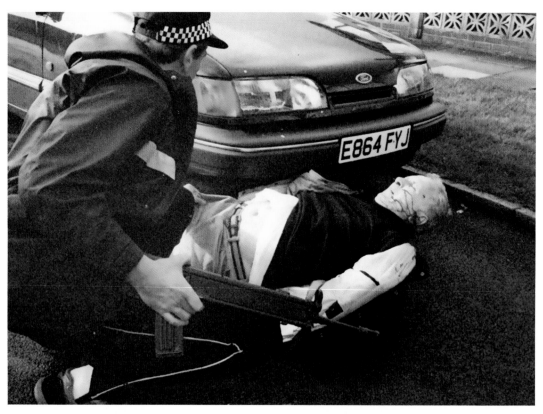

Gorman is detained by one of the PT17 officers armed with a Heckler & Koch model 93 5.56 rifle. He survived his wounds

As the facts of the story filtered out into the public domain, it became apparent that this was a heroic action by the two officers that, along with the efforts of the Flying Squad, had brought an end to a gang of armed robbers who had terrorized bank staff, security guards and members of the public for a long time.

The *Evening Standard* led later that day with a headline of: 'Flying Squad Shoot Dead Two Raiders' and a sub-heading of; 'Police ambush, and bullets fly all over the place'. The *Telegraph* the next day was a little more conservative, stating in a headline several pages in: 'Police Kill Two Robbers In Shoot-out After Bungled Raid.'

However one looked at it, the officers had acted with great bravery, the wounded officer particularly so. This was later recognized when he received the Queen's Gallantry Medal. His colleagues' actions were recognized with a Queen's Commendation for bravery. This had been the first police shooting involving officers armed with the new 9 mm Glock 17 semi-automatic pistol.

In January 1990, Gorman was sentenced to thirteen years for his part in the attempted robbery. The charge of attempted murder of a police officer was dropped. An inquest jury later that year found that Farrell and Dewsnap had been lawfully killed by police.

PART FOUR:
Coming of Age –
PT17/SO19 in the 1990s

As the 1980s ended with the bloody murder of ten Royal Marine commandos at their barracks at Deal in Kent at the hands of the IRA, so the 1990s began with a spirit of growth and anticipation for the men of PT17 (for there were, as yet, no women on the staff). Some of the recommendations from the Roach report following the police shooting of Cherry Groce and the Hungerford massacre were beginning to take effect. A huge recruitment drive was in full flow, which in 1991 would see the department more than double in size overnight. This would be a welcome boost in the struggle against armed crime and the fight against the IRA on the streets of London, in a battle that would continue in earnest for all of the coming decade at least.

The 1990s would see yet another name change for the unit, going from PT17 (Personnel and Training) to SO19 (Specialist Operations). This would mean new money for vehicles, equipment and training, funded by the larger specialist operations budget.

In this decade, the department would face some of its greatest challenges as the relentless wave of armed crime increased with the serious threat from dissident Irish terrorism and the up-and-coming increase in drug-related gang violence and gang-related shootings. In this cauldron of change the department would be moulded into a viable and cohesive armed unit worthy of progressing forward into the twenty-first century.

The Brentford Shooting: Operation 'Magdalena'
26 April 1990

After a busy start to the year with several long-running operations, the Flying Squad from Barnes once again requested the assistance of a firearms team to support them in an operation against a prolific gang of armed robbers who

A view from outside the sub-Post Office (on the right) in Enfield Road, Brentford, looking down towards where the second robber was chased

had already carried out twelve robberies in the west London area.

Owing to the imprecise information finding its way to the informant handlers of the Flying Squad, it was decided to use a level 2 firearms team, thus freeing up the level 1 teams for other duties. This proved to be the right decision as the operation lumbered on for eight weeks before there was an ending in sight. Then, on Thursday 12 April 1990, it all

Two shotguns and the discarded cash bag

changed. The Flying Squad, supported by their armed PT17 back-up, followed a three-handed team of robbers to outside a sub-Post Office in Enfield Road, Brentford, west London. While two men, both armed with sawn-off shotguns, entered the premises, the third remained in the black Ford Escort XR3i getaway vehicle.

Whilst the two robbers were holding up the staff in the Post Office, Flying Squad vehicles moved forward to block the getaway car. PT17 officers deployed from these vehicles in readiness and as the two raiders, both armed with sawn-off shotguns, left the premises with a bag containing £1,000 of stolen cash, the armed officers of PT17 challenged them.

The two men ignored commands from the armed police to stop and drop their guns and continued running towards their getaway vehicle. The armed officers gave chase, shouting again for them to stop. One of the men, 31-year-old Michael Alexander, turned and pointed his shotgun at them. This was a catastrophic error on his part as three of the pursuing officers opened fire. Alexander fell, mortally wounded. His loaded shotgun lay nearby him on the wet road. Alexander was hit three times but it later became evident that the fatal shot was fired from a Smith & Wesson model 10 revolver.

Patrick Anderson threw his weapon to the ground to avoid the same fate, before running down the street. He was pursued down the side of some houses where he was forced to surrender. He was arrested and taken into custody along with Stapleton, the driver of the getaway car.

The next day, the *Sun* newspaper featured the robbery with the headline: 'Cops Kill Bandit', showing pictures of Michael Alexander being removed from the scene by ambulance and another of the shotgun he had carried during the robbery. They quoted a New Scotland Yard spokesperson saying, 'We regret the loss of life. But those who arm themselves in pursuit of crime must face the consequences.'

Both Anderson and Stapleton, the surviving members of the gang pleaded guilty and were sentenced at the Old Bailey on 4 December 1990 for armed robbery and firearms offences, receiving fourteen and twelve years respectively.

Siege at Tokyo Joe's Nightclub, Mayfair
29 July 1990

Tokyo Joe's on Clarges Street, off Piccadilly, was one of many nightclubs in and around the popular Mayfair district of London. It was a favourite haunt of many Middle Eastern patrons and was used by the elite of the Arab world. In fact, on this night, several members of the Kuwaiti royal family were present when the ten-hour siege began.

At 1.45 a.m., as the 200 or so staff and revellers in the club enjoyed their night, a lone gunman, 30-year-old Hani Elrayes, himself from the Middle East, forced his way into the crowded club, firing his shotgun into the ceiling. He also carried with him a rifle, a replica handgun and a bayonet. Even more worryingly, he had an elaborate bomb attached to his body which he claimed contained 3 kg of explosives (although this would later turn out to be fake).

Panic ensued, which allowed as many as a hundred staff and customers to escape. Police were called to the scene, a cordon was set up and local inhabitants were evacuated. Hostage negotiators were called in, along with a PT17 firearms team, who were scrambled from home at great speed.

As the siege developed, the PT17 officers were able to provide a close containment and managed to help and negotiate for the release of many more hostages. The perpetrator, Elrayes, would not speak with hostage negotiators, instead choosing to talk with a PT17 officer on the containment. Escaped hostages told of a man, drunk and high on cocaine, who was walking around the club swigging from a bottle of Black Label whisky. Apparently, at one stage he fell over and cut his leg on the broken bottle.

There were some tense moments, as the only demand made by Elrayes was for a plane to take him to Beirut. The negotiators would have no authority to agree to such a demand, which would itself take time to consider. After ten long hours only six hostages remained, and the siege ended when Elrayes agreed to leave them, walk up the stairs and surrender. He was then arrested and taken for questioning.

Because of careful handling and clever negotiations, much of this undertaken by one PT17 officer who spoke frequently with Elrayes through one of the doors, the siege had ended peacefully.

The Princess is given an explanation of training methods, while PT17 senior instructors look on

Princess Diana receives instruction on the MP5K, a fully automatic close-protection weapon. She took to the task well and was apparently 'a natural'

HRH Diana Princess of Wales Visits Lippitts Hill Training Camp
21 September 1990

Princess Diana made two visits to the Metropolitan Police force's firearms training centre at Lippitts Hill to see first-hand the type of training that went on there. She paid special attention to the close protection training that her own protection officers would undergo.

The Shooting at Woodhatch: Operation 'Yamoto'
27 November 1990

As another year drew towards its end, down in the quiet village of Woodhatch near Reigate, Surrey, another drama was unfolding with yet more fatal consequences.

Since the late 1980s, members of a southeast London crime syndicate, along with others, had been committing high-level cash-in-transit robberies netting millions of pounds. Throughout this series of robberies, their level of violence had increased, along with their daring. The Flying Squad at Tower Bridge feared that it was only a matter of time before the gang killed someone.

The method used in the commission of these robberies was to take a custodian (usually a security guard) hostage thus gaining access to the money-laden delivery vehicle, before disabling the tracking device and driving the security van away to a quiet location where they could remove the cash at their leisure. The syndicate had eluded police for some time, and it was some good old detective work involving hours of surveillance that finally bore results.

The gang, which consisted of brothers Mehmet and Dennis Arif, Tony Downer and Kenny Baker (who was known in the circles he mixed in as 'Mad Kenny Baker'), were observed stealing vehicles and leaving them near to the service station on Dovers Green Road at Woodhatch in Surrey. All that remained was to set up an ambush for the would-be robbers and catch them red-handed.

On Tuesday 27 November, a PT17 level 1 firearms team with several level 2 officers in support, were posted in unmarked Flying Squad vehicles (gunships) with Flying Squad drivers. These vehicles were plotted up (police-speak, meaning positioned discreetly so as to cover all approaches) around the Texaco service station and its adjoining streets. At 9.55 a.m. a Group 4 security van containing £750,000 arrived and parked up in a side road next to the service station.

As the crew of the van walked towards the services to get some food, the stolen red pick-up truck containing all four members of the gang arrived. Tony Downer took the custodians hostage at gunpoint and began to lead them back to the van. Mehmet Arif ran to assist while Dennis Arif emerged from under a tarpaulin wearing an old-man mask.

Mehmet Arif, with a blacked-up face and wig, returned to the pick-up while Kenny Baker, who was wearing a Ronald Reagan mask, attempted to move cars off the forecourt to clear a route for the van. One 75-year-old driver refused to move and was threatened by Baker with a handgun. Mehmet Arif and Kenny Baker then attempted to drive through the services while the first of the armed gunships arrived on scene on the petrol forecourt.

Seeing Dennis Arif and Tony Downer in the cab of the van brandishing firearms, one officer, fearing the lives of the hostages were in imminent danger, fired at Tony Downer. Although the rounds did not penetrate the armoured skin of the vehicle the two robbers immediately indicated that they had given up. The escape hatch was opened in the roof and the officers

Top: The Woodhatch robbery: Dennis Arif (far right), runs to assist while Mehmet and Tony Downer force the custodians back into the van (just out of picture on the left) at gunpoint. Members of the public beat a hasty retreat. Out of sight, members of the PT17 attack team ready themselves for action Middle: Not interested in surrendering, Kenny Baker reaches across with his semi-automatic pistol. He is shot in the head by an officer armed with a 5.56 Heckler & Koch M93. The officer nearest him also reacts, firing two rounds from the hip with his MP5. One round hits Kenny Baker in the body, rupturing his spleen. The other hits Mehmet (who has drawn his gun) in the neck. More police arrive to block in the pick-up-truck. Both men are dragged from the truck Bottom: Mehmet is dragged wounded from the passenger door. Kenny Baker lies at the side of the pick-up. Officers attempt to provide first aid. All attention is now focused on the Securicor van just out of shot to the left. It has been contained but the suspects are still inside

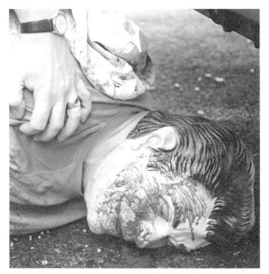

Kenny Baker, still wearing the Ronald Reagan mask, lies mortally wounded

Tony Downer is forcibly removed from the escape hatch in the roof of the security vehicle. He joins Denis Arif who was brought out first. For these two 'old-time blaggers' the game was finally up. The price of petrol indicated in the background shows just how much buying power £750,000 would have had in 1990

released the remaining hostages and retrieved Dennis Arif and Tony Downer from inside the vehicle. Before long, it was all over: the remaining two robbers were in custody and the custodians were safe.

This was a violent and determined group of individuals, who were prepared for a major armed confrontation. Only the overwhelming firepower and aggression shown could have made them surrender

In November 1991 at the Old Bailey, Dennis and Mehmet Arif each received twenty-five years imprisonment while Downer received eighteen years. At the inquest of Kenny Baker the following year, the jury passed a verdict of lawful killing.

The cache of weapons used by the gang on the day of the robbery. Mehmet Arif carried over forty spare rounds for his revolver in his jacket pocket; some gang members including Mehmet were also wearing body armour, showing their willingness to take on the police if necessary

The Advent of the Armed Response Vehicles: First Patrol on the Streets of London
1 July 1991

Following intensive selections to fill over ninety ARV places available with another fifty officers to be added within the first twelve months, the Metropolitan Police national firearms training centre at Lippitts Hill in Epping Forest was working like a sausage machine in an attempt to meet the go-live date of 1 July 1991. Some of the level 2 officers were posted to the ARVs to bolster the shortfall and add experience amongst the fledgling crews.

As it turned out, the first PT17 ARV with its three-person crew rolled out onto the streets of London on time. The event did not go unnoticed by the press, nor the fact that the first female officers had finally broken into the ranks of the firearms department. Others in high places waited with bated breath for the first ARV-related incident. Although initially few in numbers, the ARV unit would grow over the

The first-ever PT17 ARV leaves the yard of the Old Street base in east London to begin its patrol of the capital

next two decades to number over 250 officers, putting up to seventeen ARVs on the streets at once at peak times.

Along with personal equipment and radios, officers were also responsible for three Smith & Wesson model 10 .38 calibre revolvers and two Heckler & Koch MP5 9 mm carbines adapted for single shot only. The MP5s were locked in a safe in the boot with access via the back seat, whilst initially the revolvers were held in a smaller gun safe secured between the driver and operator.

The first group photo of the Metropolitan Police armed response officers, taken at Lippitts Hill training camp at the end of their training in June 1991

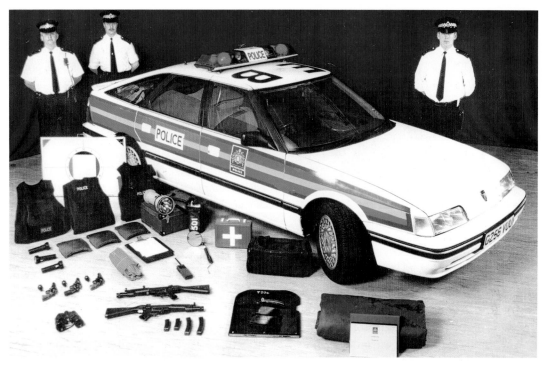

This photo shows one of the ARV crews in 1991 with the equipment they carried whilst out on patrol which included: a target identification board, personal body armour with 7.62 upgrade plates, individual torches, a seek and search torch, a first aid kit, a clipboard, an extendable mirror, a folding stretcher, a ballistic loading bag, a ballistic shield and blanket, incident logs and a portable main-set radio

These were all carried in an unloaded condition. This created a problem, which was soon identified after one crew had to deploy in great haste to give chase to an armed robber from a Post Office in Clerkenwell. The officer was attempting to load his revolver whilst giving chase. He managed to load just two rounds before confronting the man and taking his surrender at gunpoint, not knowing whether there was a live round under the hammer. Luckily, he did not have to find out.

This was rectified within the next few months and officers were permitted to carry their revolvers loaded but out of sight, i.e., covered by uniform. Over the coming months and years all new ARV officers were trained on the new Glock 17 semi-automatic pistol as well as the MP5 carbine.

Deciding which type of vehicle makes a suitable ARV has always been a headache for the engineers, who have to upgrade the brakes and chassis to account for the extra weight of three fully kitted armed officers with all the extra equipment and weapons needed in their day-to-day working capacity.

During the 1990s the role of ARV was shared between the Rover 827, the Volvo 850GLT estate and the Vauxhall Omega 3L saloon and estate. A single Ford Maverick was even tested for the role.

Each driver and crew-member had their own preferences – some favoured the solid build of the Rover 827, others preferred the handling of the Vauxhall Omega, while some liked the space of the Volvo estate. These vehicles provided the mainstay for the first decade of the ARV,

Here an ARV officer places his MP5 carbine in the specially constructed gun safe in the boot of the ARV. Loaded magazines were locked in the safe with the guns in the early days, but later carried by officers on their belt-rig. Each round would have to be accounted for at the end of each tour of duty

The infrequency of police accidents, or POL-ACs, as they were known, were a testament to the training and skill of the drivers. Most of the ARV applicants were required to be advanced drivers before applying and most three-person crews had at least two drivers who shared the driving during each eight-hour tour of duty.

Accidents aside, the prestige of joining the ARVs was attracting more quality personnel who could now hope to progress through the department either as a firearms instructor, or by applying to serve on the specialist firearms teams. The ARV detail would grow and flourish and it still remains a coveted role within the police service.

providing speed, safety and versatility. However, they were pushed to their extremes. Some of the driving across London at high speed had its own inherent dangers, which were found out to the cost of the drivers and crew. Some officers saw the car travel as an occupational hazard, and one commented, 'It's sometimes more scary getting to a call than actually dealing with the maniac with a gun.'

Female Officers' Open Day
3 September 1991

The high profile of the ARVs highlighted once again the disparity between the sexes within the firearms department. In an attempt to rectify this, a series of open days for female officers were held at Lippitts Hill. These were well attended, but the firearms department still had a way to go before it could attract female officers in any numbers. At the time there were

METROPOLITAN POLICE
ARMED RESPONSE VEHICLES

'Trojan Delta'

Watercolour of an ARV deployment, titled 'Trojan Delta', which denoted the authorization given from the information room at New Scotland Yard to deploy with loaded weapons. In time, this procedure was changed to reflect the need for officers to self-arm and deploy if the situation necessitated it. This change to procedure worked well and is still in use today

Photo taken in the mid-1990s of Sergeant Julie Colverd (one of the first female firearms instructors within the department) demonstrating use of cover on an ARV course. (Sadly Julie was killed in 2004 in a mountaineering accident)

only fifty female armed officers out of a total of over 2,000 authorized officers in the Met.

It was by virtue of the work it did that PT17 was still generally perceived by people outside the department to be one of the last male bastions within the police service. This had to, and would, change in the coming years with female officers representing every role within the firearms department including firearms instructor, specialist firearms officer and a variety of management positions.

PT17 Foreign Operations, Turks and Caicos Islands
October 1991

Up until the 1990s, it had been very rare, almost unheard of, for officers from the firearms department to be sent abroad, but there was one cry for help from the small British overseas territory of the Turks and Caicos Islands that led to a level 1 firearms team being sent out to assist with protecting a prisoner involved with Colombian drug dealer, Pablo Escobar.

The prisoner, Robert Elesi Serry (arrested earlier that year while travelling on a false passport) was awaiting extradition to the USA. He was Pablo Escobar's brother-in-law and knew the inside workings of Escobar's drug-dealing empire. He was wanted by the DEA (the US Drug Enforcement Administration) on charges of smuggling six tons of cocaine. It was feared, with good reason, that a team of mercenaries had been recruited to rescue or kill the prisoner, who had already escaped and been recaptured once. Sightings of helicopters and strange men had been observed arriving on the island. The local police, fearing it was all getting out of hand, needed help and on 19 October 1991 that help was dispatched to them.

The operation centred on the Island of Grand Turk and in essence was a protection job. The idea was to babysit the prisoner until the extradition order from the DEA could be finalized. Serry was held in the island's prison, a long whitewashed box-like building with thick clay walls and palm branches on the roof. He was kept in isolation in the building's empty female wing.

The small team of six officers was collected from the airport along with their weapons (which included six MP5K sub-machine guns), and they quickly went about their task of planning how to protect the prisoner and prevent a rescue attempt. They worked around the clock, two directly outside the cell, two patrolling in a jeep and two resting; this continued for five days. On the sixth and final day they all stayed together with Serry, delivering him early in the morning onto the aircraft that was to take him to the USA. With the operation concluded, the exhausted firearms team packed up and had a well-earned sleep on their flight home.

Within months of Serry being in the US, Escobar's hold on his cartels began to weaken and Escobar himself was killed in an exchange of gunfire with Colombian government troops. The first overseas operation for the Met's firearms department had been a great success, and the US Department of Justice praised the Home Secretary and work of the PT17 team.

ARV Shoot-out in Acton: Officer Wounded
11 November 1991

Sceptics of the armed response officer's role were soon humbled as the first ARV-related shooting took place on 11 November 1991 when an ARV was called to Old Oak Road in Acton, north-west London.

David Barfield (en ex-Territorial Army man with mental health issues) had been acting strangely and his parents had called in the duty social worker, his doctor and a psychiatrist in the hope of returning him to hospital under the provisions of the Mental Health Act. Police had also been called to assist in case of violence. Although there was no mention of firearms, Barfield had been seen in the hallway armed with a sword and so an ARV was assigned and attended to give their support if needed.

As police and the social worker moved along the pavement towards the address, the ARV kept pace, stopping near the front garden. It was then that Barfield emerged wearing camouflage clothing and armed with a rifle. This turned out to be a Lee Enfield rifle complete with a seventeen-inch bayonet, converted to fire .410 shotgun ammunition. Barfield immediately opened fire on the officers who beat a hasty retreat. The two officers in the front of the ARV deployed from the vehicle, while the officer in the rear broke out the MP5 carbines from the locked gun safe behind the rear seat.

Barfield walked towards the ARV and fired at the vehicle. Some of the shotgun pellets struck the officer inside in the head. Her colleagues returned fire with their revolvers and Barfield went back into the address.

Bleeding profusely from several wounds in her scalp the officer managed to deploy onto the street. She passed one of the carbines to her colleague and the officers began to contain the premises. But Barfield was having none of it and came out again. This time the officers were ready and in the next exchange of fire Barfield was shot in the abdomen.

Despite being hit, Barfield showed no sign of giving up until his father ran past the officers and grappled with his son. The opportunity was taken to rush him and he was restrained.

It was found that Barfield had been wounded in the stomach. He was detained under the Mental Health Act. The officer was treated in hospital and in due course made a full recovery. She eventually returned to full ARV duties, going on to have a successful career within the firearms department and later holding other specialist roles within the police service.

Formation of the Specialist Firearms Teams (SFO)
6 January 1992

The opportunity to re-define the level 1 teams and their role was given careful consideration. There was a need for additional personnel on these new teams and the obvious choice would be to select officers from the level 2 teams. So from mid-1991 the department began training these officers with a tough 'pass or fail' regime. Over the following months the level 2 officers were whittled down by half and posted to the new SFO teams with an equal spread of skills and experience. Those who did not make it remained on the ARV relief teams and would get further opportunities for selection in the future if they so wished.

From January 1992, five new specialist firearms teams would undertake pre-planned firearms operations and work hand in hand with other police agencies both locally and

Stephen Smith

Early 1992 training pictures of Green Team SFOs searching with firearms support (Trojan) dogs at a disused factory premises in Essex. At this time, ballistic helmets had not been issued; some were used but they were not widely available

nationally. The criteria would be that each officer would be skilled in hostage intervention, abseiling and rope work, maritime options, vehicle ambush techniques, covert surveillance, the use of distraction devices, helicopter deployment, methods of entry, working in nuclear, biological and chemical environments, and be expert in using specialist weapons and tactics, including the use of the shotgun for breaching doors, and deploying gas. The list of specialist skills would grow, as would the demand for their use.

In the past, the Metropolitan Police had always shied away from elitist titles such as 'SWAT' (Special Weapons And Tactics), as used in the USA, but now the term SFO was born, which stood for Specialist Firearms Officer.

These five new SFO teams were nominated as Red, Green, Orange, Black and Blue. Within the first eighteen months Grey team was introduced as a sixth team. Each team, initially formed of seven SFOs with one sergeant, covered a call-out system and the rota also allowed one week in six for training in weapons and tactics.

Ian Welsh

An artist's impression of the moment an SFO team springs an ambush on a drug dealer as he hands over £250,000 worth of heroin to an undercover buyer in a car park in Charlton, south-east London at the end of January 1992

Within the first month the new structure of ARV and SFO were working well; both were very busy and gaining in experience as they dealt with diverse and challenging armed incidents.

Already this type of work was becoming routine for the teams who supported unarmed squads and divisional officers where, owing to the nature of the offences and the large sums of money involved, the presence of firearms was always a serious possibility.

Much of the work of an SFO would be done in plain clothes, and so training reflected this, with lightweight body armour worn under clothing. The operators would learn to trust each other on and off the range, where live rounds would be fired with little margin of error.

PT17 Changeover to SO19
February 1992

On 24 February 1992, the newly formed SFO teams along with the firearms training wing based at Lippitts Hill in Epping Forest were transferred from Personnel and Training to the Specialist Operations Directorate to work alongside other SO departments such as the then SO8 Flying Squad and SO13 Anti-Terrorist Unit.

It was mainly a paper exercise but it would release extra funding from a bigger SO budget. The next month, on 4 March, the ARVs were also pulled under the umbrella of SO19 where both would remain for most of the next decade.

The firearms wing, which in 1967 boasted a total of just thirteen officers could now muster 164. It was made up of one chief superintendent, one superintendent, two chief inspectors, eleven inspectors, eighteen sergeants and 131 constables.

The unit could field five eight-person SFO teams and four twenty-two-person ARV reliefs along with an operational support team and twenty-one permanent training staff based at Lippitts Hill. It would continue to grow as the demand for ARVs and highly trained SFOs increased over the next two decades.

A Vehicle Fleet for the Specialist Firearms Teams

The six armoured Range Rovers assigned to SO19 had originally belonged to the Royalty Protection Branch, SO14, who were not keen on these vehicles, which they felt were slow and cumbersome. However, they were ideal vehicles for the work of the SFO teams, who liked their robust build and comfort along with the bulletproof windscreens and armoured doors. They were an intimidating presence on the road.

The downside of using these vehicles was that they became known in some criminal circles and so had to be used tactically, where they could be hidden from sight until the last moment, or on the more overt operations, where four bulky men in a dark four-by-four wouldn't compromise anything by standing out.

The Range Rovers were used for four years but owing to non-availability of spares and operational damage they were withdrawn from service in 1995, being replaced with a fleet of vehicles more suited to the department's changing needs.

'Suicide by Cop': a Shooting in Penge
23 June 1992

On the evening of 23 June 1992, at precisely 9.29 p.m., notification came over the main-set radios of the South ARVs (those posted to cover calls south of the River Thames) of a 'male threatening suicide'. Peter Swann had called the information room at New Scotland Yard. He

Armoured Range Rover, 1991–1995. These Range Rovers were the first of many unmarked vehicles used by the department, which now boasts the largest covert fleet in the Met

Sherpa van, level 1 kit wagon, 1984–1994. This converted Sherpa van was a remnant from the early PT17 days, but it still had its uses as a team kit wagon and ladder platform. It was used only on the overt operations or as a call-out response vehicle to get SFO operators to the scene of an armed incident or operation. Its design was mimicked in later covert types of vehicle used by SO19

Stephen Smith

Queen Adelaide Court, one of the five-storey blocks of flats on the estate in Queen Adelaide Road, Penge, where Peter Swann put SO19 officers in a no-win situation.

stated that he had a shotgun and he was going to blow himself away. A woman was heard in the background. He then became abusive over the phone. It transpired that Swann lived on the third floor of a five-floor block of flats in Queen Adelaide Court, off Queen Adelaide Road in Penge, south-east London.

ARVs attended the address and an armed containment was set up. At 9.35 p.m., screaming from a female was heard coming from the third floor. Swann was heard shouting, 'I have four shots and will kill any police officer who comes into view.' An SFO team was called out from Old Street. Hostage negotiators were also called in and attempted to establish a dialogue with Swann but he refused to talk, continuing to use obscenities and be verbally abusive.

At 10 p.m., Swann released one hostage, a neighbour, but advised police that he still had his wife. He went on to tell them that he was armed with a shotgun and an Uzi sub-machine gun. This second claim thankfully proved to be

false. It was then that Swann made his threat that, if the police didn't shoot him, he would shoot a police officer.

At 11 p.m., Swann went out onto the balcony (which ran most of the length of the block) with his shotgun and goaded the police to shoot him, saying, 'Hurry up! If you're not going to shoot me, then I will come down and shoot you.' He proceeded to parade around the balcony and descended the communal staircase down to the ground floor where he was seen with his shotgun, before returning back up the stairs to his flat.

Police faced a difficult situation. They had been unable to evacuate many of the residents whom they feared might come out of their flats and stumble into Swann as he walked down the stairs or onto other levels. They would have to position armed officers closer to prevent him moving off his level. These officers were placed on the landings of the staircase leading from Swann's floor.

At 11.35 p.m., Swann emerged once again

from his flat and walked the length of the balcony and down the stairs. After repeated challenges and commands to put the gun down an officer said, 'Don't do anything stupid.' Swann replied, 'Oh I'm gonna do something stupid all right.' He pointed his gun at the officer and was shot. He later died of his wounds despite the best efforts of surgeons at the hospital.

We do not know what triggered Peter Swann to crack and take the course of action that led to his death, although it was reported by a close family member that he used drugs and was psychotic. On the day of his death, he put SO19 officers in a no-win situation. He was not only a direct threat to them but also to the other occupants of the flats, as well as his wife, who was still terrified back in their flat.

The inquest jury at Croydon Coroner's Court in September 1993 gave a verdict of lawful killing. But this was almost certainly one of the early cases of the phenomenon known in the United Sates as 'suicide-by-cop' that was dealt with by SO19. Sadly, it would not be its last.

It is always difficult dealing with situations where, because of someone's state of mind, they do not act rationally or comply with police instructions, but the law does not currently consider it fair to endanger the lives of police by requiring them to shoot an armed suspect in the leg or arm (a disabling shot). This is primarily because it is difficult to hit the limb of a moving person and the risk of missing is high, therefore placing the officer in greater danger of being shot by the suspect.

As far as the question of the less lethal option goes, there does not yet appear to be a viable tranquillizer dart that causes instant incapacity that could be relied on to replace a firearm. The baton gun, which fires a large plastic projectile, is relatively inaccurate and can have varying effects on the person shot, from knocking them down to having no visible effect at all. Even the

Taser (the law enforcement stun gun that would be used extensively after 2003) is not recommended to replace a firearm in an armed confrontation. No doubt in the future something will be manufactured that will fulfil this role to everyone's satisfaction, but until that time the search, unfortunately, goes on.

Shots Fired in Bow
10 September 1992

Not every operation goes to plan and not every arrest ends in a conviction, but one of the main tests of the coping ability of any armed officer is how he/she copes when things go disastrously wrong. The incident at Bow Road proved to be one such operation.

In September 1992, the Flying Squad came by information regarding an armed robbery on Bow Road, east London. They were already over-committed and so passed it on to the local crime squad, who called in an SO19 SFO team to assist. The intelligence had revealed that a team of two or three robbers armed with a shotgun and an electric stun gun, using a Blue BMW motor vehicle, were intending to rob the landlord of the King's Arms public house in Bow Road, E3, as he collected cash from his local bank situated about eighty metres from his pub. The landlord was in the habit of cashing pay cheques for local builders in his pub and drew large sums of cash on a weekly basis to cover these transactions.

SO19 liaised with the inspector in charge. They agreed that owing to the lack of surveillance resources they would arrest the suspects the moment they showed up. Although this did not always provide the best evidence it was an acceptable tactic under the circumstances.

The SFO team deployed to Bow Road, near the bank, at around 10 a.m. They settled in for a long day. Their jump-off van was parked off the street within striking distance. Two plain-clothes officers concealed themselves in a nearby launderette, while the two-man crew of the Range Rover held-off a safe distance down Fairfield Road, inside the entrance to the park.

After a short while, one of the suspects was spotted on foot, near the bank. A while later the blue BMW was seen driving past the pub. The DI in charge now decided that, instead of arresting the suspects as soon as they were seen, he wanted to let them continue a while longer to see what additional evidence he could get. His intentions were not made clear to the officers on the street. Minutes later, both suspects were spotted on foot near the jump-off van (also parked in Fairfield Road). In fact, the two men stood so close to the van that the officers inside could hear them talking about the robbery. There was still no command to arrest. The two suspects then walked around the corner and pretended to use the cashpoint machine outside the bank.

What no one knew at the time was that the police informant had also tipped off the land-lord of the pub who, in an effort to defeat the stun gun, had padded himself out with news-papers and was in no hurry to test out his improvised body armour. He delayed going to the bank until the last moment, probably hoping the informant had got it wrong or that the robbers would not turn up. This delay proved to be the difference between arresting a team of robbers and the carnage that occurred instead.

While the two would-be robbers waited by the cash machine a completely unconnected marked police car drove through the plot with its blue lights on. The two men, thinking it may be coming for them, fled. They jogged away from the bank back down Fairfield road, turning into Grove Hill Park.

The DI, seeing the suspects leaving the area, made his decision to arrest and called the strike. The Range Rover, which had left the park, returned and drove up behind the two men. The driver pulled the door release catch, but as he broke sharply the heavy armoured door swung open. Both officers deployed to arrest the suspects but as the driver left the vehicle (drawing his Glock pistol as he got out) the heavy door swung back, fiercely hitting his elbow. A round was discharged at point blank range into the officer's hip. The officer later recalled how he heard the shot but did not initially register that he had shot himself. He went on to describe a strange feeling in his leg.

Both officers now secured the first suspect by the vehicle. The driver, despite his serious injury, sprinted after the second suspect. He chased him along Jebb Street and right into Wrexham Road (a dead-end street), through the bollards and out into a lay-by on the Blackwell Tunnel Approach, where he saw the man get into a blue BMW believed to be the getaway vehicle mentioned earlier. Ignoring the immense pain that was now taking effect, he stood in the road and shouted, 'Stop! Armed police!' He aimed his pistol at the two men in the car.

It was in this lay-by that the vehicle drove at the officer, who, fearing for his life, fired his Glock. He was becoming weak from blood loss. Most of the nine rounds he fired hit the car, causing the driver to duck down in an attempt to avoid being hit. The car veered away at the last moment, missing the officer, but one of his rounds struck the suspect in the passenger seat, carrying away a small part of his left ear. The car sped off, joining the fast flow of traffic on the main road and miraculously avoiding an accident.

Other officers arrived in time to see their colleague, his leg soaked in blood, surrounded by spent 9 mm cases. They quickly hailed down a car and directed the driver to take them to the Royal London Hospital. This prompt action saved the officer who had by now lost nearly two pints of blood from his right thigh.

Although the suspects were arrested and charged they were acquitted in court of conspiracy to commit armed robbery. Police could not prove the case beyond doubt; any evidence that had existed had left the scene in the vehicle and what they had left was insufficient to convince the jury of their guilt.

Even without convictions this operation demonstrated the sheer guts and determination of the officers of SO19, one of whom ran 250 metres with a serious gunshot wound to his leg. After his recovery the officer went on to have a distinguished career within SO19 and other specialist departments within the Met Police.

Operation 'Emerge': The Taking of Fox Trot Five
23 November 1992

In November 1992, SO19 specialist firearms teams along with their colleagues from Essex firearms unit were called upon to support

Regional Crime Squad officers working with Customs and Excise to intercept and seize a large cargo of cocaine with a street value of £160 million. This shipment was on a Panama-registered, 300-ton ocean-going barge named Fox Trot Five, which had been tracked 5,000 miles from the coast of the small island of Aruba, situated on the northern tip of Venezuela, to the Royal Docks at Woolwich. There, after being shadowed by police RIBs (Rigid Inflatable Boats with powerful outboard motors), it docked and unloaded at 7.30 a.m. on 23 November. Its cargo (over a ton of pure cocaine destined for the London drugs gangs) was transferred into a white van and driven to a warehouse in Deptford, south-east London. Surveillance followed on behind.

SFO officers were delivered onto the vessel from RIBs crewed by coxswains from the Royal Marines. They had hoped to arrive in time to catch some of the crew on board and retrieve evidence, but they had left it to the last minute to avoid the risk of things being tossed into the Thames and lost. The vessel itself turned out to be empty but the crew were picked up as they

Fox Trot Five, docked at Woolwich, with SO19 officers boarding her

Joyce Lowman

left in a taxi. (They managed to avoid prison after claiming they had no knowledge that the vessel contained drugs.)

Another assault team, with the aid of an armoured JCB, stormed the warehouse where the cocaine had been taken by smashing through its doors. The driver of the van was arrested as he unloaded the packages. (He would also successfully argue in court that he had no idea what those packages contained.) The main organizers of the importation were elusive too, having covered their tracks well. The evidence trail was not easy to follow or prove.

Although securing convictions in this case was always going to be problematic insofar as having to prove knowledge of the offence, the operation was heralded as a success in that it removed a large quantity of high-grade cocaine from the clutches of the London drugs cartels.

Early Maritime Training on the River Thames
1992

The SFO teams had been carrying out maritime training on the River Thames using police launches since their inception, but up until now this training had not been put to the test. Operation 'Emerge' identified the need for more training and also the need for a specialist boat unit with trained coxswains, ideally from SO19, to make the unit independent of other agencies.

In the end, it made sense to use the skills of officers already trained in working on the river. So the Marine Support Unit based at Wapping, formerly known as Thames Division, sent some of its officers away to train as coxswains to pilot the RIBs, which the Met hired at first and then purchased. The relationship between these two units grew closer as they trained together. Unfortunately, much of what they do cannot be featured in this book at the present time.

Early training with the Marine Support Unit, using RIBs hired for the purpose. It would be several years before the Met would purchase its own

Some of the training for SFO operators on the river as the RIBs deploy the teams onto one of the many wooden piers to which small ships and barges are moored

Some of the more advanced training on the river – a team board one of the many riverboat pleasure craft, which ply up and down the river

The Crouch Hill Robbery: Operation 'Odense'
22 February 1993

In February 1993, the Flying Squad had been gathering intelligence on two armed robbers who were intent on robbing a sub-Post Office cash-in-transit delivery in Crouch Hill, north London.

The two men, Steven Charalambous, aged 33, with convictions for burglary and theft, and Loukas Manicou, a 31-year-old wine bar owner,

had chosen the location because the railings outside the sub-Post Office prevented the delivery van from stopping close by, meaning the guard would have to walk the distance between the van and the Post Office in the busy street.

The Flying Squad had received intelligence that the robbery was set for 22 February 1993; a briefing was called on the morning of the day in question, attended by an SO19 SFO team. Following the briefing, the team deployed to

Crouch Hill where they were to use a jump-off vehicle and gunships to mount their ambush. The intention was to intervene quickly, thus preventing an opportunity for the robbers to threaten the guard or endanger the public. As usual, this would be a very short window of opportunity.

The officers waited either for the delivery to take place or for the robbers to appear. Then, around 10.30 a.m., the red postal delivery van pulled up at its usual spot, with the guard prepared to do his runs. Almost immediately, an urgent radio transmission came over the air. The subjects had been spotted nearby. Charalambous was wearing a plastic police helmet, a white shirt and a black tie with a fluorescent jacket and what turned out later to be a false moustache. Manicou was dressed all in black and wearing a black balaclava. From this point, things moved very quickly as Charalambous moved in on the guard of the delivery vehicle, armed with a handgun. He grabbed hold of him, placing the gun against his chest. He demanded that the custodians inside the van pass out the £250,000 on board.

Moments later, SO19 specialist firearms officers deployed from their jump-off van. One officer was faced with a terrible decision. Fearing for the life of the custodian guard, he engaged Charalambous, firing two pairs of shots from his MP5, the first pair hitting the suspect in the chest. The second pair of shots, as he spun round, were not so accurate; one round grazed his chin and the other missed, but both impacted safely against the nearby wall of an alleyway.

Charalambous collapsed to the ground, as did the guard, who had not been hit but was in shock. For one horrific moment the officer believed he had shot the guard. This was soon dispelled when the guard began moving and was clearly unharmed. The second suspect Loukas Manicou stood transfixed nearby, his handgun up in the air. He was challenged by other SFOs and had the sense to throw his gun down.

Ironically, the firearm used by Charalambous was later found to be an imitation; however, the one Manicou was armed with was very real and loaded.

Paramedics stabilized Charalambous on the street and waited for the air ambulance to arrive. A suitable road junction was found for the helicopter to land, it arrived and an attending doctor performed life-saving surgery on Charalambous where he lay in the street. Interestingly, this was the first instance of doctors from an air ambulance saving the life of a person shot by SO19.

Once stabilized, Charalambous was airlifted to hospital and placed under armed guard. (This was one of the roles given to ARV officers, that of providing armed hospital guards for dangerous criminals and those needing protection during treatment, a role they still provide to this day.) He was successfully treated for his injuries and was soon off the critical list.

Charalambous and Manicou pleaded guilty to attempted armed robbery and received five years imprisonment. Charalambous later achieved notoriety when he unsuccessfully sued police for £250,000 for committing 'unlawful assault and trespass on his person, resulting in excruciating pain, fear and shock and lasting emotional distress'.

Weaponry used by SO19 in the 1990s

Most of the weaponry used by the SFO teams had not changed a great deal from the 1980s although the MP5 SMGs had been converted to single-shot carbines with collapsible stocks and fitted torches integrated into the foregrip.

The Remington shotguns, both long and short, remained the same, along with the smoke/gas launcher and the baton gun. The

The air ambulance lands nearby

The on-board doctor was able to perform open-heart surgery in the street and save the robber's life

main change had been the Glock 17 semi-automatic pistol, which had replaced the Browning Hi Power and the Smith & Wesson revolver issued in the 80s. The Heckler & Koch M93 5.56 rifle, introduced in 1989, had now fully replaced the Ruger Mini 14 rifle. The 7.62 Steyr had likewise replaced the Enfield Enforcer in 1998.

A Steyr SSG-P 7.62 mm sniper rifle
B Heckler & Koch 5.56 mm model 93 rifle
C Night sight-mounted for use with the Heckler & Koch 93
D Glock 17 9 mm semi-automatic pistol
E L1A1 66 mm CS launcher
F L67 baton gun
G Remington 870 12-bore pump-action shotgun with extended 7-round magazine
H Heckler & Koch MP5 (Kurtz) 9 mm SMG
I Heckler & Koch MP5 (SD) silenced 9 mm SMG
J Heckler & Koch MP5 (A2) carbine fixed stock
K Heckler & Koch MP5 (A3) carbine retractable stock
L Remington 870 12-bore pump action shotgun, shortened version (Hatton gun) with 4-round magazine

Continued Deployment against the Provisional IRA (PIRA)

The IRA had been increasing its deadly efforts to attack the mainland UK since the 1970s, with a particular focus on London and its commercial and financial bases. Military establishments had also been attacked and assassinations carried out. Then, in April 1992, just two days after the general election that voted John Major's Tory government into power, a huge bomb was detonated at the Baltic Exchange in the City of London killing three people and causing £800 million worth of damage.

If these ASUs were not tracked down and stopped, the fight against dissident Irish terrorism could be lost. Happily, the first result came just four days after the Baltic Exchange bombing, when SO19 SFO teams were used to support security services on Operation 'Catnip'.

Glasgow-born James Canning (aged 37) and his mistress Ethel Lamb (aged 60) were living in Northolt, north London and acting as PIRA quartermasters. SO19 SFO teams were deployed to support surveillance on the pair, during which time Canning was seen attempting to move quantities of bomb-making equipment to another address near RAF Uxbridge.

When SFO teams were deployed to arrest them, Canning was found in possession of a Smith & Wesson .357 magnum handgun. Forty kilos of Semtex explosives and six AK47 assault rifles were also recovered. Canning received thirty years imprisonment while his partner Lamb received three years for possession of firearms and helping Canning with money and other aid, knowing it might be used for acts of terrorism.

It was mentioned in court that Lamb had fallen under the influence of Canning, who was undoubtedly using her to further his own ends. However, the court also judged that she had knowingly and willingly helped him in his endeavours.

Operation 'Brompton'
28 January–2 March 1993

SO19's success the previous year served to put the IRA on the back foot for a while. In January 1993 further attacks were made against the infrastructure of the mainland. Two suspects were identified.

On Thursday 28 January, Patrick Thomas Hayes and Jan Alexander Taylor exploded a bomb in a litter-bin outside Harrods. Six days later they bombed the 9.05 Victoria to Ramsgate train using an IED (Improvised Explosive Device) in a briefcase. Anti-Terrorist branch detectives released photo images of the suspects taken from CCTV outside Harrods and a manhunt commenced. The pictures released to the public bore fruit and on 2 March led police to an address on Walford Road, Stoke Newington.

Aware of the possibility that the IRA cell could be preparing to booby-trap the house, a specialist firearms team was deployed and rapid entry authorized.

The team moved forward and prepared to enter via the front door and the bay window. As the officers entered through the window, several shots were fired from inside the house, peppering the window frame but hitting no one. Despite the danger, entry was made. Hayes and Taylor were arrested whilst attempting to get hold of the AK47 assault rifles that were also in the premises. The full extent of the bomb-making equipment inside the house soon became clear; supplies included Semtex as well as a small arsenal of weapons.

A search of a lock-up garage revealed 567 kg of homemade explosives. It was apparent that another major bombing campaign had been averted.

Artist's impression of the SFO team preparing to make their entry into the house on Walford Road

In May 1994 at the Old Bailey, both men were sentenced to thirty years imprisonment. The mystery was why these two men, both born in England with no apparent connection to Northern Ireland, would commit these crimes. Puzzlingly, Taylor had even served as a corporal in the British army!

The IRA Suffer a Further Blow
14 July 1993

In answer to the so-called 'Ring of Steel' (a series of vehicle checkpoints around the City of London, intended to prevent another IRA lorry-bomb spectacular getting through), the IRA planned to target the City once again. Their intention was to lay a bomb down within the security perimeter in an attempt to score points in the ongoing conflict. To do this, they employed the skills of a character called Robert

'Rab' Fryers. Fryers was a 44-year-old Republican enforcer and had seen his share of sectarian violence. He was suspected of being a close-quarter assassin for the Provisional IRA.

Unaware that he was being followed, Fryers left Belfast and made for a safe house in Sauchi near Alloa in Scotland, where he linked up with IRA sympathizer Hugh Jack, who assisted Fryers as a runner and organizer. The plan was for Fryers to travel down to London and then take public transport through the Ring of Steel into the City, where he would lay down a bomb. The target was not known at this time, but the capital's financial centre or a public house would have been likely victims.

Fryers had made several visits to the City, including a dry run, formulating his plan and selecting a suitable target, but it was imperative to catch him red-handed so that no question of guilt would remain. However, such

The moment Fryers was arrested as he waited by the bus stop. The holdall to the far right of the picture contained a lethal mix of high explosives and petrol

Private source

was the danger posed by this man that consideration was even given, as a contingency, to a pre-emptive strike. A prophetic forewarning of the future!

On 14 July 1993, SO19 were briefed to effect Fryers' arrest at a place they considered to be safest for the public and themselves before he could enter his target area. Later that day, he once again made his way down from his safe house. This time it was no rehearsal. In the bag slung over his shoulder was a bomb made up of two-and-a-half kilograms of Semtex high explosive and two litres of petrol, enough to cause a huge explosion.

Fryers was followed to a bus stop in Crest Road, Cricklewood, north-west London where he was challenged by SO19 SFOs in plain clothes. His every move was controlled at gunpoint from whatever cover officers could find (still too close should the device ignite, but they had no choice in the matter). He was made to lie down and crawl away from the bag. Explosives officers then made the bomb safe.

The following day the *Sun* newspaper led with the headline, 'On Yer Knees' and featured a photo taken by a local resident of Fryers'

arrest at gunpoint on the pavement opposite.

And so ended another of the IRA's audacious attempts to turn the tables in the conflict and bring harm and destruction to the streets of London. In January 1995 both Fryers and Jack were found guilty at the Old Bailey of conspiracy to cause explosions. Fryers was sentenced to twenty-five years and Hugh Jack twenty years. As the judge passed sentence he said, 'It was a device which was of truly devastating capacity for causing death, serious injury and destruction. On explosion, the debris or shrapnel could be thrown hundreds of metres. The petrol meant that there could have been a fireball and those in range would have no chance of escaping harm, injury or possible death.'

In July 2000, under the terms of the Good Friday Agreement, Fryers was released from prison.

Abseil Training at Dartford 720 ft Cooling Tower
1993

One of the abseilers begins his 720 ft descent to the ground

During 1993 enquiries were made to the authorities controlling the Littlebrook Power Station near the QE2 Bridge at Dartford Crossing as to whether SO19 could practise long abseil drops from the 720 ft cooling tower at this location as part of advanced abseil training for their SFO officers.

Permission was granted and extra-long ropes were ordered to cover the long drop. Perhaps surprisingly, there was no shortage of volunteers willing to take part in this exercise.

Shoot-out at the Timber Yard
15 October 1993

While SFO teams had been fighting the Provisional IRA, the crews of the armed response vehicles had been trying to keep a lid on armed crime in the capital. This came to a head in October 1993 when David Stone, an ex-soldier, mercenary and legionnaire, turned his hand to robbery.

Armed with an old Colt .38 service revolver, he robbed the Barclays bank in Highgate High Street of just £1,600. Making off on foot, a young female bank clerk followed him from the bank (ignoring advice from her manager). The manager flagged down a local police car and indicated where Stone had gone; the two officers (a sergeant and a constable) left their vehicle and followed Stone on foot.

As the sergeant drew near to Stone he stopped and turned, levelling his revolver at the officer. He said, 'Stay back. You've got a job to do and I've got a job to do.' As if to reinforce this, he fired a shot over the officer's head. Ignoring shouts from the officer's colleague, who was behind a parked car, Stone calmly walked off. Undeterred, the officers followed their man, and through their radio commentary other police, including an ARV, descended on the area.

As his efforts to escape escalated, Stone attempted to hijack a traffic warden's van. He demanded the keys, threatening the driver by putting the gun to his head. The traffic warden and his colleague managed to persuade Stone that they did not have the keys. Stone continued on foot, still determined to make good his escape. His desire to hijack a vehicle came to fruition when he came across a Haringey dustcart parked at the side of the road. A council worker was shovelling rubbish into the back. After being threatened with the gun, he reluctantly handed over the keys to Stone who climbed into the cab and drove off erratically. (The erratic driving may have had something to do with the vehicle being left-hand drive, designed so that the driver could be closest to the kerb when moving slowly in the flow of traffic.) Stone collided with several oncoming vehicles and parked cars.

A patrol car driven by an unarmed police sergeant drove towards Stone but was forced to back up to avoid a head-on collision. The officer got out and ran towards the cab and Stone fired at the officer through his own windscreen, forcing him to dive for cover.

The pursuit of the dustcart continued. Stone fired at police as he passed officers on the footway while police cars followed tentatively behind. Unfortunately for Stone an ARV had now arrived, passing him in the opposite carriageway, before it turned around and took up a position directly behind him.

The ARV followed the dustcart for several hundred metres as it drove south on the Holloway Road. Stone put his arm out of the window and fired at the ARV, which quickly moved out of his line of fire. He eventually turned off the main road and after negotiating some narrow side roads ended up in Fairbridge Road where he was finally forced to stop by a parked lorry making deliveries. As the dust settled, the crew of the ARV waited to see what Stone would do. They did not have to wait long as the door of the dustcart flew open and he emerged.

The sad demise of David Stone, killed in a shoot-out with ARV officers in a north London timber yard

The driver shouted a challenge of, 'Armed police!' Stone answered by firing at him. His round missed.

Another officer returned fire, his rounds failing to hit Stone but placing him under no illusions that he was now up against armed police officers. Stone ran from the vehicle, turning through some nearby gates into a timber yard. There was now a serious risk that Stone would take hostages or shoot members of the public if they got in his way.

The ARV officers gave chase into a yard full of stacks of timber and workshops. Stone fired again as the officers followed. One of them returned fire on the move, his rounds having little effect. The officers continued shouting for Stone to give up although it was apparent that he had no intention of surrendering.

As Stone ran towards a brick building the real threat that he would stand and fight from behind the cover of the building caused the leading officer to stop and take aim. He fired one shot at Stone before he could reach the building. Stone fell to the ground. He died instantly from his wound.

This incident once again proved the effectiveness of the training of the SO19 officers. It was their first fatal shooting involving the ARVs, but it would not be their last. At the inquest into the death of David Stone the following year the inquest jury passed a verdict of lawful killing.

There was no question that Stone had come from a loving family. At the inquest, his father touchingly stated that he loved his son and apologized for the hurt he had caused. Stone had no previous convictions and it is hard to understand what drove this ex-career soldier to embark on this course of action, which led ultimately to his death.

The Holloway Siege
27 July 1994

On the evening of 23 July 1994 at Shaftsbury Road, north London, Irish barman John O'Brien, aged 34, who was said to be suffering from depression (after his wife had left him and taken their child to Uruguay), set fire to the ground floor of his house using lighter fuel. He then left the fire burning and travelled to Ireland where he visited his family. The fire caused extensive damage to the premises but was controlled by the fire service.

View of the rear garden of the Shaftesbury Road address. O'Brien left through the rear doors, walked halfway up the garden, turning to face the officers who were both behind the garden fence on the left of the picture when they opened fire

Police were keen to question O'Brien. He returned to England on 25 July and purchased a blank-firing revolver with fifty rounds of ammunition. That night he stayed in a West End hotel. He returned to his fire-damaged home on the evening of 26 July and began drinking. During the evening he visited his neighbour. She had a friend with her so O'Brien made his excuses and left. The neighbour later stated that 'he seemed nervous and strange'.

Just before midnight, O'Brien began discharging the gun inside his house. On hearing sounds of gunfire, police were called. ARVs were assigned and attended the vicinity. The location of the shots was not immediately apparent and a street search began. At around 2 a.m. on 27 July the mystery was solved when, as an unarmed uniform police inspector came to knock on O'Brien's front door, O'Brien smashed a downstairs window and began firing the gun. The inspector and his colleagues retreated to cover and called for back-up.

The ARVs responded but during the time it took for them to contain the premises, O'Brien had left by his back door and climbed over the fence into his neighbour's garden. Armed with a handgun and two kitchen knives he talked the female occupant into letting him in and then took her hostage.

By the time the ARV officers had contained O'Brien's premises, they were somewhat taken by surprise when, at approximately 4.05 a.m., O'Brien came out into the rear garden of the house next door, using his hostage as a human shield. He then bundled her at gunpoint over the four-foot high wooden fence back into his own garden.

As ARV officers attempted to reason with him, O'Brien said, 'Don't shoot me and I won't shoot you and if you shoot me, I'll shoot her', (indicating his hostage). He then dragged her back into his house.

At 4.30 a.m. O'Brien emerged into the rear garden alone. The officers pleaded with him. One shouted at him, 'Don't be silly, John, put the gun down.' He replied, 'What will you do if I don't? What will you do if I shoot you?' But the stand-off continued. Meanwhile, police had phoned his house and told his hostage to leave by the front door as quickly as possible. She took the chance and was soon safely in the hands of police.

At 4.35 a.m., back in the garden, O'Brien placed the gun against his own head. An officer

The blank-firing handgun used by O'Brien during the incident

turned the torch of his MP5 onto O'Brien, who shouted, 'Turn that fucking torch off.' He did, but sadly no amount of persuasion would talk this desperate man into surrender and in one smooth movement he brought the gun from his own head and pointed it directly at the officers, two of whom opened fire. Six shots were fired and O'Brien was hit three times. Both officers stated later that they felt their shots were having little or no effect on the suspect as he did not react, but then he collapsed suddenly. O'Brien died in hospital the next day from his wounds.

It transpired after speaking with the hostage that, during the time O'Brien spent with her, he had made sexual advances towards her and threatened her with the gun. She had managed to talk him out of a possible rape. In a later conversation (reported in the inquest transcript), just before he went out to face the police, she asked him, 'Do you want to get yourself shot?' to which he replied, 'Yes, I'm going to make them shoot me when it's light.' She then said, 'What, to commit suicide?' He said, 'Yes, but I haven't got the guts to do it myself.

If I start firing at the police, they'll have to shoot me.'

On 13 June 1995 an inquest was held at St Pancras Coroner's Court, which finished the next day. It took the jury just ten minutes to reach a verdict of lawful killing with no criticism of any police action. The officers involved were commended for their professionalism and bravery.

(By a strange coincidence, the shopkeeper who legally sold the blank-firing gun to O'Brien died suddenly on the same day as O'Brien!)

The Putney Incident
2 August 1994

It was only six days after the O'Brien shooting, on Tuesday 2 August at 4.53 p.m., when the ARVs were once again called into action. This time they were answering calls for assistance from their unarmed colleagues at an armed robbery on Putney High Street, south-west London.

Armed robbers, Robert Knapp and Kevin Gregory, terrorized the staff of Barretts jewellers in Putney High Street, firing a sawn-off semi-automatic shotgun into the safe before stealing cash and jewellery. The manager was on the phone to another branch at the time; they heard the commotion and called the police who were quick to respond.

The unarmed officers were parked on a road opposite and kept observation from their marked police van, as they are advised to do in training. (Officers are warned not to go charging into premises that may have armed suspects inside, but to keep observation and wait for armed back-up.) During this time they gave a radio commentary of the robbery in progress. Moments later, the two robbers fled from the store carrying a holdall containing jewellery to the value of £120,000. As they ran to their getaway vehicle parked nearby, Gregory

The entrance to Barretts jewellers on Putney High Street. Gregory fired his sawn-off shotgun into the safe to vent his frustration at not being able to open it; this had no other effect than leaving a mark on the door of the safe showing the spread of shot

The hijacked police car, crashed by Knapp during the pursuit

noticed the police van and discharged his shotgun at the officers, wounding both. He then casually walked over and threatened them with his shotgun, telling them to stay put.

Gregory and Knapp (who was armed with a Webley .455 revolver) drove off in their blue van, pursued by one of the wounded officers in the station van. This officer managed to give a commentary, allowing other officers and an ARV to get close. The two robbers soon became aware of the police vehicles and a chase ensued, during which the blue van crashed into a wall on Putney Bridge Road at the junction with Merivale Road.

As the two men fled from the van, Gregory made for the steps that led up to the railway bridge across the Thames. Knapp hijacked a police patrol car, which had stopped nearby, threatening the driver with his handgun. He then drove off towards Wandsworth in the police car; an ARV gave chase. Knapp crashed the hijacked police car half a mile away, hitting the brick wall of a building just off the Wandsworth one-way system where ARV officers arrested him.

The Putney Incident, Course of Events

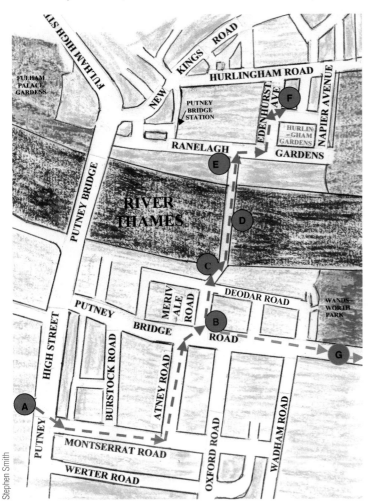

Stephen Smith

(A) Barretts jewellers, in Putney High Street, SW15. At 4.53 p.m., shots are fired in the shop and at a police van parked in Montserrat Road, wounding two police officers.

(B) The blue Peugeot getaway van chased along Montserrat Road and left into Atney Road crashes in Putney Bridge Road junction with Merivale Road. More shots are fired at the police. Knapp hijacks a police car at gunpoint.

(C) Gregory is chased onto Putney Railway footbridge. One ARV and one local officer follow him onto the bridge.

(D) Gregory fires at police, reloads and takes Jonathan Pike as a pedestrian hostage.

(E) Gregory again fires at police and makes off with his hostage, leaving the footbridge down into Ranelagh Gardens. He turns left into Edenhurst Avenue and right into Hurlingham Gardens. Builders tell pursuing officers which way he went.

(F) Gregory attempts to gain entry into a house but fails. He shoots an ARV officer and is wounded by police. His hostage escapes. Gregory commits suicide.

(G) Knapp crashes the hijacked police car near Armoury Way, Wandsworth, and surrenders to armed police.

Sketched map of the route the car and foot chase took, finishing in Hurlingham Gardens. (Map not to scale)

One ARV officer armed with a Glock 17 pistol (and an unarmed officer commentating on the pursuit) bravely pursued Gregory across the bridge. With dogged determination to escape, Gregory calmly reloaded his shotgun, turned and fired on the pursuing officers. The sound of gunfire could be clearly heard over the radio transmissions.

Meanwhile, Jonathan Pike was crossing the footbridge from the north side, completely unaware of the danger he was in. As he drew level with Gregory it dawned on him that he had casually walked into an armed incident. Gregory, seizing the opportunity, grabbed Pike around his neck and placed the barrel of his sawn-off shotgun against his head. Pike was aware that police officers were on the bridge following them, but all he could do was hold his nerve and try to keep calm.

Gregory dragged Jonathan Pike down the stairs on the north side of the bridge and out into Ranelagh Gardens, then turning left into Edenhurst Avenue and right into Hurlingham Gardens. The pursuing officers bravely

Aerial view of the Putney Railway and footbridge

Gregory lies dead after turning his shotgun on himself. (The gun was moved by police to the location shown)

followed, not knowing whether Gregory was waiting to ambush them once they turned the corners. Some builders, watching the spectacle from a vantage point high up on a building, helped to direct them. Before long, another ARV crew arrived north of the bridge and joined in with the lone ARV officer. Although they had lost sight of Gregory and his hostage they knew he must have gone to ground somewhere in Hurlingham Gardens.

Unbeknown to them Gregory had taken his hostage up the garden path of one of the big houses where he attempted to bluff his way in. The occupier wisely refused to open up, so Gregory became angry and began battering at the door. Jonathan Pike took advantage of this distraction; he managed to break free and run to safety leaving Gregory alone by the front door.

As the officers moved slowly down Hurlingham Gardens they fanned out and began checking in gardens and under parked cars. Gregory was now forced to make his stand in the front garden of the house he had tried to enter. It was from this doorway that he ambushed one officer, shooting SO19 PC Barry Oldroyd-Jones with birdshot in the lower body, causing over 140 separate injuries. Another officer quickly returned fire with his Glock 17 pistol, hitting Gregory in his thigh and catching an artery.

In time, Gregory would have died from loss of blood, but he was not done yet and he fired again at the officers. This time his aim was off, the pellets harmlessly hitting a parked car by the fallen officer. An officer bravely advanced and gave the wounded officer first aid, as another moved forward and provided armed cover.

As the remaining SO19 officers moved forward, Gregory was heard loading his shotgun.

Moments later, out of pure desperation, Gregory put the shotgun to his own head and

132

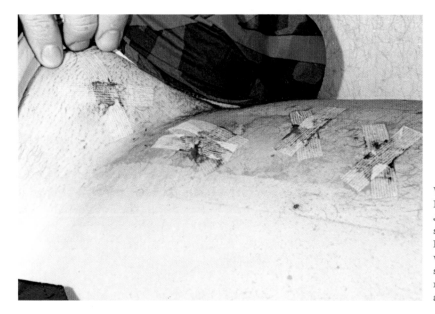

Wounds received by PC Barry Oldroyd-Jones from Gregory's shotgun. The officer had over 140 separate wounds; some of the shotgun pellets still remain in his body after 18 years

pulled the trigger. Thus ended the Putney incident. Gregory was dead, Knapp was in custody and the bravery shown, not just by the armed officers but also by their fellow unarmed colleague, had been exceptional, so much so that two officers were awarded the Queen's Gallantry Medal and nineteen others were commended for bravery.

On 27 February 1995, Knapp received twelve years imprisonment for his part in the robbery. At the inquest into the death of Kevin Gregory in the summer of 1995, the jury was told that he had served in the Territorial Army and had also served time in prison for armed robbery. After listening to the evidence the jury came back with a verdict of death by suicide.

The two officers shot in the station van recovered from their wounds; both had been active in the pursuit despite being wounded – one had even rammed the police car Knapp had hijacked. The wounded ARV officer, PC Oldroyd-Jones, made a good recovery but still carries some of the pellets in his legs. The hostage, Mr Jonathan Pike, received 'The Honour of the Binney' (a civilian bravery cita-

tion first awarded in 1947 and named after Captain George Binney, a Second World War hero) for his calmness and fortitude.

The Putney incident remains one of the ARVs most notable operations.

SO19 Foreign Operations, Saint Kitts
October 1994

In October 1994 the department was once again called to assist overseas. This time it was the small Caribbean island of Saint Kitts that required help. SO19 was asked to supply a small team of specialist firearms officers to act as a protection detail for detectives from New Scotland Yard. These detectives were from SO1 International and Organized Crime Group; they had been sent to investigate a series of murders and disappearances of officials and their families on the island and were worried that they might become the targets of the people they were investigating. This was after the island's head of Special Branch, superintendent Jude Matthews, was shot dead whilst on his way to meet these same London detectives.

The superintendent had been investigating drug smuggling and the disappearance of ten people. Six suspects were already in custody, and the murder of the police officer was seen as an attempt to disrupt the investigation.

SO19 sent four officers to give protection and watch the backs of the Met detectives as they went about their business. The investigation went on for two months and the small team of officers also engaged in training the local police in some advanced firearm tactics. They were amazed at the collection of old and rusty firearms being used by the local police.

It was later necessary for SO19 officers to return and give protection to the detectives as they gave evidence in court. The presence of these officers appeared to have done the trick, as there were no further serious attempts to harm or further disrupt the investigation.

An SO19 officer instructs the local police in some advanced weapons training

Other Events of 1994 that Affected SO19 Armed Operations

1994 had been a sad year for the Met as they had lost PS Derek Robertson in New Addington to a gang of callous robbers, who had stabbed him to death during a heist. The outrage that followed saw the armed contingent of SO19 ARVs grow from seventy-five to 120 officers, thus considerably increasing the number of ARVs, who could patrol at any one time. However, to some, this was considered to be too little, too late.

Surprisingly, that year, the Provisional IRA declared a ceasefire. Of course, some of their faction saw this as a capitulation and it was only a matter of time before breakaway groups picked up the reins again. The Met and SO19 waited for the inevitable.

Meanwhile, common sense had won through, allowing armed officers to overtly carry their weapons instead of trying to conceal them at great effort from the eyes of the general public under clothing. This new rule was even extended to the Diplomatic Protection Group.

The model 10 Smith & Wesson .38 revolver was being phased out in favour of the Glock 17 semi-automatic pistol and the training wing was running back-to-back courses to bring officers up to scratch.

SO19 officers assist local police in securing a murder scene on the Caribbean island of Saint Kitts, where a series of murders and disappearances had required the assistance of detectives from New Scotland Yard

Tactical training in what was affectionately known as 'Hogan's Alley' with the Glock 17 pistol, at Lippitts Hill

SFO Team – Close Protection Training

The training programme was always being extended to cater for additional requirements. One of these was the training of the SFO teams for Close Protection work, should they be needed at home or overseas in that role. This training would include physical conditioning, unarmed combat, emergency and ballistic first aid and, of course advance, shooting skills and tactics.

ARV Officer Wounded in Boxing Day Shoot-out in Enfield
26 December 1994

Just as another busy year was drawing to a close, officers of SO19 were once again called upon to put their lives in danger in the line of duty. This time it would be a fairly novice ARV officer who found herself, with others, taking on an armed suspect who appeared to have scant regard for his own life, or anyone else's.

An SFO team receives unarmed combat training under the watchful eye of Dougie Thompson, a former British wresting champion

The pavement area in Hertford Road, Enfield, north London, where the confrontation took place

Stephen Smith

It was on Boxing Day 1994 when Sarah, a young mother, attended the flat of her ex-partner Alan McMinn to collect their 2-year-old child after he had spent Christmas day there. McMinn's abusive behaviour had been the cause of their relationship breakdown and Sarah was trying to get on with her life, but instead of handing their child over when she arrived he became violent and attacked her, causing serious injury. She fled the flat, and he shouted after her that he had a gun and would use it on her if she made trouble. Sarah went directly to the police, arriving shortly before 1 p.m. She was, after all, very concerned for her child.

The ARVs were summoned to attend the local police station and, at 2 p.m., it was agreed that they would attend the location and carry out a tactical survey of the address to see if there was any sign of the subject or the child. It would also allow them a chance to gather intelligence around the layout of the premises to help later with formulating a plan.

Until they arrived, a 'loose containment' was maintained by local officers, who missed McMinn leaving the block with the child in a pushchair. The ARV officers carried out their survey but saw no lights on, or any signs of occupation. They began making plans to enter the address to confirm that neither the child nor his father had come to any harm.

At 2.50 p.m., as more ARV officers arrived and began containing the flats, McMinn returned. One officer spotted him walking in Hertford Road towards his flat at the junction of Albany Road. He still had the child with him in a pushchair. Armed officers moved towards him and challenged him, telling him to move away from the child and keep his hands where they could see them. His reaction was to draw

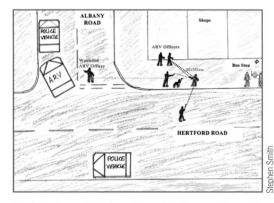

Sketch plan of the junction with the positions of the ARV officers and McMinn

Stephen Smith

136

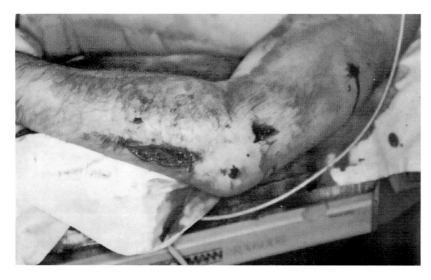

McMinn, in the ambulance with wounds to his arm

a revolver from his jacket and place the barrel in his mouth. Officers attempted to reason with him. It was a very tense situation.

As one of the ARV officers made an attempt to get the child in the pushchair to safety, McMinn moved the gun from his mouth, pointed it towards the officer and fired. The round narrowly missed him but went on to hit another ARV officer who was on containment about ten metres away in the knee. She fell to the ground.

Four ARV officers near to McMinn now returned fire. Five bullets struck him in his groin and arm and he collapsed to the ground. The child was safe and no members of the public had been injured. The police officer was rushed to hospital.

McMinn was also taken to hospital where he was treated for gunshot wounds. The *Star* published as their headlines the following day: 'Suburban Shootout' and 'Cops Gun Down Baby Row Dad'. Details of the police officer being shot featured later in the article.

McMinn soon recovered and on 22 September 1995 was found guilty of unlawful wounding, ABH and firearms offences. He was sentenced to eight years imprisonment.

The police officer shot by McMinn also made a good recovery from the gunshot wound to her leg, but this trauma, added to her previous experiences within the police service, which included being stabbed in the abdomen in 1991 as she tackled a deranged knifeman in the street and being in close proximity to an IRA bomb attack at Wood Green in December 1992, caused this brave officer to take medical retirement from the service in 1996.

The Crown Court judge at McMinn's trial commended the actions of all the ARV officers involved.

Post-Incident Procedure (PIP)

The procedure followed by SO19 after a shooting incident has changed very little since the late eighties when it first evolved. Set out below is what a principal officer (the shooter or an officer closely involved in a shooting) can typically expect to happen following a shooting incident. It is the current agreed procedure according to the following organizations: the ACPO (Association of Chief Police Officers) the MPS (Metropolitan Police Service) and the

IPCC (Independent Police Complaints Commission) or their predecessors. I have précised this for ease of reading.

Shortly after any shooting incident, someone other than the principal officer should provide an account at the scene to the post-incident manager (usually a senior police officer responsible for overseeing the post-incident procedure). This is done so that interested parties such as the IPCC can be informed in brief what occurred.

The principal officer is then taken to a post-incident location (usually police premises). The SO19 federation representative will attend and assist the officer in contacting his/her family to alleviate any worry or concern caused by live news broadcasts. The representative will remain at the PIP location and make sure the officer is seen by an FME (Force Medical Officer) who documents any injuries sustained during the incident, and assesses whether the officer is fit to remain on duty and continue with the PIP process. The officer will then consult with a lawyer to discuss their legal standing. Following these procedures the DPS (Department of Professional Standards – the police internal complaints unit) attends to supervise and record the unloading of the officer's weapons. The ammunition is counted back to confirm how many, if any, rounds have been fired. These are then preserved as evidence; any documents such as weapons booking-out logs, duty records etc. are also gathered by the DPS on an evidential basis. The officer will then be asked to make a short initial statement, noting down important facts or evidence. They will then be advised to go home and rest.

In order to provide the best possible evidence, an officer should refrain from making a full statement after a shooting for a period of time consisting of two periods of sleep. This is to give the officer time to come to terms with the shooting and allow them to return back to a state of normal functionality.

The note-writing period normally takes about ten to twelve hours and has been the subject of much controversy, mainly over officers being allowed to confer during this process. Everything conferred about is disclosed to the investigating authority – however, it has led to allegations of officers conspiring and altering accounts. All I can say in answer to this is that the statements are usually completed in the presence of a solicitor, the officers are fully aware of the restrictions placed on conferring, insofar as they are only permitted to confer on facts such as street names, locations, times, etc., and not on their own personal recollections of the incident or anything relating to justification of their actions.

These arrangements have come about following several incidents where officers who had opened fire and were in shock had been made to compromise their legal position.

The firearms officer, after a shooting, is in a strange legal place. They do not know whether they are a suspect or a witness. Even the officers investigating them often cannot decide which label to put on them.

In 2013, Schedule 3 of the Police Reform Act 2002 was amended to allow the IPCC to compel an officer who is a witness (not a suspect) to attend for an interview, be it videoed/recorded or written. What effect this new clause will have remains to be seen, but it must be stressed that all police-involved shootings are investigated independently of the force at the location of the incident and external experts assist the IPCC in establishing that the correct procedures have taken place before, during and after the incident. All officers involved are fully accountable to the law and recognize that they will have to account for their actions.

The Shooting of David Ewin, Barnes
28 February 1995

David Ewin, aged 38, was a career criminal who had over forty convictions for offences including armed robbery, burglary, firearms offences and car theft. For a time, he had the notoriety of being the Flying Squad's most wanted criminal. In 1995, he was on licence from a five-year prison term for armed robbery and after eight weeks of being free was not looking to go back to prison.

PC Patrick Hodgson was an experienced police officer of twenty years service, much of it working as a firearms instructor and 'level 1' trained officer within D11, PT17 and SO19.

On Thursday 28 February 1995, PC Hodgson was in an ARV, travelling north on Castlenau towards Hammersmith Bridge, when he and his crew-member spotted a stolen Toyota MR2 sports car driving towards them. (The car's details had been put up over the main-set radio as stolen.) They saw the car stop by a row of shops on Castlenau. The driver jumped out and went into a nearby off-licence. He was later identified as David Ewin and was high on a cocktail of drink and drugs.

PC Hodgson got out on foot in the company of another crew-member – just as Ewin ran from the shop and jumped back into the driver's seat. PC Hodgson ran around to the driver's door (in the road) and shouted for Ewin to get out. He ignored the officer and began shunting the car backwards and forwards attempting to manoeuvre out. PC Hodgson banged on the window with the butt of his pistol, shouting for Ewin to stop. He pulled open the driver's door and struggled with Ewin, trying to get him out of the car. Ewin, still in the driver's seat, drove the car forwards, dragging PC Hodgson with it. He hit the car in front. PC Hodgson was forced to let go and Ewin tried to drive out again,

crashing into a white van, which blocked his way.

The ARV drove forward, trying to block Ewin in. With tyres screeching he shunted forward again, forcing PC Hodgson to jump out of the way to avoid being crushed. A colleague managed to drag the passenger out of the car. PC Hodgson was now on the pavement. He opened the passenger door and challenged Ewin to stop. Ewin continued trying to drive the car out at any cost. PC Hodgson fired two rounds at Ewin from his Glock pistol, hitting him in his torso. Ewin was taken to the Royal London Hospital by air ambulance. He died of complications eighteen days later.

In no time at all, the incident was over, but the aftermath would see PC Hodgson arrested for murder. He would face three Old Bailey trials, two for murder and one for manslaughter, before being finally acquitted on 14 October 1997.

Patrick Hodgson continued to instruct on firearms training, but never again went on duty with a gun. He retired from the police a few years later; these events had taken a huge toll on his life, and I am sure that the memory of them will remain with him permanently.

The question that was central to this incident, and to PC Hodgson's trials, was how much force could be considered reasonable in this specific set of circumstances. One person's opinion may vary greatly from that of another, which in this case led to a jury having to decide over a period of months what PC Hodgson only had moments to act on.

It is interesting to note here that motor cars have been deliberately used by criminals to kill and maim police officers and members of the public in great numbers over the years. It is, perhaps, a fact easily forgotten by non-service personnel when examining a case such as this.

Stephen Smith

ARVs in the yard at Clapham, which became Trojan South's base in 2000

ARV Base Opened South of the River (Trojan 98)
1995

The general feeling of vulnerability following a spate of shootings of unarmed police out on the streets, both north and south of the River Thames, led to yet another increase in the number of ARVs on patrol. There also commenced a new drive to recruit more officers into the department.

The new ARV strength increased to eleven inspectors, thirty sergeants and 256 constables. This increase also led to a second base being opened at police premises just south of Lambeth Bridge in an effort to reduce call-out times south of the river. The new base took over the old B11 prisoner transportation offices and cells at the back of the police forensic laboratory in Pratt Walk. The role these offices had previously fulfilled had now been put out to private companies.

This temporary location became known as 'Trojan South'. Its call sign was 'Trojan 98' ('Trojan 99' was the north base at Old Street). Although this had been a temporary measure until better, more permanent accommodation

was found it remained at Lambeth for over five years. The location was ideal but owing to maintenance issues it was eventually necessary to find other accommodation.

By mid-2000 the ARVs from Trojan South had moved into a new temporary base at Clapham police station, Union Grove. (The police station had been closed for restructuring.) This served its purpose well. It was, once again, only a stop-gap, but it was a stop-gap that lasted another five years.

In 2005, after a decade of making do, Trojan 98 finally settled into its permanent operational south base, back at Lambeth. The new base was a converted office complex at the rear of the police forensic laboratories and remains the permanent south base for Trojan 98 today.

Although the south base ARV crews still trained and worked closely with their north base (Leman Street) opposite numbers, there has developed a healthy rivalry between the two ARV bases. And since the south base was established there has been a marked improvement in the response time to armed calls south of the river.

Stephen Smith

Stephen Smith

Above: The team practice a tactical approach up a fire escape. Right: An SFO Shotgunner in a respirator, with a Remington 870 pump-action shotgun. The shotgun was generally used by the team MOE officer. Below: Two SFO MOE (Method Of Entry) officers rehearse their drills, using the spike of the hoolie-bar and the enforcer hand-held ram to attack the lock of the door

Stephen Smith

SFO Team Training
1995

The images on the previous page are a series of training photos showing an SFO team rehearsing approach and entry drills at the rear of the SO19 headquarters at Old Street.

They are wearing the suede QRVs (Quick Release Vests) favoured at the time.

The officers had still not been issued with ballistic helmets. However, some of the early Kevlar helmets from the late 1970s were still in use.

Indoor Police Firing Ranges
Mid-1990s

Following the completion of City Road police range in 1961, the demand for further police ranges grew. Many of the small police pistol club ranges built in the basement of several police premises were extended and finished to a higher specification. These were then used to run basic firearms courses and police firearms refresher training.

Many of the police pistol and shooting clubs continued to use these ranges in the evenings. In fact, before the gun control laws (brought in after the Dunblane massacre in 1996), many potential D11/PT17 recruits were advised to join a police shooting club first to see if they were suited.

Most of the police ranges were constructed to similar specification, with four shooting points going back twenty-five metres from the turning target system (normally positioned behind a barricade to protect the machinery from stray rounds). Set behind the targets was a bullet-catcher (a system of steel troughs angled downwards to deflect the bullets into a safe area). In front of this hung a Linotex (rubberized foam sheet) curtain on rails. This prevented the bullets from ricocheting back up the range towards the officers. Most ranges were lined with wood to absorb sound, although in later upgrades sound-proof tiles were fitted.

Each range was slightly different. The fifty-metre ranges at Lippitts Hill, for instance, had sand backdrops to catch the bullets. Some of the later backdrops used tiny rubber balls reclaimed from old tyres to collect the spent bullets.

Health and Safety regulations dictated that each range had to be fitted with an extraction/ventilation system for removing dust and lead particles, and the floor also had to be non-slip. Lighting was important. The ability to change the lighting to suit the training scenario was a good feature. Some ranges were fitted with video and playback facilities for debriefing purposes.

Others featured side ranges or CQC rooms where officers could shoot 360 degrees into steel-lined walls, again with a Linotex curtain to prevent ricochets. The most modern range, constructed at the Metropolitan Police firearms training centre at Gravesend in 2003, had a drive-in facility with remote-controlled moving targets, twelve firing points and street furniture that could be moved around at the instructors' discretion.

This allowed for realistic, real-time deployment from vehicles that could be driven onto the live-fire range. It was invaluable to ARV and SFO training. Due to the nature of the firing ranges' use, regular maintenance was necessary, and they were constantly closing for refurbishments and updates. The firing range stations consisted of: Marylebone, Holborn, City Road, Croydon, Simpson Road (near Heathrow Airport), Leman Street (opened in 2001), Greenwich (closed 2005), Lippitts Hill (which had four ranges and closed in 2002), and Gravesend (with several ranges opened in 2003). The Met also borrowed range time at

The 'A' range at Lippitts Hill, a drive-in fifty-metre range partially open to the elements (photo *c.* 1997)

The modern range at City Road after its 1997 re-fit. The movable barricades create additional rooms with doors onto the targets

Bishopsgate (City of London Police) and RAF Uxbridge.

The importance of regular repairs and the dangers of a range environment were emphasized when, in March 2012, the range at Croydon blew up whilst undergoing general maintenance. Contractors had collected unburnt powder and dust in sacks and were welding the steel bullet catcher when a spark detonated the powder. In the ensuing explosion and fireball two workers were badly injured and several police officers were burnt trying to rescue them.

The Boyle/Brindle Shooting, Rotherhithe
20 September 1995

Operation 'Partake' was the result of a prolonged investigation into organized gang violence and contract killings based around south London. Over the previous seven years, a feud between gangs in the capital had been responsible for at least eight killings, three of which were of innocent bystanders.

The family gangs, or organized crime syndicates, involved were: on one side, the Brindle family (including brothers Anthony, Patrick and David), and on the other, the Daly and Arif families. The Dalys were a criminal gang who, although linked by marriage to the Brindles, had been clashing violently over their activities in south London. The Arif family were considered to be one of the top criminal gangs in south London at that time, and were heavily involved in all forms of crime including armed robbery, drug trafficking and contract killings. The Arifs had had their wings clipped when two of their family members, Dennis and Mehmet Arif, were arrested by PT17 for armed robbery in 1990 (see pages 103–5). Other members of their gang had also been arrested for drug trafficking and other related offences. The families' criminality stretched back to the late 1960s, filling the void left by the Kray twins (who had controlled crime in London's East End).

As early as March 1991 the feud had escalated when David Brindle was shot dead at a pub in Walworth. The killing was said to be a reprisal for the earlier gangland shooting of Ahmet Abdullah (cousin of Dogan Arif, head of the family) for which David's brothers Anthony and Patrick had stood trial and been acquitted.

There followed several other incidents including the shooting of James Moody in a hotel bar in Hackney in 1993. Moody had been an associate of the Richardsons and the Krays in the early days and had even escaped over the wall from Brixton prison. He was said to be friends with Peter Daly and had been in a fight with David Brindle only days before Brindle was shot. No suspects were forthcoming.

So it was into this soup of tit-for-tat killings that Michael Boyle, an Irishman with republican links was recruited. (During the Ulster ceasefire, gangs in the UK often used paramilitary gunmen to do contract killings. Both the Brindles and the Dalys had had dealings in the Irish Republic).

The south-east Regional Crime Squad's Operation 'Partake' was intended to prevent an escalation of the feud, to prevent retaliation by the Brindles and to protect the public. The main thrust of the operation was to intervene and arrest the hired assassin before he could strike. The operation was based on credible information that Tony Brindle was the target of a hired assassin from Dublin by the name of Michael Boyle who was known to have access to several firearms with ammunition, and explosives, and had served long jail sentences in Ireland for kidnapping and other related offences.

On 20 September 1995, Boyle left his safe house, wearing a wig as a disguise. He then drove a stolen van to Christopher Close, Rotherhithe, where he lay in wait near Brindles' flat for three hours in the back of his van.

As Brindle (his intended target) left his flat (just before 11 a.m.) and walked towards his vehicle, Boyle fired at him from inside the van. Brindle was hit in the elbow, chest and thigh, but still managed to run away from his assassin. Boyle left his vehicle in pursuit of Brindle, intent on finishing him off, when two SO19 officers suddenly deployed from their jump-off van parked nearby. These officers, firing on the move, discharged fourteen rounds before Boyle was brought down.

It is fair to say that the police were caught slightly on the hop on this occasion as Boyle's behaviour had led them to believe that he was only there on this day to observe his target's movements. It was also expected that Boyle would exit his van to carry out the hit at close quarters (not engage his intended victim through the window of his own vehicle), giving police time to intervene prior to any shooting. Fortunately for Brindle the two SO19 officers reacted quickly and decisively to Boyle's actions and were able to prevent any further injury.

Boyle runs towards Brindle – pistol in hand, intent on finishing the job. Moments later he is brought down in a hail of SO19 bullets. He is hit multiple times

Left: An SO19 officer standing over Boyle, his MP5 at the ready. Although wounded five times, Boyle survived the incident

Below: The cramped interior of the police covert jump-off van. Two officers spent hours waiting in here for the attack

Both Brindle and Boyle recovered from their wounds – they were lucky to have survived. Boyle was sentenced to serve at least fifteen years imprisonment for attempted murder. David Roads, the man who had supplied Boyle with his weapons, was sentenced to seven years imprisonment. He was shot dead by an unknown gunman the day he left prison. Brindle later served another fifteen years for major drug importation.

Operation 'Partake' certainly had the effect of removing a very dangerous man from the mix of escalating gang violence and vendetta.

Stephen Smith

SFO team CBRN training at Lippitts Hill

Whether it would have any effect at all on the cycle of violence remained to be seen.

In October 2001, Tony Brindle sued the Met Police for £100,000, alleging negligence and claiming that they failed to tell him his life was at risk and took inadequate steps to protect him. The High Court dismissed his claim.

PIRA Ends Ceasefire
9 February 1996

The Provisional IRA's statement of purpose was made crystal clear when they announced an end to their two-year ceasefire by detonating a huge bomb outside Canary Wharf, killing two, injuring thirty more and causing more than £85 million worth of damage.

Nine days later, an explosion on a London bus in Aldwych killed Edward O'Brien. He was on his way to plant the bomb at another location. Nine people were injured; three of them had been travelling in cars near to the bus. Miraculously no one else was killed.

CBRN Training (Chemical, Biological, Radiological and Nuclear)
From 1996

With international terrorism now bringing with it the threat of new kinds of weapons, including those with nuclear and biological potential, it would be remiss of police and security services not to prepare and train their staff for this new and hostile world. Ironically, it was D6 department (where the firearms training wing was first conceived back in 1966) that was responsible for training in Civil Defence. This included planning for a nuclear attack, which, during the Cold War, had seemed a real possibility. Civil Defence training had taken a back seat in the mid-1980s but was back on the agenda a decade later as a means of dealing with a threat from other quarters, namely the possibility of an attack by fundamentalist terrorists who might have access to a dirty bomb or even a small nuclear device.

SO19 sent a group of firearms instructors to train with the army and devise a training package for the department. These officers had the unenviable task of running all the CBRN training for SO19. Over the years, CBRN instruction has become part of the routine with regular training and exercises to test the officers, who have to complete all their specialist roles whilst wearing protective equipment.

'Just dropping in': Armed Drugs Rapid Entry, north-west London
1996

On an estate in north-west London the local police were having problems with a flat from which drugs were being sold in large quantities. It had barred windows and substantial grilles on the front door, and there was even a secondary grille in the hallway. The dealing was done through a hatch in the front door. The gang using the address felt they were untouchable and it was known locally that they had access to firearms, knives and machetes.

The problem facing the police was that any attempt to enter the flat would take time, during which the gang could dispose of evidence such as drugs and documents, etc. There was also the concern that they would have ample time to prepare to resist the entry, therefore putting the lives of the officers at risk.

SO19 were called in several days beforehand to help plan a raid on the address. During the following days, police infiltrated the empty flat above the drug den and spent time preparing and weakening the timbers in the floor. On the chosen day, armed SFO operatives broke through the ceilings in two rooms and, using 'fast ropes' (thick ropes, 40 mm in diameter, which can be up to 30 m long and are designed so users can slide down them in a controlled manner), managed to gain complete surprise, dropping in on the gang and catching them

Specialist firearms officers make an entry into a drugs den through the ceilings of two rooms, sliding down 'fast ropes' and thus gaining the element of surprise on the criminals dealing drugs below

View of the hole in the ceiling from which the officers made their entry

red-handed. A large quantity of drugs, drug paraphernalia and cash were recovered. No firearms were present but baseball bats, knives and machetes were readily at hand. Four arrests were made for conspiracy to supply class 'A' drugs (cocaine and heroin).

The ability of SO19 to think outside the box when it came to operational strategy, along with their training with ropes, had won the day. The local community and police were pleased with the action taken, as it had helped make life on that particular estate safer for residents.

Massacre at Dunblane
13 March 1996

The atrocities of the IRA were temporarily over-shadowed in the news in March 1996 by the awful massacre at Dunblane in Scotland when a deranged lone individual ended the lives of sixteen children and their teacher at a primary school in the small Scottish market town. This individual had held a firearms licence since 1977, entitling him to possess four handguns and 700 rounds of ammunition.

An outcry ensued and the result was a complete change in the law, prohibiting anyone from owning or possessing a handgun or ammunition. Private gun clubs would now be restricted to .22 target rifles only.

The Manchester Bombing
15 June 1996

In the summer of 1996, the Provisional IRA returned to the fore, continuing its bombing campaign, which had begun back in February. This campaign solely targeted the UK mainland but it needed another 'spectacular' to follow the earlier success of the attack on the London Docklands. This time, it targeted another of the UK's major cities, Manchester.

On 15 June 1996, IRA operatives set off a huge device in the city centre. The bomb was in the back of a lorry parked outside the Arndale shopping centre in Corporation Street. Following a tip-off, police were attempting to disrupt the device when it exploded. It destroyed a large part of the city centre, injuring over 200 people, mostly with flying glass. The damage was estimated at being over £700 million. A huge area of the city needed to be completely rebuilt.

Something needed to be done and quickly before the initiative, which had been won over the preceding years by the police and security services, went back over to the terrorists.

Fightback against PIRA: Operation 'Airlines'
15 July 1996

Operation 'Airlines' was the culmination of a long and protracted investigation into a seven-handed IRA cell, which was in the midst of a bombing campaign in London. SO19 were bought in by the Anti-Terrorist branch to raid three addresses believed to be the cell's safe houses and bomb factories. Plans were made to assault these addresses simultaneously. They were in Lugard Road, SE15, Woodbury Street, SW17, and Verona Court, St James' Drive, SW17. The operation involved over 300 officers across the capital.

In the late evening of Monday 15 July 1996, police convoys snaked their way to the three addresses and deployed to their forward assault points. On a given signal, CS gas (in liquid form) was fired by shotgun into all the addresses; a total of twenty-two ferret rounds were used. The element of surprise helped to ensure that the operation was a complete success.

Some officers could not believe their eyes when they saw the quantity of bomb-making equipment and explosives at one address, claiming: 'You had to watch where you stepped, these things were everywhere.' There were thirty-seven TPUs (Timer and Power Units), all ready to be connected to explosive charges, along with false identities and over £40,000 in cash. The intention had been to bomb power stations in and around London.

Six of those arrested, John Crawley, aged 40, an American ex-US Marine Corps explosives expert, Donald Gannon, aged 34, Robert Morrow, aged 37, Gerald Hanratty, aged 38, Patrick Martin, aged 35, and Frances Rafferty, aged 45, were convicted at the Old Bailey of conspiring to cause explosions. They were sentenced to thirty-five years each for offences under the Terrorist Act.

Another serious bombing campaign had been averted. This was a massive blow to an organization that was intent on bringing death and destruction to London. However, two years later, all six suspects were released under the Good Friday Agreement.

Race to stop IRA 'Spectacular': Operation 'Tinnitus'
9–23 September 1996

In September 1996, SO19's specialist firearms teams were called upon once again to assist the Anti-Terrorist branch who were gathering intelligence on a four-man IRA ASU operating in London and said to be planning another big 'spectacular'.

This ASU was suspected of carrying out the bombings in Manchester and Canary Wharf, and the attempted bombing of Hammersmith Bridge. All the stops were being pulled out by the police to prevent another such atrocity. Both sides were playing for extremely high stakes.

During the ongoing operation by police and security services, key addresses, including IRA safe houses, were located. Suspects were then followed to a domestic storage facility in north-west London where their bomb-making materials were hidden. The ASU had vehicles and enough explosives ready to carry out at least two attacks on the scale of the earlier Canary Wharf bombings. This four-man team potentially had the ability to bring London's financial centre to its knees if left unchecked.

It transpired that this storage unit contained over six tonnes of home-made explosives, known as HME, along with ten kilos of Semtex explosive, seventeen detonators, twenty-five timer and power units, a military det-cord, three loaded AK47 automatic rifles and three handguns with ammunition.

SO19 officers were held for long periods of

Stephen Smith

These SO19 Trojan support dogs were more than happy to pose for pictures in a quiet time during the operation. They always enjoyed their work and on this occasion provided some light entertain-ment for the officers as they held on standby

time at various centres in north-west London with no contact from the outside world. They were required to be in a high state of readiness. Boredom was an occupational hazard to be overcome. The first phase of the operation was to be a waiting game, while further intelligence was gathered.

Initially, consideration was given to arresting the suspects whilst they attempted to move their bomb to its final destination. This was a bold strategy that required perfect timing with no small risk but it would provide the best evidence. Plans were made and a fleet of jump-off and blocking vehicles were obtained for this purpose.

Just as the IRA cell was making its final preparations, high-level meetings were taking place. A risk assessment had confirmed that the danger to the public was too great under the current scheme so the plan was changed.

'Compromise'. A pen and ink drawing of SFO operators as they make their entry. They cover one another as the door is breached. CS gas flows out from the hotel room

The new plan involved arresting the ASU members the night before they were due to make their move and then sweeping the evidence up afterwards, hopefully linking it to the IRA men later through forensics and surveillance evidence.

Many addresses would be raided but the main address was entered by SO19. This was a hotel in Glenthorne Road, Hammersmith, west London.

The four Irishmen had all met there the night before and three of them had bedded down together in their room while the fourth suspect had returned to another known address.

A listening device in the hotel room had heard what police thought was a semi-automatic pistol being made ready. (This noise could have been made by other means but it was reasonable to suspect that these men would be armed.) They had been heard boasting earlier that they would kill any police who tried to stop them.

In the early hours of 23 September, SFO officers moved forward into the hotel and took up their positions outside the hotel room. A covert attempt to open the door failed and, as the door was breached, gas was fired into the room from the front door and a side window.

As officers entered the smoke-filled room, Diarmuid O'Neill loomed aggressively out of the darkness. Having every reason to believe that he was armed and desperate, the leading officer, fearing for the lives of himself and his colleagues, engaged O'Neill with six shots from his MP5. O'Neill died of his wounds at the scene. (It was later found that O'Neill had not been carrying a weapon at the time.) A fourth suspect was arrested later by a City of London SFO team who raided a secondary address nearby.

Along with the explosives and weapons recovered during Operation 'Tinnitus', several vehicles were seized, including a lorry intended as the bombing vehicle.

Operation 'Tinnitus' had taken over 50,000 hours of surveillance and investigation time but was money well spent in preventing yet another IRA spectacular.

In December 1997 at the Old Bailey, Brian McHugh, said to be the commander of the ASU, was convicted of conspiracy to cause explosions and sentenced to twenty-five years. Patrick Kelly received twenty years and James Murphy seventeen years imprisonment. All three were later released under the Good Friday Agreement.

Officer 'Kilo' (the code given to the SO19 officer who shot O'Neill, to protect his anonymity) had been suspended from operational duties since the incident. He underwent a full investigation by CIB2 (an internal police complaints unit) supervised by the PCA (the Police Complaints Authority – an independent body set up to oversee the investigation of serious complaints against police).

On 10 April 1998 (Good Friday), a historic agreement was signed between the governments of Ireland and the United Kingdom. It paved the way for a peaceful resolution to the Troubles that had plagued Northern Ireland and the UK mainland for decades, at a cost of thousands of lives.

Officer 'Kilo' was suspended from operations between September 1996 and June 2000, some three and a half years, during which time he was placed on restricted duties with no public contact, as per police procedure. In 1999, the PCA concluded the officer should not face any criminal or disciplinary charges. However, he would still have to wait until after the inquest the following year before he could be reinstated.

In February 2000 at the inquest into the shooting of O'Neill, the jury returned a majority verdict of lawful killing. From May 2000 the IRA began de-commissioning their weapons and in July 2005 they finally announced a formal end to their campaign.

Live-Fire, Cover and Movement Training, MPFTC Lippitts Hill
September 1996

In 1996, as part of the SFO training programme, each of the six teams was required to complete at least one full week of training in each six-week cycle. Throughout the year they were trained and tested in every aspect of their role. Although each training cycle varied, the core skills were always maintained. These included, amongst other things, advanced live-fire training in cover and movement drills using the fifty-metre range at Lippitts Hill. This training helped to develop the good working protocols around communication and weapons awareness that was so important to the role of the officers of the specialist firearms command.

Stephen Smith

Stephen Smith

Blue Team SFOs are put through their paces on the fifty-metre range at Lippitts Hill

Police Officer Deaths Lead the Met to Look at Body Armour for all its Officers

In April 1995 PC Phillip Walters was shot in the chest and killed after he and a colleague answered a disturbance call in Ilford, east London. They were in the process of detaining a suspect known as Ray Lee who had been hired by a woman to attack her boyfriend, when Lee pulled out a pistol and shot the officer at point blank range, firing twice and hitting the officer once. Lee was eventually imprisoned in June 1996 for manslaughter and firearms offences,

having been found not guilty of murder. He received ten years imprisonment.

PC Walters was the seventh Met officer to die after being shot or stabbed whilst on duty since 1990. His killing caused a public outcry for police to be armed just as PC Patrick Dunne's murder had done eighteen months earlier. PC Dunne had come across a gang-related shooting just off Clapham High Street. He had gone to investigate the sounds of gunfire when one of the gang, Gary Nelson, shot him in the chest. The murderer, along with his two accomplices, then walked away laughing. Nelson was eventually convicted of PC Dunne's murder in February 2006 and jailed for at least thirty-five years.

What makes these early nineties murders stand out is that all seven of the officers may have survived had they been wearing ballistic and stab-proof body armour. The National Police Federation for England and Wales balloted its members on the question of being armed, but only twenty-one per cent voted to carry guns. It may have been slightly higher if the ballot had been carried out in the Met alone, but it was still a long way from a majority in favour of arming the police. However, many officers had been buying their own body armour and there was even armour being sent over from the USA by fellow police officers concerned by the lack of protection afforded by the Metropolitan Police to its officers.

It was therefore agreed, after pressure from many quarters and as a direct result of the deaths of these brave officers, that the way forward was to issue body armour to all front-line officers. Unfortunately this did not happen overnight. The Met wanted to develop a purpose-built set of body armour, which was not only practical and comfortable to wear but which would afford protection to its officers against knives as well as firearms. In 1997, the Met vest was issued to all rank and file officers. This was a welcome move and has undoubtedly saved many lives since its introduction.

CS Gas Spray Canisters Issued to the Met
1997

After months of trials during the previous year, in 1997 CS gas contained in a small spray canister was issued to all Metropolitan Police officers as part of their personal safety equipment in an attempt to reduce the number of assaults on police as they encountered violent situations.

The small canisters came with strict guidelines and training. The gas, an irritant similar to that used by the officers of SO19 against armed besieged criminals, would now be available to all frontline police officers. It was not to be used indiscriminately in crowd situations but used to target violent individuals who posed a threat to the officer or the public.

If used correctly, the irritant, which is squirted in a stream of liquid into the subject's face, can incapacitate an attacker. However, if it misses or if the attacker is one of the few people on whom the gas has little or no effect, it can leave the officer vulnerable. The other drawback is, if it is used in a struggle, it can have the same effect on the officer as the suspect they are attempting to arrest.

That said, it does give the officer on the street another option when dealing with violent attackers and, along with the issue of the Met vest that same year, the Metropolitan Police were making the right moves in trying to afford their officers better protection.

Female Armed Robber Shot by Police
2 November 1997

On Sunday 2 November an ARV answered a call to Perth Road, Gants Hill, in Ilford. A woman driving a white Sherpa van was robbing people at gunpoint. An ARV was soon behind the van and the chase that followed the police's arrival ended in a cul-de-sac in Royal Close. Several other police vehicles blocked the end of the close; there was no escape.

Believing the vehicle to be blocked in, the armed officers began to deploy in the hope of arresting the driver but instead of giving up she reversed the van at speed into their ARV, causing extensive damage and narrowly avoiding cutting the legs off one officer who was in the process of deploying from the car.

Having forced the ARV out of the way, the

The white van that Jane Lee drove at the armed officers

woman then drove the van away at speed, attempting to turn into another small close off Royal Close, but the wheels became stuck in the mud after she cut across a grass bank. One of the officers, fearing that the driver of the van was preparing to ram them again, stood in front of it, pointing his MP5 carbine at the driver and shouting for her to stop and give up.

Once again, instead of giving up, she gunned the engine and, when the tyres bit, sped towards the officer who fired through the windscreen, hitting the woman three times. The van swerved past him, crashing into the side of a nearby house. Jane Lee, a 29-year-old career criminal and drug dealer, was seriously wounded, but paramedics and doctors from the local hospital managed to save her life. One round had struck her lower arm, another had entered her abdomen and the third hit her in the shoulder.

Lee, from Rainham in Essex, was found to be high on a cocktail of drink and drugs. She apparently needed cash badly to buy drugs and had been out on a robbing spree armed with a vintage black powder pistol.

In the back of the van, along with the black powder pistol, officers found a sawn-off shotgun and a replica semi-automatic pistol and also a small amount of drugs. Following a search of her house, more firearms were recovered along with a large quantity of drugs, but, most disturbing of all, was the discovery of Lee's 8-year-old son who had been left there to fend for himself during his mother's latest crime spree.

In the following PCA (Police Complaints Authority) investigation, the officers were found to have acted correctly. Jane Lee was later convicted of robbery and firearms offences and, after her release from prison in 2012, she published a book called *Gypsy Jane* detailing her life of crime and her encounter with ARV officers on that fateful day in Ilford.

Operation 'Trident' Is Born
March 1998

Following a series of gang-related shootings within the Afro-Caribbean community in parts of south London and other areas across the capital, a dedicated Operational Command Unit was set up and named Operation 'Trident'. Trident targeted the criminals within this community who were willing to use firearms within a growing gang culture to support the illegal sale of drugs. This culture had led to an increase in tit-for-tat shootings and gun-related violence, including kidnappings of other gangs' members against unpaid drugs debts.

It was inevitable that the skills practised within SO19 would be useful for the officers from Operation 'Trident'. The relationship built up over the following years between SO19 and Trident has led to many hundreds of arrests and prosecutions for serious crimes such as murder, kidnapping, possession and supply of firearms and drugs, and other related offences. This proactive operation has saved, and continues to save, many lives each year within the Afro-Caribbean community by recovering firearms and disrupting violent crime. Although the reaction to Operation 'Trident' within the community has not always been positive, in many cases it acts as a deterrent to young people thinking of joining these violent criminal gangs.

Armed Drugs Raid: Operation 'Le-Grande'
2 December 1998

Operation 'Le-Grande' was a multi-agency operation. Its aim was to shut down one of the capital's major drug supply venues. In the late nineties, the Back Beat Club off Charing Cross Road allegedly sold over £300,000 worth of cannabis and ecstasy each week to punters who took the drugs in 'chill-out rooms' within the club. It was also believed that firearms were held there.

The premises were on multiple levels, with alarms and security doors on each floor. This constituted a logistical nightmare for the firearms team planners. Because of the prob-

Stephen Smith

A light-hearted moment as the SFO team leader (right) responsible for planning the operation inspects one of his officers dressed as a vagrant (left), assigned to keep the nightclub doors open while the entry team arrive. (Note the concealed Remington short (Hatton) shotgun under his coat)

lems with gaining entry, they decided to use an assault team who would enter the club from the roof. These officers would abseil onto the sloping roof and force entry through the skylights, whilst other assault teams forced entry from the ground floor.

At 5.45 p.m. the assault was called and entry effected after an officer disguised as a vagrant held the front doors open. Over sixty specialist firearms officers deployed from a lorry on the Charing Cross Road and twenty entered from the roof. The operation was a complete success. A hundred suspects were arrested and £100,000 worth of drugs were seized along with £70,000 in cash. Because of the size of the premises and the number of people inside, the operation had needed all the resources of SO19 to ensure success.

SFOs practise on the roof of Old Street, ready for the abseil on the roof of the Back Beat Club

SFOs rehearse deploying from the back of the lorry. Here, four officers carry 'Nudge', the purpose-built door ram, to the front of the club

Greek Embassy Siege
1999

After a three-day siege of the Greek Embassy by a large number of Kurdish protesters, SO19 officers were used to clear through and check the embassy (a large modern building in Holland Park, West London) for any firearms threat still remaining, before handing it back to its Greek staff.

Thankfully, the protest had ended peacefully with the release of all the embassy staff. All the protesters were removed and processed at a local police station. Seventy-nine Kurds were charged with violent disorder. No firearms were found.

This incident, one of a number involving political targets in London, reinforced the need for specialist firearms teams to be on call and ready to support their colleagues who guard these embassies around the clock.

The Feltham Incident
28 April 1999

George Stephen Knights, aged 41, an ex-TV engineer and minder from Feltham, became obsessed with firearms after a trip to the USA. He racked up debts of £40,000 buying and collecting weapons, ammunition and grenades for no apparent reason. On 28 April 1999, at Hampton Road West, near Feltham in west London, Knights was pulled over by traffic officers who noticed that his road tax was out of date. They were shocked when Knights, who was dressed in khaki combat trousers, a green top and a dark baseball cap, pulled out a .40 calibre Glock pistol and opened fire on them. Luckily there were no injuries; the officers speedily retreated and kept their distance.

Knights sped off, followed by the traffic officers. He then pulled over a second time and took out a 5.56 Bushmaster assault rifle, using it to pepper the Land Rover patrol car with bullets. The pursuing officers managed to keep up a radio commentary, thus allowing other police assets to come to their assistance, including ARVs, who began to make their way towards Feltham.

At one point Knights abandoned his Cavalier hatchback and attempted to hijack a Mercedes dial-a-ride minibus containing three elderly passengers. The driver refused to open the door, so Knights pointed his assault rifle at him and fired. The driver ducked down and the round missed him: a lucky escape!

Knights then hijacked a white Vauxhall Astra, which he drove towards his home address, all the while pursued by unarmed officers. (Unfortunately the ARVs were attending the scene from some distance away and had still not caught up to the chase.)

In all, Knights fired at police and the public from thirteen different locations, riddling several vehicles with bullet holes. It was a miracle that no one was injured, although several police vehicles were put out of action.

Rather than trying to shake off the pursuing police on the roads, George Knights was determined to get home to his ground floor flat in Shaftesbury Avenue, Feltham, where he had a further stash of firearms, ammunition and hand grenades. When he arrived, ARV officers quickly contained the block. Hostage negotiators were called to the scene along with an SFO Team.

It could not be confirmed whether Knights was alone in his flat, but there was a family of three trapped in the flat above him, who were vulnerable to being taken hostage or being hit by stray bullets. Police managed to make contact with Knights' neighbours, but could not safely evacuate them. All they could do was to advise them to take shelter in their cast iron bath.

Knights now aggravated the situation by opening fire out of his back window, shooting half a magazine of 5.56 from his assault rifle and then throwing a live hand grenade out into the garden, where it exploded near police containment positions. Once again, the officers had a lucky escape.

Given his extreme violent instability, there was no available course of action other than to end the siege quickly before he claimed any victims. Authorization for a house assault was sought and quickly given by Commander Alan Shave. This was possibly one of the most dangerous entries any SFO team would have to make. They were coming up against a determined individual with heavy firepower and the will to use it.

The team were briefed and moved forward. CS gas was fired into the flat at the same time as the doors, front and back, were breached using Hatton rounds fired from a shotgun. Stun grenades were tossed inside as the entry was made. The element of surprise was on the

The haul of weapons and ammunition recovered from Knights' flat

side of the police and they were able to overpower Knights before he could use his weapons. No shots were fired during his arrest.

George Knights was arrested for having firearms to endanger life, resisting arrest, kidnapping and possession of prohibited weapons. A huge stash of weapons and ammunition was recovered from his flat. He also led officers to an outdoor hide in nearby woods where he had buried a further stash of weapons and ammunition. There was even an additional stash of weapons and ammunition that he had hidden at a location in Florida, in the USA!

Whilst in custody, Knights was questioned by police in connection with the murder of Jill Dando (the TV presenter who was shot dead on the doorstep of her west London home in a seemingly motiveless attack). She was murdered just two days before Knights' rampage. Police investigating her murder suspected it might be the work of a crazed individual acting on an opportunist basis. However, there was no significant evidence to link Knights to the murder and he was discounted.

(In May that year, the police arrested Barry George, a loner with no particular connection to Dando. He was convicted of her murder and in July 2001 he was sentenced to life imprisonment. George was released in 2007 after the original sentence was quashed following certain forensic evidence being discredited. He was re-tried in 2008 for the same offence and acquitted. At the time of writing the case remains unsolved.)

In March 2000, at the Old Bailey, George Knights received nine life sentences for his armed rampage. It was said by Nicholas Price, his defending QC, that he did 'not know why his client had the weapons except that he liked them'. Whilst sentencing Knights, Judge Giles Forrester commented, 'I have no doubt that you pose an unusually high degree of risk.' He went on to say, 'It is without exaggeration miraculous that no one was hit. You caused havoc, fear and distress.'

The courage of the officers who gave chase and of the officers who contained Knights' flat whilst coming under fire from guns and grenades was undeniable. The SFO team who made the entry also showed great bravery as there was a strong probability that there would be some casualties before Knights was subdued. Thanks to these officers, his rampage was ended swiftly and he was delivered into custody uninjured.

Although the bravery and restraint shown by those SO19 officers went almost unnoticed by the newspapers, and therefore the public, an armed incident in Hackney the following year would see the media baying for the blood of SO19 personnel.

Heckler & Koch 7.62 G3K Rifle Chosen by SO19

In 1999, SO19 identified the need for a more versatile, heavier calibre weapon, which could double as an intermediate sniper rifle and be used to counter the threat from terrorists armed with their weapon of choice: the AK47.

The department trialled and subsequently purchased the Heckler & Koch G3K 7.62 rifle, which was issued to SFO teams and rifle officers after training. The courses of instruction were completed at military ranges at Lydd and Hythe on the south coast.

Students lie prone for a 200-metre shoot at Lydd and Hythe military ranges

Stephen Smith

SO19 also purchased the Trijicon 3.5 x 35 ACOG (Advanced Combat Optical Gunsight) for this weapons system, which allowed the firer to shoot with both eyes open and also allows quick sight acquisition. The 'Kite' night sights already used by the department could also be fitted to this weapon. The G3K also came with a fitted bipod and adjustable butt stock and could be fitted with a retractable stock to make for easier carriage. The weapon proved to be a good addition to SO19 armoury.

The Harry Stanley Case, aka the 'Table Leg' Shooting
22 September 1999

The Alexandra, a locals' pub in Victoria Park Road, Hackney, had seen some unusual activity for a Wednesday night. Earlier that evening, armed police had stopped a vehicle directly outside the pub. They were looking for firearms, which they suspected might be hidden in the vehicle (although none was found).

Then, a short time after 7.30 p.m., a man entered the pub carrying a package around eighteen inches long. It was tightly wrapped in a blue plastic bag. The man placed it on the floor and rested his right foot on it. Although the man lived locally, he was not one of the pub's regulars. He ordered a glass of lemonade.

It would be fair to say that the other drinkers in the bar were still in a heightened state after the excitement of the earlier police activity; speculation amongst the customers was that police were out looking for an armed suspect. The staff and customers were suspicious of the man who had just wandered in. One of them, Clifford Willing, paid special attention to the package laid at the man's feet. In a statement he made to police later that night he said: 'It was in a blue plastic carrier bag. The package was wrapped so tightly that I could see it was a sawn off shotgun with the stock cut off. I could see the barrel and stock of the weapon and even the trigger. I would say it was double barrelled and side by side.' The stranger took a sip from his drink and after a short while left the pub. The worried staff locked the doors behind him and even turned off the lights in the pub.

At 7.44 p.m. on 22 September 1999, an emergency call was received at the information room of New Scotland Yard. It related to an 'Irishman with a sawn-off shotgun in a blue plastic bag', who had been drinking in the Alexandra pub. Further details and descriptions were obtained and relayed to the ARVs and local police.

Henry (Harry) Stanley, a 46-year-old grandfather, was in fact from Scotland. He was a painter and decorator who was recovering from major surgery undergone ten days earlier. That morning he had been out visiting his brother to get a table leg repaired, which had been broken during a recent family gathering. Having finished his task he made his way home, stopping in four pubs along the way.

Inspector Neil Sharman (the ARV duty officer), along with PC Kevin Fagan (an experienced SFO on attachment to the ARVs), took the call. At about 7.55 p.m. they spotted a man who exactly matched the description given of the suspect. He was walking in Victoria Park Road at the junction of Fremont Street. He gripped a blue bag in his right hand.

Both officers left their vehicle, drew their Glock pistols and approached the man from behind. PC Fagan was on the pavement with Inspector Sharman in the road slightly ahead, partially shielded by parked cars. Both officers held their pistols out in front of them. From a distance of about twenty feet, PC Fagan shouted, 'Armed police! Armed police!' Stanley stopped and, in one slow, seemingly deliberate movement, turned 180 degrees to his left. His feet were described as being in a 'boxer's stance'. The blue bag was tucked into his right hip and was pointed directly at Fagan.

As Stanley moved his left hand towards the bag (a move that PC Fagan thought was a prelude to firing the shotgun) both officers opened fire. Each fired a single shot. Stanley fell to the pavement, killed by the bullet fired by Inspector Sharman, which had hit him in the head. PC Fagan's shot had had struck him in his left hand.

Upon inspection, it turned out that the tightly wrapped blue bag contained not a sawn-off shotgun as the officers had expected but a curved, ornate table leg (see page 162). This was a terrible human tragedy, and the consequences would be grave.

It is true that Harry Stanley had not been in possession of a shotgun as police had believed. In fact, he had not committed any crime worthy of arrest, let alone being shot dead by police, so one could understand why the press championed his family and condemned the police action that night. But the media were keen to portray the two officers as liars who made false statements to cover up an overreaction that had resulted in the death of a harmless, unarmed grandfather. The police investigation also appeared to move slowly while they took statements from drinkers in the pub, family members and anyone else they felt might be able to assist.

Statements had been taken from a witness, Mrs Carpenter, who said that Stanley was holding a fifteen-inch long object in his right hand when he turned very slowly, raised his arm and pointed it at police. Although this account backed up the officers' version of events, they would have to wait until the inquest in 2002 before it could be made public. Inspector Sharman and PC Fagan always maintained that they had acted in self-defence but they would have to wait a long time before the matter could be settled.

Surrey Police investigate

Surrey Police were brought in to investigate the shooting and gathered all the available evidence. Their findings were handed to the CPS (Crown Prosecution Service) who, after careful deliberation, stated that there was 'insufficient evidence to bring any criminal charges against the officers involved'.

The crux of the allegations against the two officers was that they had shot Harry Stanley as his back was turned towards them (Inspector Sharman's round had penetrated the left rear quadrant of Stanley's head). However, both officers swore blind that Harry Stanley was facing them when they fired.

In June 2002, at the inquest into Harry Stanley's death, the coroner told his jury to return either a lawful killing or open verdict only. (This is done at the prerogative of the coroner if he considers any other verdict is not applicable.) They returned an open verdict. In April 2003, the family's lawyers, after a campaign backed by pressure groups, over-turned the earlier verdict and were granted a second inquest. In October 2004, (five years after the incident) at the second inquest into Harry Stanley's death, a jury passed a verdict of 'unlawful killing'. The two officers were immediately suspended from duty, pending further investigations. The CPS also reviewed the case, which caused the press to call for the officers to face criminal charges.

Armed police down tools

Armed officers throughout the country watched events unfold. They were fully aware of the implications this had on them and most felt great empathy for the two officers. Many SO19 officers, both ARVs and SFOs, decided that the only way of supporting their two colleagues was to hand in their authorizations

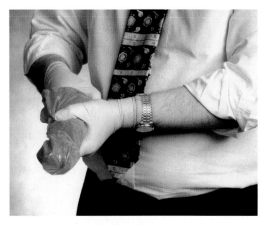

A forensic officer holds the table leg wrapped in the bag, as the officers would have seen it that night

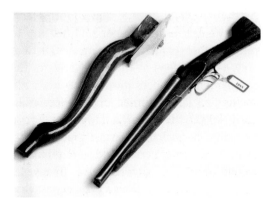

A direct comparison. The table leg alongside a genuine sawn-off-shotgun

to carry firearms. (They were all volunteers and could refuse to carry firearms if they felt they could no longer perform that role.) Now they were effectively withdrawing their labour from the service.

Over 120 officers, some from other Metropolitan Police firearms commands, took this course of action, which immediately highlighted the plight of the officers in a different way than had previously been seen. The government, and to some extent the public, were now forced to consider the implications of not having armed police on their streets, and to consider the immense strain and potential risks these officers faced in the course of their daily duties. The protest led to the commissioner Sir John Stevens attending SO19 in person. Although it was accepted that he could not intervene in the due process of law the two officers faced, he made assurances that changes in the way shootings were investigated would be instigated in the future.

New evidence

In January 2005, things got worse for the two officers after Surrey Police were revisiting some of their exhibits and found two previously missed bullet holes in the top of the left shoulder of the jacket Stanley had been wearing, which appeared to add credence to the theory that Stanley had been shot in the back. (Surrey Police found that Sharman's round had travelled through the material of the jacket before entering Stanley's skull.)

Throughout this time, both officers had been suspended from contact with the public or any involvement with armed operations. They and their families were under immense pressure and strain. This was relieved slightly when in May 2005 the second inquest verdict of unlawful killing was challenged in the high court and quashed. However, it did not affect the investigation that was still being carried out by Surrey police into the shooting.

Dave Bloxidge (the federation representative for the DPG, who had assisted Mark Williams, the SO19 federation rep, in some protracted shooting incident enquiries involving SO19 officers) suggested calling in Professor Lewinski from the Force Science Research Centre at Mankato in Minnesota in the USA. The thinking was that Lewinski (an expert on how the human body responds in high stress situations) might be able to help explain the discrepancies in the Stanley case.

Floral tributes left by family, friends and well-wishers at the scene

Visit to the USA

Bloxidge and Williams made a trip to the Force Science Research Centre in Minnesota, where they consulted with the professor on the Stanley case. After listening, he explained the probable sequence of events. He suggested that PC Fagan's round was fired fractionally before Inspector Sharman's. Fagan's round had struck the fingers of Stanley's left hand, causing him to recoil immediately and instinctively. Stanley most likely flung his arm up and simultaneously turned away from the source of the pain. Lewinski believed this positioned him so that Inspector Sharman's round, fired fractionally later, struck him in the back of the head.

Two officers arrested

Williams and Bloxidge returned to England feeling confident for their two colleagues but they then received news that the CPS, after reading the report from Surrey police, had authorized the arrest of Sharman and Fagan. The officers were held on suspicion of the murder of Harry Stanley, gross negligence, manslaughter, perjury and conspiracy to pervert the course of justice. They were released on bail.

Lewinski arrives in London

The Police Federation were quick to hire the services of Professor Lewinski and during the following weeks he travelled to London where he used hi-tech lasers to examine the scene, which thankfully had remained relatively unchanged. (He even managed to find a bullet hole from one of the rounds in a fence panel.) Lewinski then interviewed the two officers at length, walking them through the scene and taking measurements of the various angulations. Once he had a clear picture of events, he took this information away and began to construct a computer animation of what he determined had occurred. This suggested that events had occurred almost exactly the way he had explained to Bloxidge and Williams back in Minnesota.

Witnesses had stated that they had heard two shots that night very close together; the officers believed they had fired at the same moment. Lewinski proved that the audible signal made by shots fired one-tenth of a second apart would sound to a normal human as though they were two separate shots.

Lewinski concluded that the suspect 'was fully facing the officers' when they reacted to his apparent threat and shot at him.

The *Sunday Telegraph* on 23 October 2005 ran an article with the headline, 'Man Killed By Police "Had Planned To Be Shot By Marksmen"'. The story referred to a relative

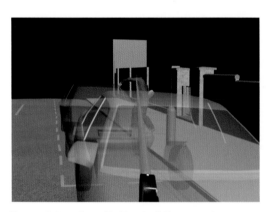

Image taken from Dr Lewinski's computer-generated video, which helped get to the truth of what happened on that fateful night (Force Science Institute Ltd, reproduced with the kind permission from the Met Police Federation of England and Wales)

who had told Surrey police earlier in the investigation that Mr Stanley had recently undergone surgery for cancer and 'wanted to die'. He had allegedly talked specifically about setting himself up 'to be shot by police marksmen'. Later in the article a spokesman for Surrey police was quoted as saying 'We did pursue a line of enquiry of what might be called suicide by police but no evidence of it was found.'

All charges dropped

Lewinski's report and animation were submitted to the CPS for consideration and on 20 October they announced that they would not proceed further against the two officers. The officers were understandably relieved at the decision not to prosecute them and thankful to all those who had supported them through this long process.

This case undoubtedly changed the way investigations into police shootings are conducted. There is now a far greater understanding of the science behind movement in stress situations and a great debt of gratitude is owed to Professor Lewinski who was able to shed new light on the dynamics of armed confrontations.

Inspector Sharman retired from the police just before the Olympics with the rank of Chief Inspector. PC Fagan still works within the firearms command. Both officers have earned great respect from their colleagues for their integrity and patience throughout this long and protracted ordeal.

PART FIVE:
A Different Kind of Game — SO19/CO19 in the 2000s

The new millennium began frantically with a hijacking, followed by several high-profile armed incidents, including a massive attempted robbery at the Dome in Greenwich. But it was the attacks on 11 September 2001 at the World Trade Centre in New York that would mark the decade as one no one will ever forget. The attacks in New York brought home to everyone that they were at risk from international terrorism, a fact that would be hammered home to Londoners in July of 2005 when their transport system was targeted.

The firearms department, meanwhile, would face tests of another nature, as it was forced to explain its actions in and out of court in several high-profile shooting incidents, one of which sparked rioting not seen in the capital since the 1980s. It would also face the busiest time in its history as it stretched itself to confront several layers of armed crime and terrorism.

The Stansted Hijacking
6–10 February 2000

The spectre of terrorism once again paid Britain a visit as the new millennium got underway, this time in the form of a hijacked aircraft. This was a rare event in British airspace, partly owing to the robust manner in which the government had dealt with terrorist incidents in the past. However, not wanting to be caught on the hop, the authorities dusted off the protocols relating to hijacked aircraft and quickly set the wheels of de-escalation in motion, hoping to bring this latest incident to a speedy and safe conclusion.

The hijackers were a group of Afghans (armed with grenades, knives and pistols) who, on Sunday 6 February 2000, hijacked the Afghan Ariana passenger jet with 164 passengers and fourteen crew members. The plane was on an internal flight between Kabul and Maz-e-Sharif when the hijackers forced the aircraft to divert to Tashkent in Uzbekistan, where ten passengers were released. After taking off four hours later, the aircraft was forced to land in the Kazakhstani city Aktyubinsk, owing to a leak in one of its fuel tanks. After a short while it was allowed to leave. It then flew to Moscow, where nine further hostages were released.

In Moscow, the hijackers were aggressive

An SO19 specialist firearms officer showing how his role had diversified through the nineties and into the year 2000, when the use of CS gas and the potential threat from dangerous chemicals in illegal drugs factories and drug-dealing dens had become commonplace, requiring such officers to work in plain clothes but still have access to additional weapons and equipment

and demanded the release of one Ismail Khan, an anti-Taliban commander who had been imprisoned by the regime in Afghanistan. They also threatened to blow up the aircraft, killing everyone on board. Following talks with Russian negotiators they were permitted to re-fuel and leave. Their final destination, although not confirmed, was believed to be a European city, possibly London.

As the aircraft entered British airspace, it requested to land at Heathrow. SO19 teams were placed on standby at this airport, but the aircraft was diverted instead to Stansted. Stansted had been identified as the most suit-able airport for this type of incident, having a secluded area where minimal disruption could be caused to the general running of the airport. The military were informed of the situation, along with the emergency services, which included Essex firearms command.

Stansted was no stranger to this type of incident. It had been used three times in the past to land hijacked aircraft, once in 1975 for a British Airways flight, then in 1982 for an Air Tanzania flight and then, in 1996, for a Sudanese A130 Airbus. All three incidents ended peacefully with the hijackers surren-dering.

The Ariana airliner landed at Stansted in the early hours of Monday morning. It was no secret that Essex firearms resources would be stretched, especially if the incident went on for any length of time. As it turned out, they coped well until later that evening, when requests were made for the Met to send an armoured Land Rover, then rifle officers and finally two SFO teams to assist with resources.

The Home Office acted as an intermediary between the hijackers and the Taliban govern-ment who were opposed to any kind of agreement, but no headway was made. The days passed by. SO19, along with Essex firearms offi-cers, continued to carry out their duties, using the armoured Land Rovers for food drops to the aircraft and supporting the remote sniper posi-tions that were in some bleak locations around the airfield. They had to snatch sleep whenever they could, using camp beds set up in the hangar nearest the hijacked airliner. The rifle officers were the heroes of the day, staying out in their hides at all hours, feeding back valu-able information to the control centre.

Stephen Smith

SO19 SFOs on standby in a hangar near to the hijacked aircraft. They were expected to sleep, eat and prepare kit and weapons in this vast, noisy hangar

There was speculation early on that the hijackers and their families (a group of about forty people also on board the aircraft) might seek political asylum, although this was still not clear as there had been no further demands made since that for the release of Khan in Moscow. The threat of blowing up the aircraft was real, as was the danger of violence towards the other passengers.

Many observations were made of the hijackers threatening cabin staff in the cockpit with firearms. On more than one occasion the hijackers, armed with pistols, had been seen patrolling around the aircraft, their heads covered with hoods.

At 11 p.m. on day four, the cabin crew (including the two pilots) took an opportunity to escape from the cockpit, sliding down from an escape hatch on ropes and fleeing into the night. The four frightened crew were rounded up and bought in for questioning. Observations were made of a man receiving a beating in the cockpit. These were times of heightened tension and all police were stood-to, along with certain military assets that had arrived early in the negotiations. The SF (Special Forces) contingent were sharing the hangar with the police and were prepared to assault the aircraft should the situation deteriorate further.

A period of high drama followed, with the hijackers demanding the return of the pilots. After a few hours things calmed down and the hijackers agreed to a face-to-face meeting with an official from the Home Office. SO19 were now sent forward in two armoured vehicles escorting a people carrier containing a Home Office representative.

The meeting took place in a vehicle a short distance from the aircraft. The hijackers' leader, his head covered with a scarf, was wearing loose clothing, which was thoroughly searched by SO19 officers. The meeting, although tense, appeared to go well, but no one except those present knew what had been said or agreed. Whatever it was did not appear to work, as later that evening things took a turn for the worse. Alarm bells rang in the police control area as the stairs under the aircraft were lowered and the limp body of what turned out to be one of the crew was tossed down the stairs onto the tarmac.

The Special Forces assets were now stood-to in full assault kit, their weapons ready. SO19 and Essex firearms officers waited to support any SAS action. An Essex police Land Rover was dispatched to collect the body. The next radio transmission was all-important – if the person thrown down the stairs was dead, a full mission to rescue the hostages would follow. After several long moments, the radio crackled into life. There were signs of life.

The victim was retrieved and sent for medical treatment. The police and military were stood down for the moment. Hostage negotiators resumed and after some skilled work on their part the hijackers were persuaded to give up.

It was in the early hours of the morning of day five that the well-rehearsed Operation 'Release' swung into action. The armed police units from Essex and SO19 moved forward, and huge floodlights were set up around the aircraft. Armoured vehicles were positioned tactically, along with cones and rolls of police incident tape. This tape funnelled the passengers down towards search areas where unarmed police staff would search them under the watchful eyes of armed officers backed up by police dogs in case anyone chose to run. The passengers would then be placed on buses and ferried to a terminal where Home Office officials were waiting to process them.

Operation 'Release' went off well. Over 140 hostages were processed through this system and finally the hijackers themselves came out

Disorientation shoots. Photo of officers firing in the inverted prone position. Although not recommended for everyday use, this type of shoot gets the officer acclimatized to any unusual position they may find themselves in: after being shot, or being hit by a car, for instance

(nine in total) under the control of armed officers. The weapons used by the hijackers were placed on the ground as they entered into captivity. How long their incarceration would be was yet to be decided. The aircraft was now searched – dummy explosives and live grenades were found, along with knives and loaded pistols. The success of the operation was greeted with relief by all involved; it could so easily have ended with great loss of life.

After two trials at the Old Bailey costing over £2 million, the nine hijackers were convicted of hijack, false imprisonment and possession of firearms. They claimed they had no choice but to take this course of action for the safety of themselves and their families. All the hijackers were subsequently released and granted asylum to stay in Britain. Of the passengers on board the Afghan Ariana airliner, seventy-seven also claimed political asylum.

Thankfully, there have been no repeats of this type of incident in the UK in the last twelve years, but SO19 still train regularly in all the skills needed to deal with this sort of situation should they be needed in the future.

Practical Pistol Shooting, Lippitts Hill
2000

The photo shows just one example of officers on an SFO course being instructed in practical pistol shooting skills on one of the twenty-five-metre side ranges. The shooting was varied and unusual to get the student acclimatized to handling firearms in testing situations. This was just one of the pistol skills taught to the students.

On a light-hearted note, the faces stuck to the target boards are those of the course instructors, done so to give an extra incentive for accurate shooting!

Kidnappings in London

In the late nineties and early noughties, there was a marked rise in the incidence of kidnapping offences in certain areas of London – from just four such offences in 1997 to thirty-one in 1999 and levelling out at between fifty and eighty offences per year in the following years. These offences were mainly carried out by criminal gangs from other parts of the globe, including the Caribbean, Lithuania, Kosovo, Albania, Russia and China (by both recent and second-generation immigrants). The practice now seems to have been adopted by other criminal gangs who see it as a fair way to extract money owed for criminal debts, even though these debts may amount to only a few hundred pounds.

The majority of these offences are committed by criminals against other criminals, but kidnapping is still (regardless of who it is perpetrated against) second only to murder on the statute books. It can also involve violence such as torture, rape and assault, leaving its victims with permanent physical and mental injuries. This sharp rise in this type of criminality sparked the forming, in 2001, of the Met's dedicated Anti-Kidnap Unit.

The kind of kidnapping with which we are more familiar, through TV drama plots and occasional news headlines, is still being committed, but is by contrast rare. These sinister crimes occur mainly where the relatives of the rich or famous find themselves targeted by highly organized criminal gangs. This was the case in November 2002 when a gang from Eastern Europe targeted the family of David Beckham, planning to claim a ransom of £5 million. Luckily this plot was foiled and the gang were arrested by armed officers from SO19 in an operation that made the front pages of the *News of the World*, who led with the Headline 'Posh Kidnap'.

Chinese Kidnap Hostage Rescue
2 August 2000

The following sequence of photos, lifted from an evidential video, was taken in August 2000 following a spate of kidnappings by Chinese gangs who were involved in the importation of illegal immigrants into the UK. This type of crime makes up around nineteen per cent of all UK kidnappings.

Aerial photo of the block of flats where the hostages were held

Officers make their entry after shooting the hinges from the back door to gain access

Caught sleeping. Two of the kidnappers are detained

The problem with detecting these offences is that, unless an informant steps forward, or a hostage escapes to raise the alarm, they will go undetected; the hostages themselves are generally in fear of the authorities and are reluctant to go to the police or give evidence. Their families also are reluctant to involve the police and draw attention to their loved ones entering the country illegally.

The gang in the photos, having already received payment for smuggling the immigrants into the country, would hold their victims against their will and demand a further payment from their relatives back in China for the release of their loved ones. They would be tortured while they pleaded on the phone to their relatives. It was a brutal and cruel trade in human misery.

On this occasion a suspicious neighbour called the police after seeing so many comings and goings from the address and hearing people in obvious distress.

After observations and intelligence gathering, the full extent of what was happening became apparent and SO19 were called in to mount a rescue.

This particular gang were arrested and their terrible trade ended, but this template is still used by other gangs and requires constant police awareness to detect and prevent it from becoming an epidemic.

ARV Officer Shoots Axe-man in Supermarket
29 August 2000

On Tuesday 29 August 2000 at 7.55 p.m., police and ARVs were assigned to an emergency call at a Sainsbury's supermarket in New Cross where a man previously barred from the store for being abusive to staff and customers had returned. Staff had just told him to leave for the second time when he produced an axe from the rear of his trousers. The staff backed off and the manager followed him around the store, while waiting for police.

The crew of the Armed Response Vehicle soon arrived and entered the store. There had been no attempt to evacuate the store; this may have been for the best as any panic may have escalated the situation. The ARV officers were directed to the freezer section. Two unarmed local officers accompanied them. They split between two shopping aisles and began moving forward.

It was at this point that one of the ARV officers saw the suspect pass the end of his aisle closely followed by the manager, who indicated towards the man. The officer drew his Glock pistol and shouted 'Stop! Armed police! Stand still.'

The suspect, Juan Barquin Braz, stopped, reached behind and produced the axe from his trousers. He turned towards the police who had emerged from the aisles nearest to him. The first officer shouted again for him to stop and drop the axe. He ignored these commands and began advancing towards the police closest to him. There was still a serious risk to other shoppers and, fearing for their safety and that of his colleagues, the officer fired one aimed shot, hitting the axe-man in the chest. This seemed to have little or no effect other than to make him turn towards the shooter and smile. He then advanced again. The officer fired once more, hitting him again in the chest. He advanced a few more steps before collapsing in the aisle. Officers administered first aid and continued until an ambulance arrived.

The axe-man survived his wounds and was committed on the grounds of mental health issues to a hospital where he received treatment. The assistant commissioner commended the officer who had fired for his actions. His intervention had prevented an escalation of violence from this man, which could have put innocent members of the public and police at risk. This incident typified the useful support for unarmed officers given by the ARVs, and proved once again the need for such an asset within modern-day policing.

Hostage Rescue – Sniper Intervention, Islington
30 October 2000

At 8.19 a.m. on 30 October 2000, police were called to a third-floor flat in Cathcart Hill, N19, after a call from the London Ambulance Service. Apparently they had answered a call to the address after a report of persons injured following a domestic incident. They were refused entry and alerted the police.

Local police attended and it soon became apparent that a man was holding two women inside the premises against their will and had armed himself with two knives and possibly other weapons. The duty officer contacted SO19 and requested urgent armed assistance. Armed response vehicles attended and soon contained the flat. Officers began evacuating other residents within the building and an SFO team was scrambled out from Old Street.

Local enquiries were made and it was soon established that one Kieran O'Donnell, aged 19, shared this flat with his 24-year-old girlfriend Nadia. O'Donnell was known to be suffering from mental illness and had been having treatment.

At 9.50 a.m. contact was made with O'Donnell by phone. He demanded that his father be contacted. He also stated that they were all going to die. It became apparent that the second female in the flat was his mother, Katherine. Police were able to speak with girlfriend Nadia, who informed them that she was unharmed. O'Donnell then grabbed the phone back and became agitated. The two women both began pleading with him to let them go.

It was becoming very tense. The ARV officers on close containment were able to speak with Katherine through the front door. She told them the door was barricaded and that O'Donnell had a knife in his hand. There was more shouting and O'Donnell was heard to say he would stab her if she tried to move the barricade.

The flats in Cathcart Hill were undergoing restoration to their façade and had scaffolding against the building on all levels at the front. Officers were therefore able to climb up and look into the flat. By 11.55 a.m. the SFO team were kitted up and ready to carry out an intervention as an emergency response if required. An SFO team sniper had found a suitable position in an adjoining flat overlooking the room where most of the activity was occurring. He was able to give a commentary of movement within the flat. He was armed with a Heckler & Koch 7.62 G3K assault rifle, more than capable of firing through both windows with some accuracy.

At 12.27 p.m. O'Donnell told the hostage negotiators on the phone that they (the police) would 'have to take him out'. The negotiators continued to reason with him but were interrupted by the women screaming and pleading with O'Donnell. At one point he threw a Stanley knife across the room. The women called out to police to rescue them.

At this rather inopportune time, O'Donnell's phone stopped working and for a period the negotiators conversed with both hostages and hostage taker through the front door. They advised the scene commander that they would continue to negotiate until they felt the situation had deteriorated beyond repair.

At 2.20 p.m. a second phone was placed on the windowsill at the front of the premises in an effort to get O'Donnell to open the window and retrieve it. He refused to collect the phone. Ten minutes later he told police he would hang himself and then threatened to set fire to the

Rear of the flats in Cathcart Hill. The SFO sniper position was from the top window on the left, looking slightly down into the double windows on the right

premises. The fire brigade were held on standby.

At 4 p.m. the phone was retrieved by O'Donnell's mother, who left the window unlocked. At 4.38 p.m. O'Donnell declared he would start stabbing people and then, as if to emphasize his erratic behaviour, he claimed he would send his mother out via the scaffolding. This was contradicted when he appeared at the window with a knife to her throat. A short time later, the SFO sniper relayed the fact that the mother seemed able to roam free in the flat, while the girlfriend, Nadia, was tied up. This was confirmed when Katherine (the mother) whispered through the door that she intended to leave the flat via a window. This was relayed to the negotiators who feared this might aggravate O'Donnell and so she was advised against this

course of action. Regardless, at 5.22 p.m. O'Donnell's mother climbed out of a window onto the scaffolding where she was assisted down and taken to the ambulance.

Meanwhile, O'Donnell was leading his girlfriend around the flat with her hands tied behind her back. He was then observed placing a noose made of electric cable around her neck. She was showing signs of great distress as he led her around the flat in this way.

At 5.55 p.m. O'Donnell was seen dragging Nadia towards the front door by her hair whilst holding an object in his right hand. This later turned out to be a corkscrew. Two SO19 assault teams moved into position, one on the scaffolding and the other by the front door. Five minutes later, O'Donnell began barricading himself into the hallway. He then took Nadia

Stephen Smith

The 7.62 Heckler & Koch G3 assault rifle as used by the SFO sniper to engage O'Donnell

into the back room; she still had the noose around her neck; it had been pulled tight. Using their scopes, the SO19 sniper and his observer could see O'Donnell and his hostage clearly. All there was between them were two single glazed windows, one covered by a net curtain. It was a distance of about twelve metres.

At 6.06 p.m., police saw O'Donnell climb on top of Nadia and begin stabbing her in the head with the corkscrew. Stun grenades were thrown into the flat and the teams began making their entries. The sniper knew he had to act immediately if he was to stop O'Donnell killing his hostage. Although the distance was small, he was firing through two windows and he knew the slightest contact could deflect a bullet. He fired; the 7.62 mm bullet punched across the narrow gap between the two buildings, hitting O'Donnell in the chest. The SFO assault teams burst into the room as O'Donnell dropped to the floor. The officers began first aid and the paramedics were called up to assist.

Nadia had received some nasty wounds caused by O'Donnell stabbing her with the corkscrew. He had also hit her with a monkey wrench. She was removed to hospital and thankfully survived her injuries. Although Paramedics worked to save O'Donnell it was not possible, and he died of his wounds.

On 8 April 2002 the St Pancras inquest jury passed a verdict of lawful killing. The action

taken by the officer in identifying the threat to life undoubtedly saved the hostage from even more serious injury or death. The SFO officer who fired the shot was returned to full operational duties within the year.

Operation 'Magician': the Dome Robbery
7 November 2000

The Dome robbery was one of the most audacious raids ever attempted – and the simplicity of the plan made its success almost guaranteed. The location was the Millennium Dome on the Greenwich Peninsula, which had been the showcase of the millennium celebrations. It had cost the country a massive £789 million and was now an open-all-year tourist attraction. It may have been overpriced and disappointing to many, but its attraction to one criminal gang was irresistible. Sadly for them, they were about to come up against the Met's Specialist Operations department, working together for a safer London.

The prize the gang were after was the Millennium Star, which was purchased in the early 1990s in an uncut state by the De Beers company. It was a staggering 777 carats, and it took six months to cut and polish down to a flawless two-inch tall 203.4-carat diamond, one of the rarest cut diamonds in the world, valued on its own at £250 million. It was displayed

Stephen Smith

The Millennium Dome, taken from the river

along with eleven exceptionally rare blue diamonds ranging from five to twenty-seven carats. This stunning collection was jaw-dropping to behold. It was set in its own life-size 'jewellery box' vault and estimated at the time to be worth around £350 million.

The gang were serious criminals from Kent with a strong pedigree in armed robbery. They had first drawn attention to themselves in February 1999 after an abortive £10 million armed robbery at Nine Elms in south London. They had intended to use a lorry with a welded battering ram to break into the security vehicle and steal the cash. But their plans were thwarted when a member of the public removed the keys, and when they came to drive it, they could not start it. They had timed the police responses and scanned police radio traffic. They had used firearms and dummy explosives to intimidate the guards and hold the police at bay, even firing shots into the air. On this occasion they made their escape empty-handed after setting fire to the vehicles and making off down the Thames in a speedboat.

The Flying Squad, realizing the threat this gang posed, pulled out all the stops trying to track them down, but they left few clues. Some names were forthcoming but no hard evidence

was uncovered as to who the ringleaders were. The press had nicknamed the gang 'The River Rats' for their preference for the river as an escape route.

Then, in July 2000, following a similar unsuccessful robbery in Aylesford, Kent, the gang slipped up. One of the incendiary devices left in a stolen vehicle used in the robbery failed to ignite properly. A mobile phone was recovered and a phone number led the Flying Squad to some farm buildings in Kent. Observations were put on these premises and the occupants were followed and identified.

On 1 September 2000, three of the gang, William Cockram, Lee Wenham and Raymond Betson, were observed separately visiting the Millennium Dome exhibition. They even took their families to see the exhibits. They were observed paying special attention to the diamond exhibit inside the Money Zone, taking video footage of the diamonds and the chamber in which they were exhibited. It slowly dawned on the officers what the gang's next target might be.

Surveillance was now stepped up on the gang and other members were identified. Officers watched Terry Millman as he obtained and tested a speedboat to be used in making their escape. Vehicles, including a JCB digger and transit-type vans, were obtained by the gang and stored in farm buildings.

After consultation with De Beers, it was decided to replace the diamonds with facsimiles – even these had cost tens of thousands of pounds to produce. SO19 were brought in to cover the removal and transfer of the diamond collection. This went off without a hitch and appeared to go unnoticed by the gang. Now planning could go ahead to catch them red-handed.

Detective Chief Superintendent Jon Shatford was leading the operation on behalf of the Flying Squad but he was happy for the planning of the ambush to be handled by the SO19 SFO office. Great effort was made to make sure all eventualities were covered. The firearms officers were told to visit the Dome to familiarize themselves with the exhibits.

All that was needed now was the date and time of the robbery, which, it transpired, would depend greatly on the tides. There were only a few days each month when they would be right for the robbers to use their boat to make their getaway. It would be a waiting game.

In the early hours of 8 September, the first of many briefings took place in Lambeth, south London. With over a hundred police officers involved, a lot of organization was required. Once briefed, the heavily armed SO19 personnel were driven to Westcombe Park police station where they were held on standby. They were to be brought forward should the gang appear to be shaping up for the robbery. On this occasion they did not make an attempt and police were stood down.

Although within striking distance of the Dome, Westcombe Park was not an ideal location. Taking into account the speed at which this gang worked, it was feared that the heist might be all over by the time police could deploy. It was agreed SO19 needed to be within

Stephen Smith

This photo shows the cramped conditions. Normally the officers were inserted at 3 a.m. and 'stood-to' at 9 a.m. when the attraction opened its doors. They were 'stood-down' when Jon Shatford was confident the robbers were not going to work that day

the Dome itself, so more phone calls were made.

After consultation with other agencies a hide was built in the basement tunnels of the Dome itself where eighteen specialist firearms officers could wait in readiness, hidden from prying eyes. From here there was just a short walk to a staircase that led out onto a landing and then onto the concourse where the jewel exhibit was situated.

Further plans involved other SFOs dressed as cleaning staff. Some were using motorcycles outside in order to respond anywhere around the Millennium site. A speedboat was hired

Stephen Smith

One of the many 'stand-to' periods; these could last for hours, waiting in full kit

(making sure it could outpace the one the robbers were using).

On 11 September, after their briefing, the SFO teams were discreetly driven into the Dome itself. They moved down into their hide and were ensconced before the staff arrived. Once inside there was nothing to do but lie down and sleep. They could not make any noise that might alert the staff. (It was imperative that the general staff were not aware of the police activity because of the inherent risk of word getting out to the press or members of the gang themselves.) A chemical toilet was positioned at one end of the hide. It was stifling in the cramped space where each hour blended into the next.

As the days and weeks progressed this ritual of briefings followed by insertion and waiting became a way of life. But if it was tough for the police, it was not all plain sailing for the gang either. Their boat had mechanical problems and so was burnt and another purchased. They had to find a new driver for it at short notice. They also had issues with some of their equipment and vehicles, causing them to postpone the date of the robbery.

DCS Shatford worried that the longer the delay continued the more risk there was of security breaches. This was compounded when a national newspaper contacted him telling him they knew about the robbery and wanted an exclusive. He could not take the risk of the press running the story and blowing all the hard work and the chance of taking this gang off the streets. He agreed to let them have an exclusive, but only if they kept quiet until the robbery had taken place. It was a gamble but one which paid off.

The gang still seemed set on doing the robbery. On one occasion, they were on their way to carry it out, and were driving the JCB near to the Dome but had to abort following a police incident outside the front of the Dome caused by a drunken driver crashing his car. There were police all over the place!

Finally the day came when all the signs looked good; the tides were right and the gang seemed keen. So that night SO19, along with the Flying Squad arrest teams, were called in for briefings. Unusually all police assets would be communicating via mobile phones as the gang were supposedly monitoring radio frequencies.

Two of the gang enter and begin smashing the armoured glass

The SO19 attack team storms the JCB and enters the exhibit

At 3 a.m. on 7 November the SO19 teams inserted into their holding areas for what would be the last time. Everyone took what rest they could before the gates opened at 9 a.m. Intelligence began to build up: the gang were busy; the JCB and speedboat were on the move. The team waited with bated breath – was this going to be another false alarm? Then at around 9.30 a.m., the JCB began its approach. The SO19 officers inside the Dome made their final kit and weapons checks in readiness. Moments later the commentary informed them that the JCB had burst through the outer perimeter and into the secure area with four gang members on board. It then went on to crash through the gates and into the main Dome complex itself. The lumbering earth digger finally came to a stop outside the diamond exhibit. The gang proceeded to throw smoke bombs onto the concourse; these ignited, letting off thick smoke.

SFOs enter the exhibit and secure the prisoners. It is dark and full of smoke

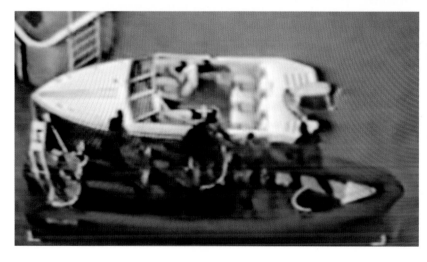

SFOs intercept the gang's speedboat while it waits by the Dome pier, arresting the driver

The adjacent photos show the course of events:

The big solid steel doors to the exhibit had been opened at 8.30 a.m. ready for the public who would be arriving at 9 a.m. The doors would automatically close if the collection was attacked – but the gang easily prevented them from doing so by wedging them open with half a scaffold board.

William Cockram and Robert Adams entered the exhibit. Cockram fired a nail gun into the armoured glass enclosing the exhibits. The shock waves caused by the impact considerably weakened the consistency of the glass. Adams then hit the glass with a sledgehammer. Using this method, the two men managed to make holes in front of each of the twelve diamonds ready to reach in and grab them. Although this action set off the alarms in the vault, the gang knew they would be long gone before any

179

security staff could interfere, and besides they had left gang members Raymond Betson and Aldo Ciarrocchi outside as guards.

The gang decided not to carry firearms on the day of the robbery, as they had total disregard for the security staff on duty, and knew they would get lighter sentences if caught. They were, however, carrying ammonia in lemon jiffy bottles, which, if squirted in the eye, could burn and cause blindness. They later claimed that this was to be used to remove any forensic traces such as blood from the scene to prevent them being traced through DNA.

When Cockram and Adams were arrested inside the exhibit, Adams remarked to the officers, 'I was twelve inches from pay day; it would have been a blinding Christmas.' They both received fifteen years (Cockram's sentence had been reduced from eighteen years on appeal). Cockram stated in court 'It would have taken a very short time from hitting the main gate to getting back across the Thames – five minutes maximum'. (Although a little ambitious, his timings would not have been far out).

Raymond Betson who drove the JCB and Aldo Ciarrocchi who rode in on it received eighteen and fifteen years respectively. Kevin Meredith, brought in at the last minute to drive the boat, received five years. Lee Wenham, who acted as a spotter and radio scanner for the gang received four years for conspiracy to rob, but was given a further nine years after pleading guilty to his part in the Aylesford robbery in Kent. Terry Millman, who was positioned across the river with a getaway vehicle, died of cancer shortly before his trial. At least six others were arrested in connection with the robbery, mainly from farm premises in Kent.

Apparently the diamonds (had the real ones been stolen) were destined for the Russian Mafia, who would undoubtedly have cut them up into smaller stones and sold them on the black market.

The facsimile Millennium Star diamond. This exact copy of the Star was commissioned by De Beers prior to the robbery and cost many thousands of pounds. It was surreptitiously substituted for the real diamond prior to the Dome raid. It is seen here mounted on a model of the Millennium Dome for display at the Metropolitan Police Crime Museum at New Scotland Yard

The national press had a great day reporting on the events at the Millennium Dome, which had already received more than its share of coverage (mostly for the wrong reasons). The *Sun* led with the headline: 'I'm Only Here For De Beers', the *Mirror* with: 'Crime Zone' (a reference to the individual entertainment zones within the Dome). Every paper carried a major feature on the robbery. The gang were likened to the great train robbers and afforded celebrity status within the criminal fraternity. The robbery was also the subject of countless documentaries, dramas and books. Even the JCB digger, made famous by the robbery, was sold at auction in 2004 for £10,200 – more than twice its market value!

Operation 'Magician' had been a major success for the Flying Squad, SO11 surveillance units and SO19, whose ambush of the robbers was timed to perfection. Their patience and planning had paid off. The fact that no one was hurt, the villains were all arrested and the irreplaceable De Beers diamond collection (including the facsimiles) were preserved made the long hours of waiting in cramped conditions worthwhile.

The Bennett Shooting, Brixton
16 July 2001

At 3 p.m. on Monday 16 July 2001, local police answered an emergency call to Loughborough Road, Brixton, in south London, to reports of a man attempting to force his way into a flat brandishing a gun. An SO19 Armed Response Vehicle crewed by two sergeants who were supervising the late-turn shift of ARVs took the call. (There were no other ARVs available at that time.)

Their ARV arrived at the rendezvous point in Villa Road, Brixton. They asked for an update as to whether the address was under observation. They were told the suspect had moved away from this location towards Fiveways Road, and were given the description of a black male aged about thirty years, around five-foot-five with shoulder-length dreadlocks, wearing jeans and a black puffa jacket.

At their request, a local officer accompanied them in the ARV. They searched the area and moved towards the nearby Angell Town Estate. As they were driving slowly through the estate, the local officer spotted a man fitting the description on the first floor walkway leading to Marston House.

The two armed officers left their vehicle and moved up the access ramp leading to the walkway where the suspect had been spotted. One officer had his pistol drawn, whilst the other carried an MP5 carbine. Both were aware of the points of danger as they moved around each corner.

Two workmen appeared on the ramp, one of them making the sign of a gun with his fingers and pointing back towards the walkway at the end of the ramp. As the officers turned the last corner they were faced with a walkway approximately fifty metres long and four metres wide, split down the middle by white concrete pillars spaced evenly every three metres, with recessed doorways leading to dwellings on the left of the walkway.

The officers became aware of a man matching the description of the suspect, walking away from them. (He was the only person on the walkway.) This man was 29-year-old Derek Bennett, a local man with a history of mental illness, who was known to local police, with convictions for drugs and violence offences.

Officer 'B' shouted loudly, 'Stop! Armed police!' Bennett kept walking and the officer again shouted, 'Stop! Armed police!' Bennett stopped and slowly turned around to face the police. Officer 'B' later commented at the inquest, 'He looked in our direction for what seemed like a few seconds and appeared to be deciding what to do. I shouted again: "We are armed police! Show me your hands! Show me your hands!"'

At this point, another workman (a painter who had been working in the flats nearby) was spotted by Bennett as he approached. This man was oblivious to the life and death scenario playing out on the walkway in front of him. Bennett lunged at him, grabbing him around the neck and shoulder with his left arm. He raised his right arm and held a silver object against the hostage's neck. Officer 'B' at first thought this could be a knife, but soon realized it appeared to be some kind of automatic pistol.

The officers moved forward, all the while shouting at Bennett, 'Armed police! Drop it! Drop it!' Bennett was now using the hostage as a human shield. The man appeared frightened and after a brief struggle managed to separate from Bennett, falling towards the wall of the

The walkway soon after the shooting, the police incident tape still in place

balcony. Meanwhile, Officer 'A' had moved out wide to gain a clear view of Bennett, all the while fearing that Bennett was about to start shooting. It was at this point, as the two men separated, that Officer 'A' fired shots from his Glock pistol. Bennett ran behind a pillar and faced the officer. He still had his pistol in his right hand. The officer fired at him again. Temporarily obscured by the concrete pillars, Bennett ran towards a recessed front door. Officer 'A', fearing that Bennett may try to gain access to a flat and endanger other members of the public, fired at him a third time. The silver handgun fell from his hand and clattered onto the balcony floor. He had been mortally wounded.

Bennett stood for a moment on the top of the steps outside the front door of the flat. He slowly sat down on a step and began to slump to the ground. Officer 'B' helped him to the ground and began giving first aid.

The confrontation had lasted less than a minute. On close inspection of the firearm it became apparent that it was in fact a novelty cigarette lighter modelled on an automatic pistol. The hostage later told the *Sun* news-

paper reporter in an interview, 'It looked for all the world like a real gun. The police were totally justified. They had no choice.' Other media sources were less sympathetic to police, implying that there was a 'shoot to kill policy'.

This shooting fuelled unrest and there were minor scenes of public disorder in Brixton. Some youths used the opportunity to riot. Three officers were injured and over thirty of the rioters arrested. Local community leaders decried the rioters' actions and helped restore peace.

The weapon in question. Is it real or is it a novelty cigarette lighter? The officers faced with this question had just moments to decide

This incident once again raised the controversial issue of armed police shooting people on the streets of London before checking that the alleged weapon was in fact a real firearm. A cartoon in a national paper at the time featured armed police around the corner to an armed criminal. The caption read: 'Hold it lads – Allow the PCA [Police Complaints Authority] members to check if it's a real weapon.'

In the *Evening Standard* of 18 July, the lawyer Imran Khan, representing the Bennett family, was quoted as saying, 'I want Sir John Stevens [Commissioner of the Met] to apologise for the fact that the actions of police officers led to the death of Derek Bennett.' He went on to call for a reappraisal of the way forces across the country use weapons.

There were also concerns raised in the national papers over allegations that officers 'shoot to kill' rather than to disable suspects, an understandable view from many of the public who have no first-hand experience relating to firearms. In movies, a gun can be shot from the hand sometimes without even taking aim, or the suspect can be intentionally shot in the leg to disable them from any further violence. Unfortunately, to do this is not only far-fetched, but leaves the officer, his colleagues and in many cases members of the public in danger, for if the officer misses what might be his only opportunity to take decisive action, the suspect may not.

Even when wounded, the suspect can continue to exert deadly force. Any police or military firearms instructor will tell you how much training it takes to hold your nerve in a high-stress situation and shoot well enough to hit a human-sized target that may be moving or even shooting back at you. Add to that innocent people moving nearby, poor lighting, restricted view caused by vehicles or street furniture, and the odds of hitting diminish greatly.

The police service trains officers to fire at the largest part of the body (the torso) to have a better chance of hitting. It does not train officers to shoot to kill. Although in many circumstances being shot in the torso will prove fatal, so could a wound to an arm or a leg if a major artery was damaged.

As always, these events are real and tragic for the family and friends of the deceased, and matters are often made worse by the length of time that must pass before their questions can be answered in full at an inquest.

On 25 March 2003, after a protracted investigation by Northumbria police, the Police Complaints Authority issued a statement concluding that, 'there is not enough evidence for a realistic prospect of conviction against any person for any offence arising out of the tragic death of Derek Bennett on the 16th July 2001'.

On 15 December 2004, almost three and a half years after the incident, the inquest jury returned a verdict of lawful killing, thus ending a long period of uncertainty for both the officers involved and the Bennett family. The family condemned the verdict, claiming it was a travesty of justice, and instructed their lawyers to challenge the ruling on the basis that Coroner Selena Lynch had deprived jurors of the option of returning a verdict of unlawful killing.

In February 2006, after a hearing at the Royal Courts of Justice, the Court of Appeal upheld the 2004 verdict. Commander Kaye, the head of CO19, stated in relation to his firearms officers: 'No one should underestimate how vital their work is to the security and safety of London. Fortunately the number of instances where they actually use their firearms remains rare.'

The deputy commissioner, Sir Ian Blair said, 'This incident and its tragic outcome only further underlines the very real dangers presented by realistic replica firearms being readily available.'

The officer who fired the fatal shots on that day in July 2001 chose to remain within the firearms unit but made a conscious decision never to carry a firearm again. He felt he could not put himself or his family through another such ordeal should he again be required to use his gun in the line of duty.

Suicide-by-Cop, Harrow
14 November 2001

On 14 November 2001, 62-year-old Michael Malsbury, who worked as a mini-cab driver, assaulted his wife after a domestic argument. She fled the home and informed police that Michael was a member of a gun club and had ready access to firearms, particularly a .22 pistol. Armed Response Vehicles were deployed and arrived at his address in East-leigh Avenue, Harrow (a mid-terraced house divided into two flats) at 4 a.m. They soon contained the flat.

Hostage negotiators began communicating with the suspect who had barricaded himself in a bedroom in his second-floor flat. He refused to give himself up or co-operate with police in any way. At around 2 p.m. Malsbury fired a shot in his bedroom to attract the attention of the police before shouting, 'Get your guns ready, I'm coming out.' He opened the bedroom door and walked out pointing his silver .22 semi-automatic pistol at the armed officer in the bathroom across the landing. The ARV officer shot him, firing one round from his Glock pistol. Officers provided first aid at the scene and Malsbury was removed to hospital where he died of his wounds.

The *Evening Standard* dedicated their front page to the incident with the headline: 'Man Shot Dead By Yard In Siege'. This incident received little further press coverage and the officer was returned to full operational duties within a short space of time.

During the inquest in May 2003, the coroner heard from officers how Malsbury had adopted a 'cowboy attitude' and repeatedly made reference to the film *High Noon*. The inquest jury at Hornsey Coroner's Court returned a verdict of suicide. This was the first time a coroner's jury had ever given a verdict for a man shot dead by police as suicide or, as we know now it, suicide-by-cop.

Maritime Patrols
September 2002

In 2002, on the back of international terrorist alerts and the constant threat of attacks on London, it was considered prudent to form a response to prevent and deter terrorist activity in which the River Thames was used as a direct route into the city.

A specialist search dog is winched on board to assist in the search of the vessel

So in September 2002, SO19, in conjunction with the Thames Division Special Operations unit and other agencies, began a series of armed operations on the river.

A small fleet of police craft would intercept their target in the estuary and board her. Once the vessel had been boarded and secured by SO19 officers, specialist dog handlers with their firearms and explosives search dogs would assist in checking the ship for evidence of terrorist-related activity. These patrols on the River Thames were seen as yet another weapon in the fight against terrorism and armed criminality.

The Hackney Siege

26 December 2002–10 January 2003

Eli Hall, aged 32, was born in Jamaica, moving to the UK with his father and two brothers and settling in Battersea, south London, where he became no stranger to crime. In August 2002, Hall became wanted by police after his involvement in two shooting incidents. The first was in Old Compton Street, Soho, when his behaviour aroused the attention of an unarmed police unit carrying out anti-crime patrols. Officers stopped Hall, who became aggressive and violent, so much so that an officer deployed his CS gas spray. However, the CS gas had no apparent effect on Hall, who produced a firearm and began shooting at the officers. The officers, on seeing the firearm, had dived behind cover and were fortunately unhurt.

Hall used this opportunity to run off. He hid in his vehicle by lying across the back seat. ARVs were called and searched the area. They noticed one parked car was steamed up and, as they moved towards the car, Hall climbed across to the driver's seat and sped off, managing to ram his way out of the street by knocking over a police motorcycle. Although

Hall was identified by the officers, his present address was unknown to police.

The second incident occurred four months later, when local unarmed officers on an estate in Hackney saw a man leaning into a car talking with the driver. They suspected he was drug dealing and moved in to stop him. It was Eli Hall who once again pointed his handgun at the officers and said to the man in the car, 'Which one shall I shoot first?' The officers reacted and ran for cover. Hall fired once, missing them. It was another lucky escape.

Around the time of this incident, both Eli Hall's father and older brother were serving long sentences for drug offences. Another factor, which may or may not have affected his mind-set, was that his 17-year-old brother had been the victim of a fatal shooting in Mitcham, Surrey, and a man was awaiting trial for his murder.

On 26 December 2002 in Marvin Street, Hackney, police located the Toyota Celica that Hall had used in the Soho shooting. Two ARVs were called and observations maintained on the vehicle in the hope that Hall would come back to it. After eight hours and no sign of Eli Hall, the decision was made to recover the vehicle for forensic examination. A vehicle removal lorry was employed, but just as the operator was attempting to lift the car, a man leant out of a nearby first-floor window and shouted aggressively for them to leave the car alone and go away. Fearing it was Eli Hall and that he may be armed, police and removal officers retreated into cover.

Police quickly contained the rambling Edwardian building that had been converted into flats and bedsits. After waiting a while with no further contact, it was decided to move forward and carry out a limited entry into the building, hoping to establish which rooms were occupied by Hall and whether he was still there. Information had become available from some

A rifle point from a bedroom overlooking the side of Hall's bedsit in Marvin Street. The vehicle removal lorry can be seen abandoned in the road, its doors still open

old plans of the building that a certain door in Marvin Street led up to the rooms from which the man had appeared. ARV officers moved forward along the building line with a Trojan support dog bringing up the rear.

Luckily, officers missed the door leading into the enclosed yard accessing Hall's rooms and passed on to another door, which, although it had once been the main door to the building, was now a blocked-off façade. As they began forcing open this door, Hall, alerted by the noise, put his arm out of the window and discharged several rounds from a pistol. These bullets peppered the area around the yard, narrowly missing the dog handler at the rear of the police team and fortunately hitting no one. (This may have been a different story had the officers entered the yard through the correct door!)

Several officers returned fire as the team made a rather hasty tactical withdrawal. They had established that Eli Hall was still in the building and that he was armed. The longest siege in British police history had begun. Local residences were evacuated and SFO teams were placed on standby. ARV officers containing the building were supplemented with an armoured Land Rover and rifle support positions, one of which was situated on the roof of a nearby building, where it was exposed to the elements and the shutters of the press cameras.

The reluctance of Hall to co-operate in any way with the police made this a big challenge to even the most experienced police negotiators. The initial contact was made using loudhailers, and then mobile phones. Hall had, from the

186

Possibly the last-ever photo taken of Eli Hall, as he appears briefly at his back door to collect food

start, stated in no uncertain terms that he was not going back to jail and that he would not be taken alive. Officers reported the strong smell of petrol early on in the siege, leading to fears that he might set a fire.

As the days passed by, the police dug in, accepting that they would be there over the New Year. Technical devices were installed; these included listening devices and cameras but even these failed to identify a second person within Hall's bedsit. Eli Hall's hostage, Paul Okere, was a Nigerian student who lived in a bedsit in the same building as Hall. After three days he managed to call the emergency services on his mobile phone but some confusion regarding the address he gave delayed police in realizing he was with Eli Hall. Apparently Okere had awoken to find himself barricaded

inside the building with Hall. He later identified himself as the suspect's hostage.

Hall never made any demands or threats in relation to Okere and the reason his existence was not confirmed until day three of the siege remains a mystery. Okere admitted he got on well with Hall, and that they even cooked meals together but, as the siege wore on, Hall's behaviour began to scare him.

The hostage negotiator, DCI Sue Williams, spoke with Hall for many long hours trying to assure him he would not be harmed if he gave himself up. He asked for a written guarantee that he would not go back to prison. However, he must have known this could not be given. He also asked for Kentucky Fried Chicken to be delivered to the building. He specified that police should allow a friend of his to buy the food and that he only liked it when it was twenty-four-hours old. Although this was thought strange at the time, it was agreed to in the vain hope that Hall might be won over and surrender.

The KFC was duly delivered to his door under the cover of armed police with ballistic shields. This was repeated many times over the following days. Then, after a week had passed, an officer checking the food package made a strange discovery. Inside the chicken he found that, along with the Colonel's special recipe, the chicken had been stuffed with cannabis!

The deliveries of chicken stopped then and there and a harder line was taken to end the siege. (No charges were ever brought in relation to the cannabis as the police had enough on their plate at the time.)

Things now stepped up at the siege; helicopters flew low overhead and sirens were sounded throughout the day and night. The block's electricity and water were also cut off (the other residents had already been evacuated) in an attempt to make life uncomfortable and sleep difficult for Hall.

A view towards the containment position at Graham Road's junction with Marvin Street. An armoured Land Rover provides ballistic protection while the blue tarpaulin provides some shelter from the elements

After eleven days Hall's hostage, Paul Okere, walked out of the building unharmed, claiming to have escaped at his earliest opportunity when Hall had gone upstairs.

Hall was still displaying a reluctance to communicate with police or surrender and he stressed time and time again that he would not be taken alive. On one occasion, he said that he had 'a bath full of ammunition and plenty of guns'. He goaded police, saying, 'The man in the street with a gun will always be top dog.' He added, 'Bring it on, this is war.'

Negotiators contacted Hall's father in prison and he agreed to speak to his son in an attempt to persuade him to see sense and surrender. When this call was made, Hall's father shouted down the phone, 'Don't do what they say, don't let them take you alive.'

Further days passed and the siege was turning into a marathon of endurance for both the police and the local residents who were being kept from their homes and workplaces. Their long wait began to end on Thursday 9 January, when Hall appeared at the window and began shooting at police positions, narrowly missing the officers. Police returned fire and Hall retreated back inside the room. A police bullet had found its mark, passing through his cheek and lodging in his neck. Shortly after this, police spotted smoke emanating from parts of the building occupied by Hall.

Then, as the fire took hold, several bangs were heard coming from the building. Efforts were made using loudhailers to communicate with Hall, demanding his surrender, but it was to no avail. Water was poured through the building from above and SO19 officers fired baton rounds (normally reserved for riot control) through the windows to break the glass thus allowing the fire hoses to pour water on the flames. CS gas was fired into the rooms in the vain hope of forcing Hall to surrender.

An atmospheric night photo, taken during the fifteen-day siege, of Graham Road looking towards the junction with Marvin Street on the left, the floodlights giving police a good view of the block

The following day, on 10 January, after the flames had been extinguished, SO19 officers used ladders to gain vision into the charred rooms. (The building was now declared to be structurally unsound.) A slow, laborious search was made under the directions of structural engineers and firefighters. The inevitable discovery of Eli Hall's body was made in the hallway. He had been extensively burned; a handgun was found lying on his chest and, as well as the wound to his cheek, there was a gunshot wound to his temple. The pathologist later confirmed that this wound was the cause of death and had been self-inflicted.

Later that day, under full glare from the lights of TV and press cameras, the undertakers wheeled the remains of Eli Hall from the burnt-out building.

A forensic search was made, finding several handguns, along with a large quantity of ammunition and gun-making equipment. Eli Hall had been prepared for a small war.

This was a tragic end to the longest recorded police siege in the UK. It had lasted fifteen days and the police bill was estimated at over £1 million. (Prior to this, the longest-lasting police siege had been in Hull, in 1995, when Steven Wood had taken two women hostage. The siege had lasted fourteen days, ending peacefully after all services to the premises had been cut.)

Although the police were criticized in some quarters for their 'softly, softly' approach, it was generally considered the safest tactic in the circumstances. Eli Hall could have used his weapons and supply of ammunition to inflict casualties on police had they forced their way in. He was given every chance and encouragement to surrender but chose in the end to take his own life. At the inquest held later that year the coroner Dr Andrew Scott-Reid said the only verdict that could be returned was suicide.

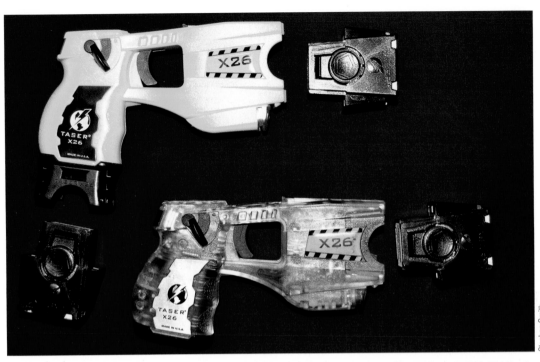

Stephen Smith

The **X26** Taser with red dot laser sight. The one below is a covert model used by SFO and TST (Tactical Support) teams. It does not carry a spare cartridge in its grip

Taser: SO19's Less Lethal Option
January 2003

In 2003 the Metropolitan Police took the Taser on a twelve-month trial basis. It was given to SO19 to use operationally and its results were closely monitored.

Initially treated with scepticism, it slowly won over its critics. The first few occasions it was used generated a lot of interest. Its use was initially treated the same as the discharge of a firearm, with a full investigation and temporary suspension from firearms duties of the officer who discharged it. After a while, a more realistic approach to its use was taken. Now all discharges of the Taser are recorded and reported to the DPS (Department of Professional Standards – the internal complaints commission) who look into each case on its merit. The officers are not removed from oper-ational duty as a matter of course unless there is evidence of wrongdoing.

During the Taser's twelve-month trial period it was discharged only fourteen times, but this was considered enough to judge it safe for use in other forces. The concept of the Taser is a simple one. It uses an electric current to disrupt the voluntary control of a person's muscles, making them tense up, and causing incapacitation. If the current is maintained then so is the incapacitation. Most people will also experience discomfort in varying degrees during its application. When loaded with a cartridge it is a fire-once device. Two small prongs with seven metres of trailing wire attached are shot at the suspect; the prongs penetrate clothing and into the skin where 50,000 volts pass through, causing almost instant incapacitation. The Taser can also be used to 'dry-stun' a suspect. With no cartridge fitted the device is pressed against a person's body and discharged. It will have the same effect for as long as it is applied.

The advantage of the device is that it has no apparent long-term effects on the human body. All usage is recorded in a chip fitted inside the device and these readings can be downloaded later onto a laptop. The Taser was never intended to replace conventional firearms but work alongside them. In this capacity it has undoubtedly saved many lives during the years it has been in use and it has also prevented injury to countless members of the public and police. The Taser is now carried on every armed operation attended by the firearms department and is finding use with other unarmed police units.

Although Taser is the word people use readily to describe any stun gun, it is worth mentioning that Taser is a brand name and is just one of numerous electronic, less than lethal devices available to police forces throughout the world. Other brands include Panther, ZAP, Scorpion and Streetwise to name but a few. However, Taser is one of only a few that use a cartridge system, as required by the Met Police.

Interestingly, the Taser was apparently named after a 1911 novel by Victor Appleton called *Tom Swift and his Electric Rifle*. A middle initial of 'A' was added to make the product name sound better.

Metropolitan Police Specialist Training Centre, Gravesend, Kent
Opened 2003

In May 1996, the Metropolitan Police purchased the National Sea Training College just outside Gravesend in Kent, and the military firing ranges nearby at Milton, for the purpose of constructing a firearms training centre on the site. It was then agreed that a joint training facility taking in public order training would be more realistic. Plans were drawn up and the contracts awarded. The original estimate of £8.8 million had spiralled with the addition of the POTC (Public Order Training Centre) to £55 million.

The combined firearms and public order training facility was completed and opened on 15 April 2003. It boasted state of the art ranges and classrooms and residential blocks for students to stay on courses. It also boasted mock-ups of suburban streets, with shops, a pub, a bank, working traffic lights and other street furniture. A versatile fieldcraft house was constructed on two levels, with a balcony and many windows and doors where multiple entries could be made. A ninety-foot abseil tower was also built. Other features included an aircraft fuselage, and train and Tube train carriages along with several dedicated search houses and judgement rooms with live-fire screen-shooting facilities. A range with movable walls for changing the layout of rooms and corridors was provided too. This was ideal for practising room entries and searching.

The public order training site also featured realistic street scenes, road junctions and buildings along with classrooms and everything needed for the important training it delivered. Both developments shared the same restaurant.

The MPSTC (Metropolitan Police Specialist Training Centre) hit the ground running with hundreds of courses and thousands of students passing through its doors within the first year.

The other obvious advantage to the site was its close proximity to the ex-military rifle ranges at Milton (also purchased by the police) which boasted a 600-metre rifle range and a hundred-metre carbine/pistol range. Finally, it was situated far away from any residential areas (proximity had plagued the training site at Lippitts Hill – the residents objected to the noise of gunfire and explosions along with the

Aerial view of the Metropolitan Police Firearms Specialist Centre at Gravesend in Kent. The facility opened in April 2003

Looking over the building façades, ideal for training purposes including search and street scenarios

One of the many fake buildings, which include pubs, banks, shops and houses

other ancillary disturbances that a training site of this nature brings).

It would be impossible to show all the facilities available at MPSTC so those pictured are just some of those that are used all year round for training and maintaining the firearms skill levels of all Metropolitan Police firearms officers. The facility is also a nationally accredited firearms training facility; it receives students from other firearms units around the country and, in fact, other parts of the world.

Operation 'Dido': Police Shooting in Thornton Heath
Wednesday 12 May 2004

On Wednesday 12 May 2004, specialist firearms officers from SO19 were engaged on Operation 'Dido', in support of South Norwood's Crime Task Force in south London. This was a pre-planned armed operation to effect the arrest of one Nicholas Palmer, wanted in connection with firearms offences. Palmer had not only broken his bail conditions after being arrested in possession of a firearm, but had got hold of yet another firearm with ammunition. Palmer had a history of violence and unpredictable behaviour and it was suspected that his intention was to make use of this weapon in the very near future.

The plan was to follow Palmer to a safe area where an arrest could be made in a controlled environment with minimum risk to the public. The firearms officers carry out this type of arrest many times across the capital each week, mostly with the suspect's compliance. On rare occasions this does not go to plan. Nothing can be taken for granted.

Surveillance officers from the Specialist Crime Directorate, SO11, followed Palmer. He was identified in the company of another male in London Road, Thornton Heath. He was then observed entering Raymead Passage at the rear of the High Street shops. A decision was made by the officer in charge to take this opportunity to arrest him. SO19 officers entered the passageway whilst others blocked the exit. SO19 officers, shouting, 'Armed police! Stand still! Show us your hands!', challenged Palmer.

Palmer, not wishing to be caught for a second time in possession of a firearm, ran towards the exit, but realizing his escape was

Armed officers attempt to stabilize Palmer after he has been shot attempting to pull a revolver from his jacket pocket during an armed police stop. His associate is detained in the background

blocked, stopped and turned back, facing the officers who were still shouting at him to stop and show his hands.

It was then that he made a fatal error by putting his hand inside his jacket. One of the officers, fearing Palmer was about to draw a weapon and shoot at them, fired his MP5 carbine. The bullet hit Palmer the just below his neck. He collapsed to the ground; he had been fatally wounded. Meanwhile, his associate complied with police and was detained unharmed.

The officers went to great lengths trying to keep Palmer alive until help arrived. When a HEMS (Helicopter Emergency Medical Service) team landed nearby, the doctor and paramedics attempted open-heart surgery at the scene. Sadly, after all these efforts, Palmer was pronounced dead on arrival at hospital. The single gunshot wound to his neck had damaged major blood vessels. The pathologist later commented that because of the severity of the injury, Palmer would never have been able to survive his wound.

Even the efforts of the HEMS (Helicopter Emergency Medical Service) team could not resuscitate Palmer

A detective examines the loaded revolver after removing it from the red sock in which it was carried

A loaded revolver was recovered from Palmer's jacket pocket wrapped inside a red sock. This was a common way for criminals and gang members to carry firearms. The weapon could still be fired through the sock and they believed it prevented the transfer of forensic matter between the weapon and its firer.

At the inquest in 2005 the officer recounted to the court, 'When you open your jacket and pull away from it, you make room to draw a weapon.' He later added, 'I feared for my life so I shot him.' The jury at Bromley Magistrates' Court passed a verdict of lawful killing. The coroner praised the actions of the officers, particularly the officer who had fired the fatal shot as his actions undoubtedly prevented injury and/or death to himself and his fellow officers.

SO19 Tactical Support Teams (TST)
Commenced November 2004

As early as 2002 the need for additional, specially trained firearms officers was identified, as the workload of the SFO department was becoming unmanageable.

It was decided to select and train a team of twelve officers taken from the ARVs to ease this workload. These officers would be trained to work in both uniform and plain clothes, using specialist weapons and munitions with their own fleet of unmarked vehicles. They would specifically carry out the long protracted operations, which required a commitment to providing armed support to surveillance. Some of these operations could go on for many months at a time and were draining the SFO resources.

The first Tactical Support Team went live in November 2004 and was followed by a second team in May 2005. It was originally intended that there would be three or four of these teams – however, selection processes and training commitments made this impractical. Instead, the department was only able to sustain two such teams.

Since their inception, both Tactical Support Teams carry out hundreds of firearms operations each year and have achieved outstanding results, recovering firearms and arresting armed and dangerous criminals. The level of training of the TSTs has developed as their role has expanded. Like all SO19 units, the TSTs use the facilities at the MPSTC in Gravesend to perfect their core skills around containment, building search and armed vehicle and foot interventions. The pictures overleaf show some of that training in progress.

TST officers deploy in a vehicle interception training exercise

A TST officer contains the rear of a building in an armed containment exercise

TST officers firing Glock and H&K G36 at an open-air range

SO19 Becomes CO19 Central Operations
April 2005

On 1 April 2005, after a merger with the Central Operations Directorate, SO19 became known as CO19. This coincided with giving up the very early title of force firearms unit to become the specialist firearms command.

The Mac 10 Threat

The Mac 10 sub-machine gun had originally been developed by Gordon B. Ingram in the early 1960s for use in the military. It had a rate of fire of 1,090 rounds per minute, and was capable of emptying the thirty-round magazine in seconds. It was undoubtedly a devastating weapon and a great danger to the public.

Although the laws in the UK prohibit the importation and possession of prohibited weapons such as the Mac 10, there has sprung up an underground cottage industry that makes money by converting and supplying these types of weapons to feed the ever-growing demand of drug dealers and criminal gangs. One such armourer, Grant Wilkinson, aged 34, was to have a dramatic effect on the supply of this type of weapon to the London underworld.

In early 2004 in Middlesex, Wilkinson purchased ninety blank-firing Mac 10s under a false name from a registered gun dealer for £55,000, claiming they were to be used on the set of the new James Bond film. He then set about converting these guns and selling them to criminals up and down the country.

These weapons began to surface when CO19 raided a house in Whitcomb Street, London, where one of these converted Mac 10 sub-machine guns was recovered. Over the following weeks, months and years this batch of converted weapons was used in forty-eight shootings in London, four in Birmingham and one in Manchester. Eight people died in these incidents – the majority of them in London. The gang who murdered PC Sharon Beshenivsky in Bradford in 2005 used one of these weapons in the robbery during which she was shot dead as she tried to arrest them. CO19, SFO and TST teams worked tirelessly on armed operations to recover these weapons and arrest those involved in the shootings.

In August 2008, Wilkinson, who had been arrested earlier that year, was found guilty of conspiracy to convert imitation firearms, conspiracy to sell or transfer firearms, conspiracy to sell or transfer ammunition; two counts of possession of firearms with intent to endanger life and two counts of possession of ammunition with intent to endanger life.

He was sentenced to life imprisonment with recommendations that he serve at least eleven years. His co-defendant Gary Lewis who faced the same charges was cleared of them all. During sentencing, Judge Zoe Smith said, 'The scale of this criminal enterprise is unprecedented in this country. The roll call of deaths and injuries is horrific. Some thirty to forty of these weapons are still unaccounted for, and the roll call of death and serious injury will continue to rise.'

Scotland Yard followed this up with an offer

Stephen Smith

One of the Mac 10 sub-machine guns recovered by CO19

197

of £10,000 to anyone with information leading to the seizure of these weapons or to the arrests of criminals using them. CO19 continue to carry out operations to recover these weapons, ever mindful of their capability.

The London Suicide Bombing Campaign and Operation 'Theseus'
July 2005

Background

It's easy to forget as we bask in the afterglow of the successful 2012 London Summer Olympics just how ecstatic we were as a nation when, on 6 July 2005, the Olympic Council awarded the honour of hosting these games to London. There was both national and worldwide media coverage of the celebrations. The Olympic Games were returning to the capital after sixty-four years.

Then, the very next day on 7 July, the cruel and deliberate actions of a group of Islamist terrorists, most of whom were home-grown

Britons, three from Leeds and one from Aylesbury, shattered the mood of joy in the city. These bombers were to make the date 7/7 synonymous with the atrocities they committed that day. To understand the actions of the Metropolitan Police during Operation 'Theseus' one must first recall the catastrophic consequences of the attack on 7/7.

Once in London, the four terrorists entered the London transport system at King's Cross. Three went into the Underground while one boarded a No. 30 bus at Tavistock Square. All were carrying rucksacks, which contained homemade organic hydrogen peroxide-based explosive devices. Nails and other metal objects had been added to act as shrapnel in the hope of maximizing the number of potential casualties. The three Tube bombers detonated themselves at 8.50 a.m. in the middle of the rush hour.

The casualties were as follows (this list does not include the terrorists) – Edgware Road: seven dead and 185 injured, Aldgate: six dead and ninety injured, Russell Square: twenty-six

British Transport Police

The four suicide bombers enter Luton Station where they travelled together on their way to London to cause murder and mayhem

dead and 180 injured. The lone bomber on the bus, after failing to detonate his bomb, purchased and fitted a new battery and succeeded in detonating himself an hour after the Tube bombs. He killed a further thirteen, injuring seventy-three. In total the terrorists killed fifty-two innocent commuters and injured 528 more. This was by far the worst attack in one day on the British public since the Blitz.

What made matters worse was the fact that the police and security services had been caught 'on the hop', as the attack had come from quarters not high up on the security radar.

The justified public outcry was felt throughout the land. The misery caused to the families of those who died and the life-changing injuries of those who survived made this and any future attacks the main priority of the police. The fear of future attacks and the belief that further such terror cells existed within mainland UK sent the security services into overdrive.

Failed Bombing Attempts and Police Investigation
21 July 2005

CO19 were little used in the enquiry following the 7/7 attacks, owing to the nature of the investigation (the suspects had died in the attacks and most of the work in London was intelligence gathering and forensic recovery). Although there were police raids and further arrests made in the Midlands, the car the bombers had used to drive themselves to Luton railway station on their final journey to London proved to be a veritable treasure trove of bomb-making technology. Several different types of smaller bombs and hand grenades were recovered, showing these bombers had planned for other options. Why this material was never used remains a mystery.

Whilst the work up to this point had largely precluded CO19's involvement, things were about to change when, on 21 July, just two weeks after the earlier attacks, the unspeakable happened once again. In an attack almost

The Russell Square Tube bomber detonated himself, killing twenty-six and injuring a further 180 commuters in the middle of the rush hour

identical to the first, another group of Islamist terrorists, this time from more diverse backgrounds, sought to attack the London transport systems.

One of the men, Manfo Kwaku Asiedu, had second thoughts and discarded his device in Little Wormwood Scrubs, near Shepherd's Bush. The other four persisted with their attack – while three of them entered the Underground system one boarded a bus in Shoreditch High Street, east London.

Between 12.30 and 1.30 p.m., these men attempted to detonate their devices made from similar material to those of the previous attacks. The targeted Tube stations were Shepherd's Bush, Oval and Warren Street. In each case, only the detonators exploded and, although a great deal of panic was caused, there were no serious injuries. The would-be suicide bombers discarded their rucksacks and fled the scenes. One was pursued heroically by a passenger but managed to evade capture. The manhunt for the 21/7 bombers was on. Sir Ian Blair, the Met commissioner, called it, 'the largest investigation that the Metropolitan Police has ever mounted'.

Unstable hydrogen peroxide, found on the floor of the Tube after the detonators failed to ignite the mixture. The HME (Home-made Explosive) was mixed incorrectly. London's commuting public had a very lucky escape

It is fair to say at this point that hundreds of lines of enquiry were being followed up. There had been over 800 calls from the public with information following these attempted bombings and dozens of smaller operations were being carried out, both armed and unarmed. Every available surveillance team in London was engaged one way or another, gathering intelligence or following subjects and associates, hoping they would lead to the bombers.

One line of enquiry amongst many focused on a gym membership card found in one of the discarded rucksacks found on the Tube. It led detectives to an address at Scotia Road, Tulse Hill in south London, which was believed to be the address of one Hussain Osman (the Shepherd's Bush bomber).

From the early hours of Friday 22 July this address was kept under observation. Although no clear image was available for Osman at that time, the surveillance teams were working from descriptions and a poor quality CCTV image. As the CO19 specialist firearms team mustered at their Leman Street base that day none of them could have imagined what lay in store for them in the hours that followed.

The team had already loaded their personal weapons with the heavier 124 gr, 9 mm hollow-point ammunition, which had been made available to them for the first time that day. This ammunition apparently had better stopping power and in theory should not over-penetrate. (This had always been a worry when working in busy areas of London: if a round fired at a suspect passed through that person, it could still have enough power to injure or kill an innocent member of the public.)

As the team gathered in readiness by their cars in the basement car park the team inspector called them over for a briefing. He told them they would be assisting a Special Branch surveillance team in an operation to

Stephen Smith

The premises in Scotia Road, south London, under police observation. This was believed to be where Hussain Osman had been staying

apprehend one of the failed suicide bombers from 21 July. During this briefing they were advised that they 'may be called upon to use unusual tactics'. They were also told to trust the information they were given, as they would not be aware of the whole picture.

At 7.45 a.m. the team attended a further briefing in south London with a view to assisting the surveillance at an address in Scotia Road. They were given a comprehensive update, which included a run-down on the types of bombs used and other types of devices available to the bombers. It was also explained that the bombers might diversify their methods by using hidden body-borne devices, triggered by touching two wires together or by a third party detonating the bomb they were carrying. The team were also told that the failed bombers were still 'up for it' and would martyr themselves if given the chance. They were shown grainy photos of the suspects believed to be involved in the failed suicide bomb attacks including one of Hussain Osman. The specialist firearms officers were left in no doubt that they were up against dangerous and determined

men who were still intent on causing death and destruction.

The plan was a simple one. CO19 would work in support of the Special Branch surveillance team at Scotia Road. They would only be deployed if one of the failed bombers was positively identified leaving or arriving at the address – otherwise they would remain in the vicinity of Scotia Road in a state of readiness in case they should be required. Meanwhile, surveillance officers would follow and identify every person leaving the address in question. To aid this, the local bus stop had been temporally suspended to stop any potential suspects from getting on a bus near to the address. This would give the surveillance teams longer to have 'eyes on' and make their identification.

By 9.27 a.m. the SFO teams' assets began to arrive at a holding location at a Territorial Army base only minutes from Scotia Road. One of the five CO19 vehicles was delayed at the briefing location sorting out radio problems and never made it to this holding location. The address in Scotia Road was on a modern housing estate serviced by side roads and cul-de-sacs with alleyways leading to Upper Tulse Hill. Scotia Road led out onto Tulse Hill Road, which ran down towards Brixton.

The block in question was made up of several bedsit flats, serviced by one communal entrance. Apparently most of the residents had already left for work and had been discounted by those keeping observation. Then at 9.33 a.m. a subject left the Scotia Road address. The officers in an observation van parked in a street nearby were unable to take a photo of this man owing to the fact that their photographer was out of the vehicle answering a call of nature. However, the Special Branch surveillance officers were asked to have a closer look and see what they thought. A few passes were made and he was put up as a 'good likeness' for the subject. Further attempts were made to positively identify him but the officers could not confirm or deny whether it was Osman. This may have been down to the quality of the image they were using at the time. The decision was made to follow this subject in an effort to confirm his identity one way or another. For the time being, the CO19 resources were instructed to remain near Scotia Road.

The sad fact was that this man was not Hussain Osman but Brazilian electrician Jean Charles de Menezes, who was working for his uncle in London. Finding the nearest bus stop suspended he walked to the next stop in Tulse Hill where he arrived at 9.39 a.m. He then boarded the No. 2 bus towards Marble Arch and was followed onto the bus by surveillance officers. There was still no positive identification as the bus continued down Tulse Hill and into Brixton. It was at this point that a decision was made to send the SFO team from Scotia Road to back up the surveillance officers following the subject towards Brixton. This decision came from the control room in the heart of New Scotland Yard, where operational commander Cressida Dick had been monitoring developments since 7.15 a.m. Commander Dick was one of the DSOs (Designated Senior Officers, trained to take responsibility for very high risk decisions). A senior CO19 tactical adviser was also on hand to advise on firearms options.

The firearms team still did not have the authority to deploy but as a safeguard control they were wanted nearer to the surveillance team in case a positive identification was made and a decision could be taken whether to stop the subject.

Meanwhile, Jean Charles de Menezes alighted the bus near Brixton Tube station, but after a short while got back on the same bus. It had been held in heavy traffic and had not moved. (At the time, the police found it suspicious that he had got off the bus and returned so quickly, but it eventually transpired that Brixton Tube station had temporarily closed because of a security alert.) De Menezes' change of plans were interpreted as evidence of anti-surveillance, i.e. trying to throw off a tail by drawing surveillance off the bus. Surveillance officers described the subject as being 'very jumpy'. The decision to 'establish ID and hold' was relayed to the surveillance team from the DSO. This piece of surveillance speak means to hold off and continue the pursuit, whilst seeking to gain further intelligence as to identity and what the subject is doing.

The Stockwell Incident
22 July 2005

The bus moved slowly through Brixton, turning left towards Stockwell on its journey into central London. There was as yet no indication that the subject would leave the bus at Stockwell station. The CO19 vehicles maintained a discreet distance from the bus, awaiting instructions. As the bus moved slowly

Stockwell Tube station as it was on 22 July 2005, with scaffolding at the front

along Stockwell Road towards Stockwell Tube, the surveillance team were being asked over the air to confirm whether the subject was or wasn't 'Nettle Tip' (the code name for Osman).

Although some of the surveillance team later stated that they had doubts, these were not forthcoming at this time. In fact, the general consensus, relayed to the surveillance control, was that it was understood to be the subject Nettle Tip. This was translated as a positive identification over the radio to control (although at the inquest in 2008 Commander Dick stated that although at that time it was understood to be him, she still had room for doubt and wanted more information).

At 10.02 a.m., the subject got off the bus and walked towards the entrance of Stockwell Tube station. (It was known that this was the same Tube station the attempted bombers had used to enter the system the previous day.) Some of

the CO19 vehicles discreetly moved closer in anticipation of being deployed. The missing CO19 vehicle arrived and joined the others near the station.

Two of the armed surveillance officers were already in the station foyer and asked their control if they wanted the subject stopped. They were apparently unaware that CO19 officers were nearby. They received no instructions to stop the subject. (It is possible that these transmissions were not received by central control at the Yard.) Meanwhile, the CO19 control was still awaiting instructions from the main control room at New Scotland Yard.

By 10.03 a.m., the subject was in the station, passing through the barriers. The CO19 control was told over the radio, 'He must not get on the Tube. Stop him getting on the Tube.' This was relayed over the back-to-back radio system. It must be remembered that officers had been

British Transport Police

The down escalator, showing the officers as they ran down to the platform

instructed earlier that they would only be deployed if a subject had been positively identified and that they should trust the information and be prepared to use unusual tactics.

Within twelve seconds of receiving these instructions, nine specialist firearms officers deployed from their vehicles into the station. These officers moved fast; one vaulted the barriers, others pushed their way through. They knew the subject could well be on the platform waiting for a train. This was a critical time; they were all aware that any delay could result in massive loss of life.

The covert radios used by CO19 at the time did not receive signals inside the Tube system so any contact with the outside world was lost the minute they entered the system. They would have to rely on direct contact with their colleagues, and their training. These officers knew that any decisions they made when they found the subject had to be based on their assessment at that time, drawing on all the information they had been given up to that point.

As the officers reached the foot of the escalator a surveillance officer indicated that the subject had boarded the train stationary on the northbound platform. The stakes had just been raised.

The train was held in the platform. There were many people already on board and most of the seats were taken. Some passengers were standing. As officers moved onto the platform,

View looking towards the front of the train. De Menezes had boarded the nearest carriage and was by the second set of doors

the officer given code name Charlie 5 (code names were later given to all the officers involved to protect their anonymity) entered the carriage at the rearmost door and began moving forward. He began scanning the passengers, looking for the subject who was described as having a dark complexion, short black hair, and who was wearing training shoes, jeans and a denim jacket. The jacket had been described as being padded, or lined.

Other officers, including Charlie 2 and Charlie 12, moved along the platform where a surveillance officer identified where the subject was sitting. Jean Charles de Menezes was sitting in the second seat along, facing the platform in the upper third of the carriage. A surveillance officer had been sitting near him but, on seeing individuals he correctly believed to be plain clothes CO19 officers on the platform, he moved across and stood in the open doorway, diagonally facing the subject. Coincidently this officer was dressed in similar clothes to those worn by the subject, including a denim jacket. He also had a swarthy complexion and carried a small rucksack.

He had been spotted by C5, who was in the carriage moving through and trying to make an assessment as to whether this could be the subject they were trying to locate. At this point, C2 and C12 stepped into the carriage through the open doors near to where the subject was sitting. Jean Charles de Menezes, for reasons unknown, now stood up and began to move forward.

The surveillance officer (code named Ivor), thinking this man was about to detonate himself or go for a weapon, grabbed him in a bear hug. The two men tumbled back into the seat. This flurry of activity only added to the CO19 officer's belief that the subject was about to detonate a bomb. C2 and C12 moved forward. Both men knew that in order to stop this happening they needed to act decisively and with enough force to stop him having the chance of setting off an explosion that would have wrecked the carriage, killing and maiming most of the people in it.

The decision was made and both officers opened fire at point blank range. From their training they knew the most effective method was to fire directly into the subject's head. This was done quickly, with both officers believing they had no alternative. (This may seem dangerous to the public, but owing to the ammunition the police were using there was little risk to other passengers from over-

British Transport Police

CCTV image showing the panic caused as passengers flee the station fearing a terrorist attack

The aftermath on the Northern Line train after a tragic case of mistaken identity leads to the death of Jean Charles de Menezes

penetration. The construction of the carriage itself also made the risk of ricochet minimal.)

The third officer, C5, along with other officers who had arrived, managed to pull Ivor out from the mêlée. It soon became apparent to C5 that Ivor was a surveillance officer. Meanwhile, panic and fear spread through the carriage, the recent bombings still fresh in people's minds.

The carriage emptied in no time at all. The surveillance and CO19 officers evacuated the remaining carriages. The train driver, who had fled down the tunnel, was identified and gently persuaded back onto the platform. The explosives officer was called down to examine the subject. It was soon confirmed that there was no explosive device. Even after this discovery it was still believed that this man was one of the failed bombers from 21 July. First aid was attempted for a short while until the air ambulance crew arrived and confirmed there were no signs of life. The scene was handed over to detectives and after what seemed like a long wait the CO19 officers were removed to another location. Their part in this operation had been brief and the consequences had been tragic.

Contrary to what was reported in the newspapers, Jean Charles de Menezes did not jump the barrier; he walked into the station, took a copy of the Metro and used a ticket to get through the barrier. It is true that, like many people trying to catch a train, he ran down the last half of the escalator to make sure he got on before taking his seat, but this was all normal behaviour. None of this could be relayed to the firearms officers, as police radios did not work in the Tube.

The aftermath

The following day it was confirmed that the subject was in fact trainee electrician Jean Charles de Menezes, a 27-year old Brazilian who was unconnected with any involvement in the bombings. The Met issued an apology and correctly described the incident as, 'a tragedy, and one that the Metropolitan Police Service regrets'. The individual officers and the rest of the CO19 team were devastated. They had gone from thinking they had shot a terrorist to realizing that they had taken the life of an innocent young man.

The two firing officers, C2 and C12, would take no further part in armed operations for a considerable time and accepted that they would be the subject of a thorough investigation by the IPCC (Independent Police Complaints Commission).

In the Stockwell Two report (the result of the second investigation into the incident) published in 2007 by the IPCC, one of the conclusions reads as follows: 'During July 2005 following the suicide bombings of the 7 July and attempted bombings of the 21 July, the MPS were operating under tremendous pressures which stretched resources and staff resilience to levels unprecedented in recent times. The MPS accept that management information structures were severely tested, errors were made and lessons learned.'

This tragedy was a serious blow to all concerned, not least the family of Jean Charles de Menezes, but with the suspects still adrift and a clear and present danger to the public remaining, SO19 had to pick itself up and dedicate itself to the task in hand.

Theseus II
29 July 2005

On Friday 29 July after the biggest UK manhunt ever, CO19 SFO teams were deployed in several co-ordinated raids on premises across London. The main target of the operation, code named 'Theseus II', was an address in west London, a flat in Dalgarno Gardens, where two of the failed 21/7 bombers were believed to be

Stephen Smith

The memorial from family and friends to Jean Charles de Menezes outside Stockwell Tube station

hiding. The raid was played out in broad daylight as an armed containment was put in around the block of flats. As the CO19 team moved forward to the address, the memory of the Madrid bombers who blew their building up just as the police were about to enter was forefront in their minds.

A TV and news blackout was maintained and at 12.45 p.m. CS gas was fired inside the flat and the front door was breached. After a tense time, two naked bewildered terrorists were captured in the full glare of TV and press cameras as they chose the surrender option over any thought of martyrdom. Muktar Said Ibrahhim, the Eritrean asylum seeker who had been given UK citizenship in 2003, was responsible for the attempt to set off the bomb on a London bus. Ramzi Mohammed

The team prepared to enter the target address

was a Somalian asylum seeker who had tried to detonate a bomb at the Oval Tube. Both were talked out at gunpoint and taken into custody.

Other addresses were also being searched, including one in Tavistock Crescent, west London, and one off the Old Kent Road in south-east London. Two female associates were followed with heavy cases to Liverpool Street station where senior officers held their breath as CO19 specialist firearms officers moved onto the concourse and quietly apprehended the two women as they queued at a ticket machine. The element of surprise allowed them to restrain the two women before they knew what was happening.

Manfo Kwaku Asiedu, the 32-year-old from Ghana who had discarded his device, gave himself up to police in London. Yasin Hassan Omar, the 22-year-old Somalian was picked up at an address in Birmingham. And finally, after

dressing in a burqa to fool border police, Ethiopian Hussain Osman was arrested by Italian police in Rome. This part of the operation had been a success.

The conclusion

On 9 July 2007, the four main conspirators were found guilty of conspiracy to commit murder. They were each sentenced to life with a minimum of forty years imprisonment. After a retrial Manfo Kwaku Asiedu was sentenced to thirty-three years imprisonment for his part in the attempted bombings. (Although this lengthy sentence sounds harsh as Asiedu did not go through with his bombing, one cannot underestimate the nation's strong feelings towards these atrocities. Also it was recognized that, even if Asiedu had second thoughts, he still did not warn the authorities or try to stop the others.)

Stephen Smith

The 7 July memorial, unveiled on 7 July 2009 in London's Hyde Park by Their Royal Highnesses the Prince of Wales and the Duchess of Cornwall, in memory of the fifty-two innocent victims of the bombings of that day. Each of the fifty-two steel posts is inscribed with the date, time and location of the explosions, and a nearby plaque names each victim

Five other men faced a total of twenty-two charges in relation to assisting the bombers before and after the attempted bombings. These men, who were all originally from Africa, were convicted, receiving sentences of between three and ten years. Yeshi Girmi, Hussain Osman's wife, was sentenced to fifteen years for having prior knowledge of the attacks.

On 7 November 2007, an Old Bailey jury found the Metropolitan Police guilty of failing in its duty of care to Mr De Menezes and fined them £175,000 with £385,000 costs. In October 2008, the commissioner Sir Ian Blair resigned from his post following sustained criticism of his handling of the media after the incident and a very public vote of no confidence in him from the newly elected mayor of London, Boris Johnson.

On 12 December 2008, the inquest into the death of Jean Charles de Menezes (which lasted three months) ended and after a week's deliberation an open verdict was returned. After a thorough investigation by the IPCC no criminal or disciplinary charges were bought against any of the CO19 officers, although many recommendations were made for changes, including some relating to command structure, radio communications and inter-departmental training.

In the following years, the survivors of the 7/7 bombings would have to live with horrific memories of that day, some with disabilities affecting every aspect of their lives. One brave victim who lost both her legs in the attack went on to represent Great Britain in the Paralympic Games of 2012, showing an indomitable spirit.

Stephen Smith

A suspect is led from the flat by an SFO

The front door of the flat, bearing the scars from the Hatton gun used to gain entry

Hostage Rescue, South London
2006

Another day and another hostage rescue for CO19's specialist firearms officers when SCD7(1) (the Anti-Kidnap unit) called in their services after receiving intelligence that a 32-year-old Ethiopian man had been kidnapped by a gang of criminals made up of West Indians and Ethiopians who believed their victim owed them £30,000.

The gang, it turned out, were heavily involved in credit card fraud and other related criminality. After failing to recover the alleged debt from their victim, they proceeded to contact his family, hoping that threats to harm their son would bring forward their money. The family, having no access to that amount of cash and fearing for their son's life, called the police and the Anti-Kidnap unit swung into action once again.

There was no luxury of time, as the unit strongly believed the hostage's life was in imminent danger. The gang would have no qualms about murdering their hostage if they believed the police were involved. Using detective ability, along with some technical assistance, the police established that the stronghold was located on the third level of an old block of flats off Brixton Hill in south London.

Permission was granted for a full hostage rescue with specialist munitions to be carried out, and at around 11 p.m. a fully kitted SFO team moved up to the corridor outside the address. On a given signal, Hatton rounds fired from a shotgun were used to disrupt the front door lock. Once entry was made, the team fanned out into the rooms of the flat. Distraction stun grenades were deployed creating noise and smoke, giving the entry team the time to move in and dominate each room and everyone inside. As the smoke cleared, the hostage was located tied up on a bed. He was relieved to see police, in the knowledge that he would soon be reunited with his family. Eight suspects were arrested inside the flat.

SFO officers wait outside the address in Forest Gate after the raid. They are wearing full CBRN protective equipment

The Forest Gate Raid
2 June 2006

On Friday 2 June 2006, police acting on specific intelligence raided two houses in Lansdown Road, Forest Gate, believing that there were terrorists in possession of a chemical weapon and other terrorist-related paraphernalia staying at one or both addresses.

Operation 'Volga' was a massive operation in police terms and was sanctioned at a very high level within the security service. CO19 SFO teams were chosen to carry out the raids because of the risk of firearms being used to resist or delay the entry of police. The obvious danger of a chemical bomb being detonated during any delay was also high. A large number of unarmed TSG (Territorial Support Group) officers were used in support to cordon off a large area and help evacuate other members of the public, in case this was required.

The SFO teams would carry out the raids wearing CBRN (chemical, biological, radiological, nuclear) protective clothing, which included respirators and thick rubber gloves.

All SFO teams train each year wearing the clothing and work and shoot under testing training environments, but this was the first-ever live operation in which it had been worn.

The main address was occupied by brothers Mohammed Abdul Kahar, aged 23, and Abul Koyair, aged 20, along with other family members. In the early hours of Friday morning, after extensive briefings from the anti-terrorist branch, the teams moved into position outside the address. The quiet environment of the street was shattered by a loud detonation as the front doors were simultaneously breached.

The specialist firearms officers at the main address moved purposefully into the house controlling the downstairs whilst others moved to the upper levels. They were shouting, 'Armed police!' although this would have sounded muffled when shouted through their respirators. As one officer, code named 'B6', arrived on the half-landing he was aware of two figures approaching from his right at speed. They came into contact with him, forcing him against the wall. His safety catch was off and his finger was on the trigger as per his training. His right arm was taken hold of and pulled and a round was unintentionally discharged from his MP5 carbine, hitting Kahar in his shoulder. 'B6' later stated that he feared they might have been attempting to get his weapon but he had not fired intentionally. The wound received by Mr Kahar, although serious, was not life-threatening and he was treated by paramedics at the scene.

After the address had been secured and handed over to the Counter-Terrorist branch, SO15 officers were withdrawn. The two brothers were held in custody but later released with no charges. After searches taking many weeks, which involved parts of the house and its very fabric being dismantled, no terrorist-related items were found. The family were placed in a hotel and the police picked up the £30,000 bill. A full apology was made to the family and an investigation was initiated by the IPCC into the shooting.

Two months later the IPCC released their findings, maintaining that the shooting was an accident. They stated, 'There is little doubt that the bulky clothing and gloves had an effect on the officers' mobility and dexterity and that the respirator muffled sound', but added that, 'The equipment was, however, the most up-to-date currently available for use by the Metropolitan Police service in such circumstances. Officers were trained in its use. In the circumstances, I conclude that the officer has committed no criminal or disciplinary offences.'

In reaction to the IPCC report, Prime Minister Tony Blair gave the police his full support on the BBC news, saying, 'Without detracting from what the report says, I hope people understand how difficult that job is when they are faced with the prospect of protecting people from a loss of life that could be dreadful, as we saw on July 7, 2005.'

This operation and its aftermath had cost the police/taxpayer in excess of £2 million, and so ended another uncomfortable episode in the UK's fight against terrorism. As the security agencies went off to check sources and place safeguards in position to prevent any similar occurrences happening in the future, CO19 accepted the findings of the report, which was quick and fair, and acknowledged that there was probably nothing the firearms department could have done at the time to have prevented this accident.

Senior Officers Training Day, MPSTC Gravesend
August 2006

Periodically, CO19 provides open days to which senior police officers are invited to observe the various facets of the firearms department, including the most up-to-date equipment, vehicles, weapons and tactics. This is done so that they can be aware of the service that can be provided to them should the need arise and to instil their confidence in CO19.

SFO teams assault the fieldcraft house at MPSTC Gravesend in a display laid on for senior police officers. The idea is to engender a better understanding of the capabilities of CO19

212

Above left: Police stooges act out a cash-in-transit robbery. This demonstrates the speed of events and the need for quick level-headed judgement when calling the right time to stage an armed intervention. Above: The suspect is talked from the premises and secured ready for a search by the team. Note the use of the Taser with its trailing copper-coloured wires leading from the suspect. Below: SFOs demonstrate an entry into a building using an assault vehicle and a lot of pyrotechnic distraction devices

Operation 'Broadoak', New Romney, Kent
31 October 2006

In October 2006 the Flying Squad were investigating a series of armed cash-in-transit robberies going back nearly ten years. These had been committed across south-east London and the Home Counties, in particular Kent and Essex. They believed that Robert Haines, aged 41, a keen body-builder and giant of a man who had worked as a doorman, was the leader of the gang. The squad also believed that he recruited from friends and associates in that industry.

Information obtained by the Flying Squad led them to believe that Haines and his gang intended to rob a cash delivery at one of two locations: one was in south-east London, the other at the Nationwide Building Society in New Romney High Street, Kent.

The robbers had targeted the same building society in New Romney successfully on a previous occasion and so it was the more obvious target for the gang who it was believed were becoming overconfident. They had no idea that, because of their propensity for violence, the Flying Squad had called upon the assistance of a CO19 specialist firearms team to help plan and carry out an ambush on them.

Permission was granted for CO19 to operate in Kent and plans were made for suitable holding locations for the firearms team. These would include a rifle position overlooking the target premises and suitable off-street locations from which armed officers could deploy. CARVs crewed by SFOs would be responsible for sweeping up other gang members in the area and blocking any getaway vehicle used by the gang.

It was Halloween night, Tuesday 31 October 2006. Groups of trick-or-treaters passed by the armed officers sitting in their unmarked cars waiting patiently for any sign of the gang. Fireworks went off with bangs and flashes, lighting up the black sky. It was an almost perfect cover for a robbery of this kind.

At around 7.30 p.m., Haines was spotted as the passenger in a silver Mercedes saloon, which was driven by a man later identified as Dean Jenkins. This vehicle was seen to drive around the area before stopping in a small car-parking area, which serviced the high street shops (including the Nationwide Building Society). It was joined to the High Street via an alleyway called Church Close. Other known gang members had also been observed driving through New Romney High Street. The scene looked set for the law to finally catch up with Robert Haines and his gang.

At around 7.45 p.m., the blue cash-in-transit van arrived and parked in the High Street across the end of Church Close – just metres from the door to the Building Society. A commentary crackled over the police radio sets from the observation/rifle point. The custodian began his delivery with boxes of cash to restock the cashpoint.

Haines, who was well over six feet tall and of intimidating stature, left his accomplice, Jenkins, in the car park, with the engine of their Mercedes running, ready for a quick getaway. He made his way purposefully up Church Close, heading towards the building society. He pulled a black balaclava down over his face and attempted to conceal a sawn-off shotgun. Haines timed his walk well and forced his great bulk in behind the custodian.

As he entered the glass-fronted building society he proceeded to threaten the terrified guard with his sawn-off shotgun. There was no clear shot from the rifle position, so all the officers in the observation point could do was to continue their commentary as the guard passed over the money cassettes containing £105,000. Haines slipped the cassettes into a green sack and nonchalantly exited the door into the dark alleyway, heading back the way he had come.

A still taken from
surveillance footage
of the cash-in-transit
delivery to the
building society

Up until this point, police could not inter-vene because of the risk of the custodian becoming a hostage or being shot by Haines, so they had no option but to call the attack when he left the building society.

Haines jogged slowly down the alley towards the car park and his waiting getaway car. He still wore the black balaclava and was carrying the bag of cash in his left hand while clutching the sawn-off shotgun in his right. Four SFOs had been concealed in a building overlooking the car park. They quickly exited into the bottom end of the alleyway. They could see the huge form of Haines running towards them. Between Haines and their position was a gap in the wall, which led into the car park. The offi-cers began shouting challenges of 'Armed police! Stand still! Drop the gun!' He continued towards them, reaching the gap in the wall and, as if in answer to their challenges, discharged his shotgun towards police.

In the darkness the flash was almost blinding. The nearest officer, using the torch on his Heckler & Koch G36 carbine to illumi-nate Haines, opened fire. This return of fire took the big man down. Haines collapsed in the car park just metres from his getaway car,

which had now been blocked in by SFO vehi-cles. As officers approached Haines, he appeared to be trying to get up. One officer, unable to see his hands, fired his Taser. Owing to the heavy clothing worn by Haines the barbs failed to deploy properly and the Taser was inef-fective. It then became apparent that Haines had been shot.

The area was secured and once Dean Jenkins, who witnessed his conspirator collapse to the ground, had been handcuffed, the specially trained SFO medics went to work. They managed to stabilize Haines who had been hit three times in the torso.

In the meantime, Ben Grehan, aged 21, was arrested in the High Street by SFO officers, and David Jenkins, aged 60, was arrested some distance away in the nearby village of Hamstreet.

Unfortunately, once Haines was removed to an ambulance his condition deteriorated, and he died of his wounds on arrival at William Harvey Hospital in Ashford.

In November 2007, Haines' three accom-plices were given prison sentences of between ten and seventeen years for conspiracy to commit armed robberies. Jailing them, Judge

The bag containing the £105,000 cash stolen by Haines

Phillip Statman said, 'Until that occasion you the robbers had enjoyed rich pickings. You came back for more. You were playing for high stakes and probably felt, after your earlier successes, a degree of invincibility.'

In January 2010 at the inquest into the death of Robert Haines, convicted armed robber Dean Jenkins gave evidence confirming that Haines had pointed his shotgun at police and opened fire. The jury passed a verdict of lawful killing with no criticism of police action.

Operation 'Wondoola' for Trident
15 May 2007

Terry Nicholas, aged 52, lived with his family in Acton, north-west London. He apparently ran a gym business locally. For reasons still not clear to police, he became embroiled in a feud with local criminals, who were possibly members of a gang. This came to a head on 20 April 2007 when gunmen opened fire on his house in what is known colloquially as a drive-by shooting. Police now became involved.

Two days after this incident, Nicholas was outside his house with a detective, answering some questions, when a hooded man walked up and opened fire on him with a pistol. Although Nicholas was wearing a bulletproof vest underneath his clothing he received gunshot wounds to his abdomen and legs. The officer who had dived for cover now radioed for assistance. The suspect ran from the scene. Nicholas was taken to hospital; his wounds were not serious and amounted to bullet grazes and a flesh wound but he was detained in hospital.

The investigation was not progressing well. Nicholas was refusing to co-operate with police. He informed investigators that he would sort matters out himself and police would know when he had his revenge because he would leave the 'mark of Zorro'. It was never understood or ascertained what he meant by this comment. However, police took his threat seriously, fearing that he might attempt to take matters into his own hands. Operation 'Trident' (set up to investigate 'black on black' shootings) became involved.

This operation was given the name 'Wondoola' (all operation names are generated randomly from a database at New Scotland Yard) and on Tuesday 15 May 2007, surveillance was maintained on Terry Nicholas after information was obtained that he might be taking possession of a handgun at some point during that evening. Trident officers called upon CO19 specialist firearms teams to back up the SO11 surveillance officers who were behind Nicholas.

It later became apparent, when evidence was given at the subsequent inquest, that Nicholas had engaged an associate to collect a package and hold it until after he left hospital. Nicholas

The car park and garage area, in the shadow of Park Royal Underground station. Note the paramedic ambulance in the background

then arranged for this same associate to meet him with the package at the rear of Paolo's restaurant near Park Royal Underground station at Hanger Green in west London.

Nicholas was followed to the restaurant, where he met his family for a meal. At about 9 p.m. he briefly left the restaurant and took delivery of the package, which was strongly suspected to be a firearm. He returned inside. A decision was made not to arrest him inside the restaurant as it was too busy and would cause unnecessary danger to other members of the public. Then, at around 10.20 p.m., Nicholas got up and left, walking on his own around to the rear of the shops, where he had parked a moped.

Acting on this development, Trident decided to initiate the arrest phase of the operation, sending in the CO19 SFOs. Two CARVs were sent to the rear and two to the front to act as cut-offs. The vehicles pulled up into the car park, and the officers began to deploy. But as this happened Nicholas opened fire on the nearest vehicle using a CZ semi-automatic pistol. A round penetrated through the rear

quarter light window, narrowly missing the officer as he exited the vehicle. The officer later said at the inquest, 'I was aware of a shot being fired, a loud bang and a rush of air going past my face. I knew immediately I was being shot at.'

One officer from the front seat of the leading CARV returned fire at Nicholas who retreated with his gun into the dark recesses of the car park, pursued by three officers. The arrest phase of the operation had been turned into a fight for survival. Nicholas was armed and had proved he was dangerous. The officers were taking no chances; they advanced into the service area with the odd parked car and industrial bin as their only means of cover. The officers continued shooting at Nicholas, believing he was still firing at them. He refused to comply and throw down his gun. Instead, he went behind one of the industrial wheelie bins. The officers strongly believed that if they didn't get Nicholas soon he would shoot one of them.

Eventually, in the darkness, amid all the shouting and sounds of gunfire, Nicholas was hit multiple times. These included gunshot

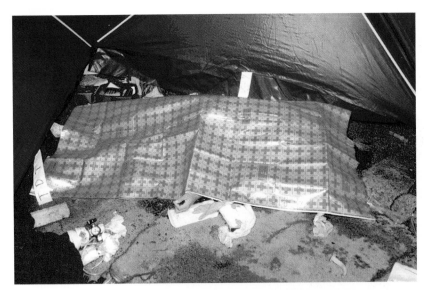

Left: The covered body of Terry Nicholas, following attempts to revive him by the paramedics

Below: The 9 mm CZ100 self-loading pistol with fully charged magazine, and the sock it was inside

wounds to his neck and head. He collapsed behind the bin. The shoot-out in the restaurant car park was over. Paramedics were quick to arrive on the scene and went to great lengths to save Nicholas's life, but it was to no avail. He died of his wounds in the car park.

It transpired that the semi-automatic pistol Nicholas had taken delivery of was inside a sock, and that, after firing the first round at police, the weapon had jammed. It's possible the ejected round had failed to clear the ejection port and caused the weapon to malfunction, but we shall never know. He had been attempting to clear the stoppage when he was shot.

In September 2009, the inquest jury came

back with a lawful killing verdict and no criticism of the police or their tactics. Nicholas's associate who delivered the gun to him was cleared at court of knowingly supplying the firearm.

Operation 'Trident' continues to carry out hundreds of proactive operations each year, but they are fighting an uphill battle. In 2007 alone there were thirty gun-related murders, with victims under 18 making up almost one third of the total. This, along with over 3,000 gun-related crimes that same year, makes Trident's job a difficult one and they frequently require the assistance of CO19 and other agencies to make the arrests.

Operation 'Hurlock', Chandler's Ford
13 September 2007

Operation 'Hurlock' was an operation instigated by the Flying Squad. It targeted a gang of prolific and violent armed robbers, whose preferred victims were banks and cash-in-transit deliveries in small villages and towns in the Home Counties where they anticipated the police response would be slow and limited. The gang were growing ever more confident, having committed robberies over an eighteen-month period and netted hundreds of thousands of pounds. They had fired shots at bank staff and members of the public who had got in their way and apparently had no compunction about taking on police if the need arose. The two main gang members were Mark Nunes and Andrew Markland. Both men were in their early thirties and lived in Brixton, south London.

Their luck ran out when the Flying Squad received information that the gang were aiming to rob a cash-in-transit delivery vehicle outside the HSBC bank in the beautiful Hampshire village of Chandler's Ford. This village was no stranger to violence. It had been the scene of many battles in the 800s between the Saxons

and the Danes fighting over the river crossing that the village was named after. It would now be the setting of another, more modern, confrontation, this time between armed criminals and police.

The Flying Squad brought in an SFO team from CO19 to assist in the arrest of these violent criminals. Intelligence passed on by the Flying Squad stated that Mark Nunes was in possession of at least one firearm along with armour-piercing ammunition. It was apparently the gang's intention to fire rounds into the delivery van if the guards did not comply.

A team briefing was held in the early hours of the morning at the CO19 base in Leman Street. A decision was made to take team snipers from the dedicated sniper team in order to provide cover for the specialist firearms officers as they deployed onto the robbery. It was noted by the Flying Squad that they would need very strong evidence to convict the gang, as all they had so far was circumstantial evidence.

At 4 a.m. the CO19 assets followed the Flying Squad down to Hampshire to find locations to 'hold up' near the bank. Suitable positions were found for the team snipers and at observation vantage points overlooking the bank.

At 6 a.m. information was received that the gang were travelling down towards Hampshire in a stolen Land Rover. The SFO team were mostly positioned in a public toilet block about fifty metres from the bank. They would be called to the robbery from the observation point overlooking the junction. It would be a crucial time as they approached, as they were relying on the team snipers to cover them. Throughout the morning there were regular updates relating to the movement of the criminals and the delivery vehicles, which were both converging on Chandler's Ford. The two rifle officers, one armed with a 7.62 calibre Heckler & Koch G3 rifle, the other with a 5.56 calibre Heckler & Koch G36 carbine, had a difficult role. Not only were they acting as the eyes and ears of the attack team but they also had a duty of care to the security guards and would need to act if they feared their lives were in danger.

At around 9.15 a.m. Markland was seen at the bus stop directly opposite the HSBC bank. He looked completely out of place wearing a bulky ski jacket, with a ski mask rolled up on the top of his head. His right hand remained inside the shoulder bag he was carrying.

Other gang members had been seen driving past the bank in the stolen Land Rover Discovery. Just before 10 a.m. a stolen Volvo was seen parking up, facing the expected parking spot of the cash delivery van. A few tense minutes passed before the arrival of the Group Four security van, which parked at the junction near to the bank. The custodian guard got out, moving to the rear door in full view of the sniper observation point. This was the moment the police would make their move. Their radios crackled out a commentary, following the movements of the guard and the robbers.

It was at 10.05 a.m. when Mark Nunes made his move. Nunes, the self-elected leader of the gang, moved towards the guard, pointing a 9 mm pistol at his chest. The guard was frozen to the spot.

Nunes advances towards the guard aggressively, his pistol pointing directly at his chest

The movement was followed with concern by the snipers, one of whom, fearing Nunes was about to shoot the guard, opened fire. He fired one shot at Nunes from his G36 carbine, hitting him in the chest. Nunes collapsed to the ground at the feet of the stunned guard.

Almost instantly, Andrew Markland ran across from the bus shelter where he had been waiting and stooped down, foolishly picking up the 9 mm pistol dropped by Nunes. (What he imagined had happened to his accomplice we shall never know.) The CO19 SFO team were already deploying from their holding point in the public lavatories nearby and were moving towards Markland as he rose up with the pistol, appearing to level it at them. The second police sniper, fearing for their safety, fired one shot from his rifle, hitting Markland in the chest. Markland fell to the ground where, although wounded, he was still moving. The officer considered he was still a potential threat to the approaching officers, and believed he still had control of the pistol. He therefore fired a second time, hitting Markland again in the chest. This time he stopped moving.

Once again, the speed of the incident and the danger to the guard, the public and fellow officers from a dangerous man in possession of a firearm left very little time for consideration to be given to, for instance, shooting the gun from the suspect's hand. As mentioned before, this goes against the officer's training and is fraught as a tactic in case the shot misses its target. A high-velocity bullet can travel miles and still have enough energy to kill.

The officers arrived and began administering first aid. Meanwhile, two other gang members in the stolen Volvo, seeing what had become of their accomplices, made off at speed. They were arrested later.

Andrew Markland, aged 36, died at the scene after the second round struck him in the chest, while Mark Nunes, aged 35, died of his wounds later that morning in hospital. The following day, the *Sun* newspaper featured a headline with the words 'Bang Bang To Rights' showing the aftermath of the scene of the shooting. The IPCC immediately opened an investigation into the incident.

Over the next few days, many homes were raided in south London and seven more members of the gang were arrested. Three later pleaded guilty to conspiracy to commit armed robberies and a further four were convicted at Kingston Crown Court later that year. The jury heard that the gang had been involved in eighteen armed robberies using varying degrees of violence. The jury were also told, 'Nunes luck ran out when he was gunned down as he held a pistol to the head of a security guard close to a branch of the HSBC bank.' The surviving members of the gang received prison sentences of between five to seventeen years.

At the inquest held in Hampshire over October and November of 2011, the jury were shown video evidence and the officers gave their testimony. The jury were later directed by the coroner, Graham Short, to give a verdict of lawful killing on both counts. (The coroner

SFO team members secure the firearm and check the two fallen suspects, rendering first aid where necessary. The guard also lay on the ground; he was understandably in shock

makes his decisions based on the evidence laid before him; as mentioned before, he has the right to direct his jury but he must be fair to all interested parties and be aware that any decision he makes can be open to judicial review, or an application to quash on the grounds of insufficiency of enquiry, disclosure of new facts, or if it is in the interest of justice that another inquest should be held.)

The IPCC found that the two officers had not broken the law or committed any offences for which they could be prosecuted. However, they commented in their report that they believed there had been a window to arrest the pair safely. The Met said it would look into the report. Many of the recommended changes had already been adopted after the incident, prior to the report coming out, for instance having a separate firearms commander (who was not also the officer in charge of the operation).

The shooting was widely reported and the public response to the action of the police was varied. Some felt that another outcome should have been more keenly sought, while others felt the quick thinking and decisive action of the officers could well have saved the life of the guard and fellow officers or members of the public in that quiet Hampshire village. (It is interesting to note that over the next few months this type of cash-in-transit armed robbery almost stopped completely.)

CO19 Training with the Air Support Unit on the new Eurocopter EC145
October 2007

The officers of CO19 have always enjoyed a close relationship with their colleagues in the ASU (Air Support Unit), who have assisted on many occasions with aerial reconnaissance and even helped deliver advanced firearms parties near to the scenes of sieges and other major firearms incidents.

The specially trained ASU dispatcher prepares for the first descent on the 'fast rope'

Pilot leads 4 SFOs to his aircraft under the instructions of the dispatcher

However, it was not until July 2007, when the Met took delivery of three of the new versatile Eurocopter EC145s (costing £5 million each), that CO19 could make use of the full potential of the ASU's helicopter fleet. With their larger capacity and payload EC145s were able to do much more than the previous aircraft. They could also be fitted with rails from which ropes could be attached, allowing fully kitted firearms officers to 'fast rope' (deploy by sliding down a thick rope) and 'abseil' (rappel down a rope using a metal descender). Another method of delivery is the hover jump (stepping off the helicopter skids onto a roof, balcony or open land space without the aircraft having to land). Alternatively, the aircraft could land and deploy its officers. These methods of delivering officers at, or near to, a firearms incident allowed a firearms commander more tactical options. For CO19 this meant more specific training with the ASU and with the Olympics on its way this soon became a matter of urgency.

ARV Armed Stop on the Street
27 October 2007

The versatility of the Armed Response Vehicles is one of their major strengths. To have a highly trained and experienced armed presence patrolling the streets of the capital 24/7 with the capability of being directed to any incident at any location at any time is a great asset in the fight against armed crime.

Here we have images lifted from CCTV footage of an armed stop being made by the crew of an ARV to apprehend a suspect who has just taken possession of a firearm for criminal purposes. The suspect with the bag is with a second male who may or may not be an accomplice. He must be treated in the same way as the suspect until his status can be confirmed. Once again, the stop must be done with the

The ARV officers deploy; the rear officer provides cover as they move forward. The second ARV arrives in support

The two ARV crews detain and secure the two suspects

correct level of force to avoid any misunderstandings, which can put the lives of the public, the officers and the suspects at risk.

CO19 Hostage Rescue, East London
2008

In early 2008, CO19 were called in to assist SCD7(1)(the Anti-Kidnap unit) to perform a hostage rescue at an address in east London, where a West Indian gang had targeted the son of a wealthy Indian businessman.

The gang, who specialized in kidnap and extortion, had lifted the 19-year-old whilst he was out shopping in an east London super-market. They were in the process of demanding £50,000 for his safe release, but unbeknown to them the hostage's family had informed the police who were using every means available to them to track down where the young man was being held.

Their enquiries led them to a first-floor flat in a newly constructed estate in Barking. The stronghold was located at a critical time when the gang were threatening to cut off one of the hostage's fingers as proof they meant business. There was no time to delay and a hostage rescue was authorized.

SFO officers stand in the hall after securing the premises

An explosive charge was used to help the team gain entry. The methodology and tactics around this subject are still secret, but at 5.40 p.m. after a rifle team had moved into cover near the railway track at the rear of the address, the entry team moved up to the front door.

On a given signal the door was blown in and the SFO team made its entry. Although the initial entry was quick, the team encountered a second locked door. Whilst this was breached, three suspects jumped from a first-floor window at the rear. These men were quickly detained by the cover group. Three more suspects were detained inside the flat. The bound-up hostage was located unharmed on a bed in the lounge. Two of the suspects were subdued using the Taser. A total of six suspects were arrested and later charged with serious offences including kidnapping. A large semi-circular bladed knife was recovered from the kitchen, believed to have been intended for the threatened amputation.

The Chelsea Siege: Markham Square
6 May 2008

Mark Saunders, a 32-year-old lawyer, lived in a multi-level maisonette in Markham Square, Chelsea, west London. He had been suffering from depression for some time and had been using alcohol and controlled substances to cope. His relationship with his wife was also under severe pressure. All these things would contribute to the tragic set of circumstances that would ultimately lead to his death.

Despite his troubles, it would appear that Mark Saunders gave no obvious signs that he had finally reached breaking point prior to the that fateful day in May. What made him go one stage further we shall never know, but the point at which he stepped over that undrawn line was defined at 4.30 p.m. on Tuesday 6 May 2008 when, in the kitchen of his luxury flat, he took

224

it upon himself to begin firing his shotgun out of his window into his garden and towards the windows of the houses opposite.

One lethal load of lead pellets from his shotgun easily cleared the thirty-metre gap between the two buildings and penetrated through the window of a child's bedroom, embedding in the plaster of the wall at the back of the room. Fortunately the room was empty but had the pellets hit the next window along things may well have been different.

At the sound of gunfire, Mark Saunders' neighbour, who lived in the basement, came out to investigate and claimed he fired at her; she retreated back inside her apartment and called the police who dispatched an ARV to the address. Upon arrival at the scene, the ARV put in place an armed containment of the three-storey block, which effectively restricted Saunders' movements and reduced the potential threat he posed to those residents nearby if he was to come out onto the street.

It later transpired that Saunders, who was the lawful owner of two shotguns and ammunition, had been in touch with a friend, informing him that 'he had been firing his gun and that the police were coming and he was in trouble'. (Saunders had served a period of time in the Territorial Army and would have had knowledge of the destructive power of firearms).

At 4.50 p.m., ARV officers moved into premises overlooking the kitchen where Mark Saunders was situated with his shotgun. On seeing the police in the buildings opposite he fired at them from the window. The shot narrowly missed one officer and the householder who had shown him into the bedroom. In response, this officer exchanged further shots with Saunders, firing three rounds from his Glock pistol. This made Saunders retreat from the window back into the kitchen. He then began texting the same friend, informing

him, 'This is the end my old friend, the end', an apparent reference to the movie *Apocalypse Now* of which they were both fans.

The officer who had fired was replaced (he would be taken away to begin the PIP process). The replacement officer placed a ballistic shield up against the window to afford some protection should Saunders fire again. By 7.00 p.m. police negotiators, who were in contact with Saunders on his mobile phone, were aware that he had been drinking heavily and was very drunk. He informed them that he was scared and could see police snipers outside. The negotiators heard him vomiting and drinking from a bottle and tried to reassure him that he would come to no harm.

At short while later, Saunders' condition had deteriorated and he was continuing to drink heavily. He subsequently appeared at the window with a note, which could be read by those observing. It simply said 'Mum'. At 8.00 p.m. he said to the police negotiator, 'Who is going to employ me as a barrister now?' and 'I don't want anyone to shoot me', followed by a further appearance at the window when he produced another note saying, 'Kill Myself'.

Police negotiators continued in their efforts to try to calm the situation down and reassure Saunders that he would not be harmed. His response was to threaten to 'blow out the windows and finish the thing'.

Shortly after 9.00 p.m. Saunders again fired the shotgun out of the window and once again an armed officer returned fire from the containment with no one being injured as a result. Saunders would not speak to the negotiators again. (During this last exchange, pellets fired by Saunders had struck the ballistic shield sheltering the officers in the house opposite and knocked it down. The shield had undoubtedly saved the officers from serious injury.)

Saunders was heard to shout out of the window, 'I want to speak to Bradley [referring

The rear of Mark Saunders' apartment and gardens; the open window is the one from which he fired most of his shots

to his friend Michael Bradley]. I want to speak to my wife.' But it was decided that this would not be allowed. The police negotiators, who decide how best to manage contact with the subject, would have made this decision based on many factors. For one, the prospect of talking to family and friends can sometimes be used as an incentive for the subject to surrender. For another, if contact is allowed it can sometimes escalate a volatile situation and any good work done by the negotiators can be lost in an instant. There is also the risk in cases where suicide is a potential threat that any conversation with a loved one could be a prelude to that suicide.

Despite the continued efforts of the negotiating team to try to re-establish communications with Saunders, he now refused to engage with them. At 9.25 p.m. high-intensity spotlights were used to illuminate the property. Shortly after this, Mark Saunders appeared at the kitchen window and leant out. He waved the barrel of the shotgun in the air and then brought it down, pointing it directly at the police officers on the containment.

Fearing that Saunders was going to fire directly at them again and fearing for their lives and those of their colleagues, seven officers from the containment returned fire, resulting this time in multiple injuries to Mark Saunders, from which he died.

The five-hour stand-off was over and tragically it had ended the way Mark Saunders had predicted – with his own death. Firearms officers in the Metropolitan Police are trained to the highest standard and none more so than those in CO19 who have to make split-second life or death decisions. The fact that all seven officers perceived the threat to be so great that they had to engage Mark Saunders to mitigate it gives a clear indication of how dangerous they considered his actions to be at that time.

During the siege, Mark Saunders had fired his shotgun eight times, six times out of his kitchen window and twice out of a window in the dining room passageway. He had a further

Mark Saunders leans out of his kitchen window and, after waving his shotgun around, lowers it into a position where it is pointing at the police. He is shot by several officers and falls back into his kitchen fatally wounded

203 live shotgun cartridges in his flat. Westminster Coroner's Court was told that traces of saliva were found on the muzzle of his Beretta shotgun.

The court also heard that a mother and her two children had locked themselves in the bathroom of their flat next door to Mr Saunders for the duration of the siege, too afraid to come out. Police negotiators had been patient and prepared to play the waiting game, while the armed officers had a duty to protect the public and each other. In the end, the police action was a direct response to Mark Saunders' actions on the night. The inquest into the death of Mark Saunders held at Westminster Coroner's Court ended in October 2010 and the jury found that the actions of the officers were lawful, proportionate and reasonable.

Man Brandishing AK47 Shot by Police, Harold Hill
29 October 2008

On Wednesday 29 October 2008, at around 1.40 p.m., several urgent calls were made for police assistance at a housing estate in Harold Hill near Romford. The initial call related to a fight in progress, a female being attacked, and an attacker on the scene threatening to kill himself and others. Reports stated that this man (later identified as Andrew Hammond, aged 40) had left the address in Honeysuckle Close and was walking around the estate with what appeared to be an AK47 assault rifle. Later calls stated that the five-foot-eight male, who was sporting a shaved head and wearing a black bomber jacket, was pointing the weapon at children on the estate and threatening members of the public. Hammond even made a call to police himself, stating that he was armed with guns and was willing to use them.

As ARVs arrived on the estate near Honeysuckle Close an RVP (rendezvous point) was established and an incident control set up. It was now around 2.10 p.m. and a woman attracted the attention of two ARV officers, stating that the armed suspect was down a passageway on the estate. The officers, fearing for the safety of the public, moved off in an attempt to locate and contain the suspect.

As they moved towards the vicinity of Honeysuckle Close, where the call had originated, they could hear the voice of a man who sounded agitated. The two ARV officers sped up in an effort to contain him in his current location. As one of the officers checked around a corner, he could see the suspect clearly over a distance of between twenty to thirty metres. The man was holding an AK47 assault rifle by its pistol grip; it was pointing down towards the ground. He was holding a mobile phone in his right hand and was talking loudly into it. He was rocking from side to side and seemed very agitated.

The other officer now also had eyes on Hammond and shouted a challenge of 'Armed police! Drop the weapon.' Hammond slowly raised the weapon in his left hand until it was waist height and pointing horizontally

Aerial view of the scene of the shooting at Honeysuckle Close

outwards, and he began turning to face the first officer who was now aiming his MP5 directly at Hammond's torso. Hammond was heard to say into the phone, 'Here we go.' He continued to turn until he was pointing the AK47 directly at the first officer who, fearing that he was about to be shot, fired twice. Hammond flinched, but apart from this the bullets seemed to have no effect and he began to walk towards the officer who fired two more shots. Again, nothing seemed to happen. Hammond now began turning back towards the second officer. Fearing the man was wearing body armour and about to shoot at his colleague, the first officer now aimed at his head. He fired once and Hammond fell backwards onto the pavement. Another officer now joined them and between them they administered first aid. Andrew Hammond was heard to say, 'Let me die, let me

die.' As well as the AK47 assault rifle, he also had a semi-automatic pistol tucked into his waistband.

The ambulance crew were unable to save Hammond who had received fatal wounds and was pronounced dead at the scene. Three firearms were later recovered (the third being an MP5 carbine) and sent for forensic examination to establish whether they were capable of being fired. (In this case the weapons were found to be realistic replicas, which can be purchased legally on the internet.) Apparently Andrew Hammond had gone out with these weapons after a domestic dispute had come to a head.

On 14 June 2010 at Walthamstow Coroner's Court the inquest jury returned a verdict of lawful killing and also determined that Mr Hammond intended to kill himself by provoking the police to shoot him. This incident had all the signs of a 'suicide-by-cop' shooting, the consequences of which the officers who fire the fatal bullet have to live with all their lives.

Operation Makepeace
2008

Operation Makepeace was set up in 2008 within CO19 firearms command with the intention of reducing incidences of young people carrying guns and knives and becoming involved in gangs. It seemed an obvious step for experienced firearms officers to take the message into schools and youth clubs, particularly in areas of high gun crime.

The Makepeace officers are specially selected to deliver their important message by way of short presentations explaining the consequences of carrying guns and knives and the effect these crimes have on their victims, along with the important message that armed police treat all guns (including imitations) as real.

Since its inception in 2008, Makepeace has reached over 40,000 young people in over 300 locations and continues to be an important tool in the Met's fight against the growing trend towards violent crime amongst young people in central locations in London.

Motorcycle Jewel Snatch – Operation 'Cassian'
14 December 2008

It's not particularly unusual to leave your Christmas shopping until eleven days before Christmas, but this group of individuals were no ordinary shoppers. In fact, they were becoming a thorn in the side of the Flying Squad detectives who were trying to catch them.

The robbers' modus operandi was to rob high-class jewellers of expensive watches and jewellery. They would use excessive violence to dominate the staff and customers, then smash their way into the display cabinets using sledgehammers and crowbars. The gang would then use powerful stolen motorcycles to make good their escape. These bikes would dominate the pavement outside the shops, keeping any curious people or 'have-a go-heroes' at bay. It was great news for the Flying Squad when a tip-off came in, giving the gang's next target as a high-class jewellers specializing in designer watches in Brompton Road in London's busy West End.

The gang were not expected to use firearms but it could not be ruled out. They were dangerous enough armed with their heavy wrecking tools, which they would not hesitate to turn on the staff or the public if the mood took them. Their level of violence had been escalating and it was only a matter of time before someone was seriously hurt or killed. This was why CO19 were called in to help plan and carry out the ambush of what was, in effect, a glorified 'smash and grab' crime.

On Sunday 14 December 2008, CO19 assisted the Flying Squad to set the trap that would hopefully catch this gang once and for all. CO19 would take on the robbers within the store just in case the robbery developed into a hostage rescue situation, while the Flying Squad would deal with the getaway bikes.

The CO19 SFO team filtered into an office above the shop next door and waited. Their patience was rewarded when at 11.30 a.m. the sound of high-revving bikes came from the street below. Two high-powered motorcycles had delivered their pillion passengers to the front of the store. The two men, later identified as Billy Stewart, aged 18, and Wole Osinlaru, aged 20, smashed the front door with a sledgehammer and terrorized the staff inside, smashing the displays with hammers.

The SFO team, holding in nearby premises, prepare to move in and make the arrests

The SFO team enter and dominate the robbers

The team moved down the stairs and out onto the pavement. As they entered the jewellers they threw stun grenades in to disorientate the robbers. Already the bikes were attempting to get away as the Flying Squad gunships moved in. Inside, the shop was a mess. Glass and wreckage from the cabinets lay all over the floor. The terrified staff were motionless behind the counters. The robbers were caught with their bags full of stolen jewellery. They could do nothing but surrender, going down on the floor to be handcuffed. One customer (an ex-New York cop) had looked on throughout the whole incident and as the smoke cleared was heard to say, 'Jeez, you guys must have known they would be here!'

The operation was a success. The two robbers who entered the store appeared at Blackfriars Crown Court where they both pleaded guilty to robbery. Stewart received five years imprisonment for robbery and two years for a previous burglary to run concurrently. Osinlaru received six years for robbery.

Detective Sergeant Rhys Willis, of the Finchley Flying Squad, said: 'This offence and others like it have a substantial impact on the business community. Just as important is that staff and customers at these offences are often terrified by these individuals' actions. The sledgehammer used by Stewart narrowly missed the security guard present.'

Helicopter Sniper
2008

The role of the CO19 sniper had changed dramatically over the years but at no time more so than in the build-up to the London Olympic Games of 2012. Most of our European colleagues have been using snipers in helicopters to combat armed crime and terrorism for many years. But up until the purchase of the Eurocopter EC145, which entered police service in 2007, this had not been possible within the Met. However, the new aircraft lent itself well to the role of a rifle platform with its ability to hover almost in the same spot with very little vibration.

In 2008, CO19 began training its specialist rifle officers to operate from these helicopters. The aim was to provide a versatile response to policing problems in the twenty-first century and to provide tactical options for the fast-approaching 2012 London Olympic Games.

Above: An SFO sniper on board the Eurocopter EC145 armed with a SIG 5.56 high-velocity carbine. The CO19 sniper has access to many types of rifle and optical sights. Right: View through the ELCAN 1-4 Power Scope. This type of scope allows the sniper to identify and neutralize an armed threat from a reasonable distance. Below: Team training photo with Eurocopter hovering above SFO teams mounted on ladder vehicles

Death of ARV PC Gary Toms
11 April 2009

On Saturday 11 April 2009, north base ARVs answered a call to an aggravated burglary in Dagenham. The crew included 37-year-old PC Gary Toms. Following a short chase, which ended in Ashlin Road, E15, the ARV blocked in the suspects' car. As the officers were deploying to arrest the suspects, it became apparent that Gary had sustained a serious head injury (possibly whilst exiting the vehicle). He remained critically ill for six days and died on 17 April.

Gary had been with CO19 for less than a year. The inquest found that he had died of accidental injuries sustained whilst attempting to arrest escaping suspects.

Of the four suspects arrested for the robbery, three received sentences of between six and eight years. The driver, Temitope Iyiola, aged 20, was given ten years, one of which was for dangerous driving.

Gary Toms was the first officer from the firearms unit to lose his life whilst arresting suspects.

CO19 Firearms Recovery

One of the duties of the police is the recovery of illegally held firearms and by far the safest way of recovering these is to utilize the resources of CO19 who, by using their training and experience, can detain the suspect(s) thus creating a safe environment for their unarmed colleagues to search and retrieve the weapons.

The unveiling of the memorial to PC Gary Toms at Ashlin Road, E15, by Prime Minister David Cameron

Firearms recovered on operations – just a fraction of those recovered each year by CO19

Stephen Smith

One of the new telescopic ladders of the type used in this incident, now carried on all ARVs

Suicide By Appointment: Shooting in Holloway
4 October 2009

Richard Hiorns, aged 43, a former psychiatric nurse and at the time the assistant director of the Highgate Mental Health Centre, himself had a history of instability. This had manifested itself previously in brushes with the law, resulting in his arrest for impersonating police, assault on police and possession of an imitation firearm. He also had a strange fascination with all matters involving police. Sadly this led to him forcing a course of action on 4 October 2009 that would bring him into a direct confrontation with CO19 officers.

On that day, Hiornes had been drinking heavily even before 10 a.m. when he phoned 999. He spoke with the operator, demanding that police attend his address in Kiver Road, Holloway; he threatened to 'shoot dead the first

police officer who arrived'. As if to emphasize his point, he discharged a firearm near to the phone receiver four times, almost deafening the police operator.

Not knowing whether the public were at threat or whether there were hostages involved, the information room had no choice but to dispatch an Armed Response car to the call. They would need to approach with caution and try to establish the nature of the threat. Was it a genuine crisis or some elaborate hoax? Either way this was a call that would have to be taken very seriously.

At 10.30 a.m. two ARVs arrived in the vicinity and made tactical approaches to the address. One crew worked their way around to the rear of the property whilst the other contained the front aspect. The intention was to make contact with the occupant of the ground floor flat and ascertain from there what was needed. The rear containment officers used a telescopic ladder to gain vision over a wall into the rear garden. One officer climbed up and took a position covering the back door with his MP5 carbine. The double-width French doors were open and he had vision into the kitchen.

No sooner had he reported his position to the control than he saw a man roll onto the floor into the opening of the French doors. He lay prone, with his arms pushed out in front of him holding what the officer recognized as a Glock 17 semi-automatic pistol. It was pointed directly at him.

The officer perceived the threat and fired twice. Hiorns did not have time to discharge the weapon, but instead rolled across the doorway out of view, leaving the pistol in the doorway.

Believing he had hit the subject who possibly lay wounded and dying in the kitchen, the officer and his colleagues made the brave deci-

sion to enter the premises to protect life. Hiorns was discovered in the kitchen, wounded. He had been hit in the hand and the groin. The wound to the hand had led to him dropping the pistol, which turned out to be a blank-firing replica of the same type of pistol carried by the ARVs.

It later transpired that Hiorns had consumed up to four bottles of vodka prior to his confrontation with armed police. He survived his wounds and in May 2010 at Blackfriars Crown Court he pleaded guilty to possession of a firearm and intent to cause fear of violence. He was sentenced to three years in prison.

With unprecedented speed, the officer who fired the shots was returned to full operational status in just twenty-five days. The officers involved were also commended for their swift action resulting in getting Richard Hiorns the medical treatment he needed.

PART SIX:

On the World Stage —
CO19/SCO19 in the 2010s

The main focus of CO19 for the early part of the decade would obviously be the London 2012 Olympics and all the challenges that this would bring to a firearms department. However, in every other area of CO19, it was business as usual. With a recession in full swing, armed crime was expected to rise. Spending cuts were also on the horizon and CO19 was expected to field its fair share and still maintain the cover needed to keep the capital safe for the years to come.

Trojan Support Dogs
2010

CO19 has always trained with and used Trojan support dogs on its numerous firearms operations. In fact, they were used back in the days of D11, when the handlers were all armed. This was not considered appropriate and was stopped in the early 1980s. The training has gone from strength to strength over the years and Trojan dogs are called out on a regular basis to assist ARV, TST and SFO teams for armed searches of buildings, open country operations or static ambushes where a suspect may have the opportunity of escaping on foot.

The dogs will find hidden suspects under beds, in cupboards and loft spaces or other difficult spaces where access is a problem. The dogs are also trained to search on board ships, abseil while attached to their handler, be comfortable when travelling in helicopters and, most important of all, to keep quiet and not get excited on firearms operations. They have undoubtedly saved many lives and go into dangerous places where it would not be safe to send a police officer.

Over the years, several police support dogs have lost their lives on duty. The most notable was Yerba, the German shepherd shot dead while tackling a bank robber at Petts Wood in 1985 (see page 64). Yerba was honoured with a citation for bravery from the RSPCA. Trojan support dogs continue to give an excellent service to CO19, whose officers respect and admire their work, which makes a dangerous job a little safer. Below and opposite are photos showing their diverse training with CO19 officers.

ARV officers train with Trojan support dogs searching buildings and outbuildings

Bread and butter work for any support dog. These dogs are trained to go after and attack an armed suspect attempting to run away. They will latch onto an arm and bring the suspect down, holding on until the person becomes submissive

Below: Trojan support dogs all train with their handlers in abseiling should the need arise to deploy into an enclosed area

SFO Course Final Exercise, Essex
2011

Since 1991 each twelve-week SFO course finishes with a final exercise. This exercise should test the skills learnt over the course's twelve-week period, and will always encompass a 'hostage rescue' scenario followed by plain clothes, covert, vehicle and foot interceptions. The exercise is always planned and briefed by the students under the scrutiny of the instructors. The SFO operators of all ranks have their preparation, leadership and teamwork skills assessed before, during and after the scenarios. The final exercise will be at a training site unknown to the students, maybe a derelict or disused hospital or commercial premises.

Realism is an important factor. It is the only way to properly test a student's reaction. If the student passes this stage they graduate on to their SFO teams doing the job for real. There can be no room for mistakes.

The entry team prepare to make their entry behind a ballistic training shield

CO19 Becomes SCO19 Specialist Crime and Operations
January 2012

In January 2012 the Metropolitan Police firearms department underwent its final name change (at the time of writing). In another service restructuring Central Operations (CO) merged with the Specialist Crime Directorate (SCD) to become Specialist Crime and Operations (SCO19).

The change in name did not affect the day-to-day running of the unit which still focuses on its training and operational commitments. Forty-five years since its inception the department strength now stood at one chief superintendent, two superintendents, four chief inspectors, twenty inspectors, over 500 constables and seventy-nine civilian support staff.

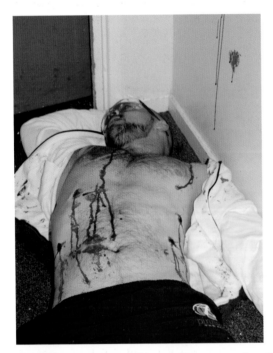

Make-up artists are used to provide a sense of realism with the casualty's wounds. This helps the officers understand what they may face during a real firearms operation. It also helps with the student's ballistic first aid skills, which are also assessed during the exercise

These numbers were divided between the SFO teams (which had now increased in number and included two TST teams). There were also six ARV reliefs and a proactive ARV team. The department additionally boasted a permanent training cadre of over 100 officers along with fifteen civilian firearms instructors, Operation Makepeace (the proactive community-based unit) made up of five officers and the firearms enquiry (licensing teams), consisting of thirty-two civilian enquiry officers. These were supported by admin staff, armourer's weapons-issuing officers, stores personnel and vehicle fleet garage hands.

The firearms command had grown beyond recognition from its early days and no one could have imagined the vast workload it now took on both in terms of firearms operations, training and its myriad other responsibilities.

Of the total strength mentioned above, there are now thirty-four female officers within the SCO19 firearms command of which twenty-six are authorized to carry firearms on an operational basis – a vast improvement from days back in 1987 when there were none!

ARV Officers Shoot Knifeman, Forest Hill
19 February 2012

Shortly before 6 a.m. on 19 February 2012 local police were called to Elsinore Road in Forest Hill, south-east London, to reports of a man attempting to break into motor vehicles. As the officers arrived, the 25-year-old suspect, George Asare, held them (a sergeant and an inspector) at bay with a machete and a large knife. Several times he attempted to slash and stab the officers.

Following a call for assistance, an Armed Response Vehicle that was close by attended. The ARV crew deployed and attempted to use their Tasers. These had little or no effect. (Sometimes one or both barbs do not stay in the subject. In order to deliver the charge they must both have contact. When a subject is moving quickly or struggling one or both of the barbs may miss.)

The incident was becoming desperate as the suspect seemed intent on inflicting serious injuries on the officers as they attempted to detain him. Now the ARV officers were in fear for their lives. They were being forced back, their Taser was not effective and, after several near misses with the knife and machete, three officers opened fire with their weapons. In all, five shots were fired, hitting Asare three times in the abdomen, leg and hand. He was taken to King's College Hospital in south London where he survived his wounds and was later charged with causing criminal damage, attempted GBH and affray.

On 2 November 2012, at Croydon Crown Court, Asare pleaded not guilty owing to temporary insanity. This defence was supported by three independent psychiatrists. The jury returned a verdict of not guilty by reason of insanity. Asare was remanded in hospital care under the Mental Health Act where he would receive mental health treatment.

Mental illness can be debilitating, both for the sufferer and their loved ones, and it can affect people in many different ways. It is fair to say that only a minute number of people with mental health issues will ever display any violent symptoms, but when this happens it can have devastating effects on the community and the individuals that come to harm. Sometimes there is no alternative other than turning to our police to protect us in these instances and on these occasions it is not always safe or practical to use less lethal options to incapacitate a person armed with a knife. It's easy to forget that in the UK more people are killed or injured each year by knives than by firearms.

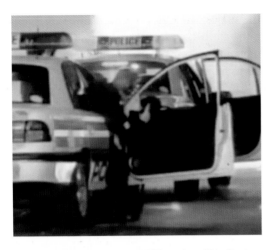

Officers deploying from ARVs onto a 'live-fire' range. Concentration and awareness of others and their own weapons must be paramount

Advanced Firearms Training at MPSTC Gravesend
2012

All SCO19 personnel will at some point in their firearms careers undergo advanced firearms training at some level. Whether it be ARV training or an SFO course, these skills need to be maintained on a regular basis. The training facilities at MPSTC Gravesend are well suited for this task, with specific ranges designed to fit each training requirement.

Pre-Olympic Training with the SIG 5.56 carbine
June 2012

An SFO advances down the range using the new SIG 5.56 carbine

A multi-weapon cover and movement shoot on the fifty-metre 'A' range at MPSTC Gravesend

SCO19 ARV Fleet, Leman Street
2012

Since the introduction of the Armed Response Vehicles back in 1991, there has been a steady flow of vehicle types from the first Rover 827s, the Volvo 850 GLT estate, the three-litre Vauxhall Omega and the Mercedes E270. But since 2005 BMW has provided the backbone of the fleet with their 530D series, which has proved to be one of the most successful ARV workhorses ever, popular with both drivers and crew alike.

As we go to print the BMW 530 series is coming to the end of its effective operational life, mainly owing to continued increase in the weight of equipment it is required to carry. After assessing many likely replacements, the one chosen as best suited to the needs of the new ARV has been the four-wheel drive diesel automatic BMW X5.

A contemporary photo looking down on the back yard at the SCO19 base at Leman Street. Some of the ARV fleet of BMWs packed into the yard ready to go out and patrol the streets of London

A new ARV support van fully equipped to be called to any firearms incident where extra equipment is required

A Modern Breed of Weapons: SCO19 Firearms
2012

As well as improvements to the pistols and carbines available to the officers, another important addition to the department's armaments was the introduction of the Benelli M3 automatic/pump-action shotgun, which replaced the Remington 870 shotgun. The Benelli has been in use with SCO19 since 2004 with a seven-round magazine, and is also available as a shortened 'Hatton gun' version with four-shot magazine (as seen in the Kev Lyles painting at the front of this book). This weapon can be fired in 'automatic' or pump-action mode by twisting the selector at the end of the foregrip. The Benelli complements the other weapons shown here and is used on a daily basis.

The family of Glock 9 mm pistols.
Top: Glock 17 (17-round magazine).
Middle: Glock 19 (15-round magazine).
Bottom: Glock 26 (10-round magazine)

Stephen Smith

Stephen Smith

An old favourite – the MP5 carbine. Shown here with retractable stock and picatinny rails to accommodate the foregrip and torch/laser

Stephen Smith

The new SIG 5.56 carbine with retractable stock, aim-point sights and picatinny rail to accommodate foregrip and torch/laser

2012 Olympic Preparation: Combined Response Firearms Teams

The armed contingency planning for the 2012 London Olympic Games was a massive undertaking. The Metropolitan Police called upon the help of outside police forces to provide the extra presence needed to host a successful games. This was also the case for the firearms department. In the year preceding the event, SCO19 provided training for these officers at MPSTC Gravesend. They were also responsible for training hundreds of visiting protection officers, ARV officers and SFOs. The need for a versatile reserve of specialist officers with their own command structure was identified.

These specialist teams, of which there were to be three, were known as CRFTs (Combined Response Firearms Teams). They were structured to be self-sufficient and able to deploy anywhere at a moment's notice. Each CRFT had its own command structure and the authority

CRFT officers training for deployment from a Chinook helicopter prior to the commencement of the Olympics

The CRFTs are put through their paces in unarmed combat techniques

One aspect of the training was hostage rescue on aircraft. The London airports were considered a possible target throughout the games

A combination of Met and Constabulary CRFT practising CQC

Stephen Smith

The CRFTs out on the River Thames during maritime training

to work at any of the Olympic venues. Each consisted of one Met SFO team and one Constabulary police SFO team, along with all the necessary support elements. They were equipped with both covert and armoured vehicles and had the capability of being airlifted to any location in the country should the need arise. It was imperative that these mixed firearms assets were given the opportunity to work together before the games began.

By the end of 2011, training had begun and each member of the CRFT attended at least three combined training sessions. These were intense and testing for the officers, who were all well aware of the responsibilities put on them for those three weeks in the summer of sport. The training focused not only on the core skills of the SFO, such as hostage rescue and live-fire CQC, but additional skills, some of which were new to many of the Constabulary force SFOs such as aircraft intervention, maritime boarding techniques, helicopter deployment and high-risk convoy protection.

A Safe and Happy Olympics: 2012 London Olympic and Paralympic Games
27 July–9 September

The London 2012 Olympic and Paralympic Games were held in the summer of that year under a terrific security blanket. They succeeded mainly owing to a great collaboration between several agencies tasked with the massive responsibility of providing a safe environment in which the Games could thrive. The role of SCO19 was to supply and maintain armed firearms cover throughout the period of both Games. The firearms cover was at several levels including an armed uniform deterrent patrolling the venues and the surrounding areas and an armed plain-clothes presence able to respond anywhere in the Olympic parks and other satellite venues. There were also teams of specialists ready to counter any terrorist or other armed threat, which might impact on the event, the public or the participating athletes.

The opening ceremony, as seen from the dizzy heights of one of several sniper observation points around the stadium. These individuals helped provided a safe environment for the Games to flourish. The rifle officers from SCO19's sniper team had direct contact with squads of plain clothes SFOs who worked in pairs mingling with the crowds of spectators

247

An SCO19 sniper/observation point, high up in the stadium superstructure. By using powerful scopes and optical aids they can pinpoint an armed individual or pass valuable intelligence down to their colleagues on the ground

The London 2012 Olympics is a fantastic place to finish this book. The Games were an unadulterated success in terms of organization, logistics and public relations. The number of visitors to the capital and the Games during that period made them a massive target for terrorism in its many guises, but the collaborative effort of the security services involved meant this opportunity could not be seized.

The firearms department, although busy at the Games and around London during the summer of 2012, recorded no Games-related shooting incidents and were able to use this time to build some valuable bridges with the public they are sworn to protect. Sadly, that success has been followed by the long-awaited cuts to funding and finance as Britain wallows in a recession. How these cuts will affect the future of SCO19 and the way it polices London remain to be seen, but Londoners can rest assured that the brave men and women in this unit will continue to go out there, day in and day out, and put themselves between the innocent and those willing to use violence against them.

Postscript

This book is not about facts and figures but about the people behind the guns. However, it would be remiss of me to leave anyone under the misapprehension that our armed police are going around London shooting people at every

The sheer volume of people created its own problems for the firearms officers on duty at all the Olympic events. Once a potential threat was identified the crush of people made it difficult to get to the flash point, or locate an individual picked out by an observer

Mark Williams

Met ARV personnel on duty at the London Olympics take time to pose with a young spectator

opportunity. This couldn't be further from the truth.

Throughout the period covered by this volume, the operations carried out each year by the firearms department have continued to rise. There does not exist a comprehensive list of the total number of armed incidents it has dealt with over this period but, when looked at in the round, the number of incidents where shots have been fired is infinitesimal when set against the total deployments.

Since 1966 the department has had five officers wounded by hostile fire and one killed during the arrest of armed suspects (not as a result of gunfire). From recent firearms department figures between 2005 and 2012, London's ARVs have responded to 19,517 spontaneous armed incidents. The firearms teams have also dealt with 14,187 pre-planned armed operations. During this period they have discharged firearms on just eighteen occasions, resulting in nine fatalities. This record is second to none when compared to other major cities around the world with similar dense populations.

Although the department still strives to improve safety for the public, the criminals and its officers, the record this extraordinary unit has achieved is outstanding, as is the volume of training that the department provides each year to its staff and the training it carries out overseas for countries that request its expertise. I hope this book goes some way to giving these incredible men and women of not just the Metropolitan Police firearms unit but all the nations' firearms departments the recognition that they so rightly deserve.

Glossary

ACPO — Association of Chief Police Officers
Leads development of policing practices in England, Wales and Northern Ireland

AFO — Authorized Firearms Officer
Officer who has completed a basic firearms course

ARV — Armed Response Vehicle
An overt police vehicle containing a crew of three armed officers

ASU — Air Support Unit
Police helicopter unit based at Lippitts Hill in Epping Forest

CARV — Covert Armed Response Vehicle
An unmarked police vehicle containing up to three armed officers

CBRN — Chemical, Biological, Radiological and Nuclear
The term used for equipment and training in those fields

CIB2 — Complaints Investigation Branch Two
Took over from A10 branch in the mid-1970s, investigating internal complaints against police. Restructured in 2003 as the DPS.

CIT — Cash in Transit
Money moved between locations by security companies in security vehicles

COBR — Cabinet Office Briefing Room
Crisis briefing rooms used for civil contingency committee meetings

CO19 — Central Operations Department 19
Firearms department title used between 2005–2012

CPS — Crown Prosecution Service
Government department responsible for public prosecutions in England and Wales, headed by the director of public prosecutions

CQC — Close Quarter Combat
SCO19 term used to describe fighting through a sequence of rooms and corridors. Military usage of the term is CQB (Close Quarter Battle)

CRFT — Combined Response Firearms Teams
Large, highly mobile self-contained firearms team made up of Met and Constabulary SFO teams for use in the London 2012 Olympic Games

CS — Mild irritant gas
Used on armed besieged criminals

Custodian — Security guard
Employed to protect and deliver cash in transit

DEA — Drug Enforcement Administration
United States federal drug enforcement agency

DPS — Department of Professional Standards
Internal police complaints unit who investigate police shootings

D6 — Department 6
Police training department in which the firearms wing belonged between 1966–1967

D11 — Department 11
Firearms department title between 1967–1987

FBI — Federal Bureau of Investigation
United States Government agency set up for counter-intelligence and to investigate federal crimes

Green Meanie — Early D11 Schermuly stun grenade
So-called because of its colour and its extremely loud detonation

Gunship — SCO19 or Flying Squad Covert Armed Response Vehicle
Police term to describe a Covert Armed Response Vehicle

Hard Stop — Enforced vehicle stop
This tactic usually involves multiple police vehicles blocking a suspect's vehicle

Hatton — Shotgun or shotgun cartridge (Hatton gun, Hatton round)
Name taken from its Special Forces inventor. Used to disrupt locks and hinges, and to deflate car tyres

HEMS — Helicopter Emergency Medical Service
Air ambulance capable of landing at or near incidents, includes a doctor

HME — Home Made Explosives
Term used to describe non-military or industrial explosives usually produced locally, for use in terrorist attacks

IPCC — **Independent Police Complaints Commission**
Independent government body formed to investigate serious complaints against police

Jump-off — **Vehicle or building used as a forward assault point**
From which armed officers can deploy

Levels 1 and 2 — **PT17 firearms teams**
Firearms department's two-tier operational system

Makepeace — **Name given to SCO19 community educational programme**
Set up to tackle the issues around gun and knife crime in the capital for youths aged between 11 and 19 years

MOE — **Method Of Entry**
Title given to the team 'breacher' or breaching equipment both mechanical and non-mechanical, used to gain entry to premises by force

MPFTC — **Metropolitan Police Firearms Training Centre**
Located at Lippitts Hill in Epping Forest, the main firearms training centre until 2003

MPSTC — **Metropolitan Police Specialist Training Centre**
Located at Gravesend in Kent, this is the main centre for firearms and other specialist training, opened in 2003

OP — **Observation Point**
Normally manned by unarmed detectives who give a radio commentary

PCA — **Police Complaints Authority**
Forerunner to the Independent Police Complaints Commission

PIRA — **Provisional Irish Republican Army**
An Irish republican terrorist organization

Plasticuff — **Nylon ties for handcuffing prisoners**
Convenient, cheap and lightweight for restraining multiple prisoners

PT17 — **Personnel and Training department 17**
Firearms department title used between 1987–1992

Q CAR — **Unmarked police crime car**
Old police term for an unmarked crime patrol car, from the Second World War term 'Q boat'

QRV — **Quick Release Vest**
Equipment vest, with pockets and pouches worn over body armour

RCS — **Regional Crime Squad**
The RCS dealt with serious and organized crime across the country, which was divided into regional areas. It was replaced by SOCA in 2006

Respirator — **Gas Mask**
Carried by SFO teams for use in gas or CBRN environments

RIB — **Rigid Inflatable Boat**
A fast assault craft used for maritime operations by SCO19 and the military

SAS — **Special Air Service**
British Army elite special forces

SCO19 — **Specialist Crime and Operations department 19**
Firearms department title from 2012

SFO — **Specialist Firearms Officer**
An SCO19 officer who has completed the SFO twelve-week course and has worked on an operational firearms team

SO19 — **Specialist Operations department 19**
Firearms department title between 1992–2005

SPG — **Special Patrol Group**
Mobile police task force – sometimes armed. Disbanded 1986

Taser — **Police stun gun**
Trademark name of the company who produce police stun guns in the UK.

Trident — **Operation 'Trident' SCD8**
Set up in 1998 to combat the growing number of black-on-black shootings

Trojan — **Radio call sign of all PT17/SO19/CO19 and SCO19 assets**
Each Trojan unit is allocated a number i.e. Trojan 805

TSG — **Territorial Support Group**
Mobile police task force, replaced SPG in 1986

TST — **Tactical Support Team**
Made up of SCO19 officers trained above ARV standard and formed into firearms teams to provide support to the SFO teams. Formed in 2004

Select Bibliography and Further Reading

Arden, Michael R., Fletcher, Eleanor and Taylor, Christopher, *Metropolitan Police Images – Motor Vehicles* (Phillimore, 2008)

Artwohl, Alexis and Christensen, Loren W., *Deadly Force Encounters* (Paladin Press, 1997)

Ashcroft, Michael, *George Cross Heroes* (Headline, 2010)

Collins, Steve, *The Glory Boys* (Century, 1998)

Collins, Steve, *The Good Guys Wear Black* (Century, 1997)

Doyle, William and Shatford, John, *Dome Raiders* (Virgin, 2004)

Firmin, Rusty and Pearson, Will, *Go! Go! Go!* (Weidenfeld & Nicolson, 2010)

Force Science Institute, *Force Science News* No. 33 (December 2005)

Gould, Robert W. and Waldren, Michael J., *London's Armed Police* (Arms and Armour, 1986)

Gray, Roger, *The Trojan Files* (Virgin, 2000)

Kemp, Anthony, *The SAS Savage Wars of Peace: 1947 to the Present* (John Murray, 1994)

Mason, Gary *The Official History of the Metropolitan Police* (Carlton, 2004)

Squires, Peter and Kennison, Peter, *Shooting to Kill* (Wiley-Blackwell, 2010)

Waldren, Michael J., *Armed Police* (Sutton, 2007)

Index